LA
AND ANGUISH
IN THE CYCLADES
CAROLA MATTHEWS

LAUGHTER AND ANGUISH IN THE CYCYLADES

CAROLA MATTHEWS

First Edition.
Book designed by Zac Matthews
Paperback ISBN: 979-8-9910117-6-1
eBook ISBN: 979-8-9910117-7-8

Front cover photograph by Catherine Bicknell
All other images from the Matthews family collection

Published by VRAX Productions
Glendale, California

VRAXProductions.com

CHAPTERS

Foreward VI
Author's Note VIII
Chapter One 3
Chapter Two 29
Chapter Three 45
Chapter Four. 67
Chapter Five 93
Chapter Six 121
Chapter Seven. 143
Chapter Eight 159
Chapter Nine. 183
Chapter Ten. 197
Chapter Eleven 223
Chapter Twelve. 235
Chapter Thirteen 251
Chapter Fourteen 273
Chapter Fifteen. 285
Chapter Sixteen. 303
Chapter Seventeen 321
Chapter Eighteen 341
Addendum - The Magic Muletrack 348
Additional Addendum - Cubby's Wedding 356

Foreward

In the autumn of 2020, my aunt, Carolina, died peacefully in her Langatha home, having been lovingly cared for by her Amorgian compatriots. Her life well lived, and her adventures well chronicled brought her to her last breath in her late eighties, still walking the donkey path down to her un-electrified home in the almost deserted village of Strombos, the most remote village on the far end of a distant Cycladic island. She liked it that way. And despite the cruelty of age that painfully bent her spine, she made the perilous trek repeatedly against the protestations of… well… just about everyone. A life lived deliberately.

Covid travel restrictions kept the family away, and without us, the village managed a marvelous processional and burial in the traditional manner, treating Carolina as one of their own as they carried her on her last journey through the village of Langatha. The village she called "The One." My family and I finally arrived in Langatha in the summer of 2021 to find Carolina's house and spare belongings well cared for by dear friends, generous people who loved Carolina and honoured her legacy. In her belongings, I found these two books in manuscript form and on an unlabeled cd-rom, the manuscripts typed in by a friend.

These books told the real-life story surrounding her best-known books, *The Mad Pomegranate Tree* and *At the Top of the Muletrack.* Reading these manuscripts for the first time felt like watching a vivid movie about making a vivid movie, a picture within a picture. Compelling and slightly obtuse in the way that only Carolina could be, these books are a window into a time she refused to put in print until certain characters had passed on. Her mother, the author C.M. "Molly" Matthews, might not have approved of some of the more salacious details, therefore Carolina's decorum bade her wait.

Carolina saved few belongings but treasured her photographs of the era. Looking through those images, I saw a vision of Mykonos before it became "Mykonos" and Amorgós before Aigali had roads and electricity. A handful of those photographs can be found in these books, and a few more can be viewed on a web page dedicated to Carolina and her Amorgos homes: www.amorgosrental.com/CarolinaMatthews.php

Finding print copies of Carolina's published books becomes more difficult as time passes, and if you find used copies somewhere, you should grab them while you can. I do hope that this book, and its companion, bring you some joy and a view into the life of a truly unique character, Carolina, The Mad Englishwoman at the Top of the Muletrack who taught Amorgós to speak Αγγλικά.

- Zac Matthews, June 2024

Author's Note

`Now' in this book means around 1980, during the time of writing.

Accents on proper nouns and Greek words where the stress may be unexpected: afendikós; Amorgós; Demosthénes; Elefthería; Evangelía; Kaliópe; Katápola; kyría; kyrios; Lakí; Langátha; Langathianí; Nikouriá; Panayía; Phanís; Potamós

Boundless thanks to my dear friend Jaap Jansen who worked long and doggedly to turn the aged typescript of this book into presentable form.

To Julian

Chapter One

T he house is nineteen thousand drachmas,' wrote Mr N. `I can't beat the old woman further down. Just write to me if you want it - yes or no.'

Nineteen thousand! That was over two hundred and fifty pounds, a high price in 1972 for a semi-ruin in the village of Langatha on an island such as Amorgos, and high for me. Mr N's guess had been fifteen. The way my budget habitually worked, four thousand made a weighty difference.

And yet, `It's now or never.' He had been right in the autumn in so badgering me. `They'll be building the road soon, and when we have a road and then the electricity...' One day that road, the wires and pylons, would be real ones, and the old refrain turn into lamentations on what had not been done before. And yet it was difficult not to go on looking on such wonders as only a little more realistic than talk of Judgment Day.

If I wrote the one word on a postcard, Mr N could go ahead and buy the house for me. He'd have to - at least it would have to be in a Greek name, so why not a local one? Amorgos is technically a frontier island, where property may not be owned by foreigners, even though the straight line that could theoretically be drawn from its coast to the coast of Asia Minor would be eighty miles long. Physically it is a natural frontier, falling with hair-raising abruptness over one thousand feet into the sea, but when you have turned the corner at the end of a long mountain walk and reached the precipice on the north-eastern rim, it is only at the end of the Cyclades that you are standing, with the Dodecannese ahead. I would have thought that you could draw a straight line to Turkey from some point of any island east of the mainland, but the law is the law and I was not much concerned.

At thirty-three and single I was thinking of my lifetime and could not see the inhabitants of Langatha changing their philosophy towards foreigners before the end of that. The village belongs to the area called Aiyiali around the second port of Amorgos, and Aiyiali was so neglected, or unspoilt - whichever you might choose to call it - until a lonely bulldozer was landed to represent Public Works in 1978, that the attitude of its people appeared as safe as its lifestyle. If we had been divided from the main port and the capital by a stretch of sea and not a mountain range, the powers that be in Athens might less belatedly have noticed Aiyiali on the map. As it was, its people had as good reason for complaining as I had for fleeing to it from the big traumatic world.

Langatha, the lesser capital, is one of three hill villages looking out over the bay. If your boat arrives in daytime you can see it all mapped out. You are inside the curling tail of a long thin island, like Crete in miniature, with those three white splashes in the mountains, Tholaria on the left, Langatha in the middle, Potamos above Ormos, the lazy little port. The highest peak above them is eight hundred metres, which is not a foothill in the Alps, but the difference between a mountain and a hill depends on character, and our range is unarguably mountainous - you can look down on the sea on both sides from the top. Inside the curve, behind a long beach, olive trees cover the plain and lower slopes. The outside coastline would not tempt an optimistic pirate.

There is no longer the hustle and excitement of scrambling into a caique from an arriving steamer in the middle of the bay - nowadays you walk off onto a spacious quay and very likely get into the village Landrover. But the old mule track is still there, still useful, only once intersected by the great S of the new road, and still a good way of switching off the journey if you should ride or walk. The silence is so startling here that you may wonder if you're having a mystical experience. Even a cavalcade of mules and donkeys makes little sound on this paved way, where dung like the dry husks that it virtually consists of lies in carpets round the stones. I cannot call that mystical, but I do know that I am in confusion at the bottom and truly in Aiyiali half-way up.

I had just come off a boat when I first met Mr N, or rather I did not remember him when he stepped out of the dark. During my first summers on the island he was being a sailor round the world but he must have dropped by at some time while I was there, for he recognised me and knew everything there was for a villager to know about me, the little that there was. That is to say, I was the annual tenant of Langatha's only habitable house for rent, that being my answer to what to do in the peak tourist season when Mykonos, where I began my Greek life, was being St Tropez. I taught English to half a dozen village children, and wrote books. *At the Top of the Mule Track* had been displayed about the cafés, with photographs of several of the villagers including a full plate of the old priest. So much was common knowledge. I was slightly enigmatic because I was the village's sole foreigner, and female, and liked living by myself.

Mr N was enigmatic too, the only villager who was. That was the only reason for his title, awarded to him by one of the few foreigners who were to come into my island life. Nobody is much of a `Mr' in Langatha, but he's a weasel and it suits him, the slightly sinister proprietor of an evening drinks-shop, convivial and talkative, taciturn and dour.

He was not dour that night when I was heading for Langatha and he was riding up. He took me on the saddle by him and talked from the bottom of the mule track to the top. Altogether I was less comfortable than concentrating. My Greek was strained by his vocabulary which seems to come from Appendix C of an off-beat dictionary. He also leaps at metaphors and tangents, circling every point, so that unless you are alert you may well miss the moment when suddenly he aims at the bullseye and throws his dart. Meanwhile it takes two thin people to ride the way that we were riding, which means side-saddle, and even so we were squashed. I was aware of bones. The island men do not have the plump bottoms of the Athenians and Mr N has none at all - nothing is big about him but his nose, and that seems so in contrast to his other features, especially the receding cheeks. We were squashed, but he did not behave like any normal sailor. He had left the big bad ports of the wide world and turned back into an emphatically proper villager.

The mule track to Langatha is less than a mile and a half long, but seems more if you are unused to it, or are being talked to non-stop by a Mr N. The gradient begins gentle with olive trees, and steepens with figs towards the top. At the point where you might start complaining you are on the second to last lap, so take it easy, look about you, make the walk a dawdling hour if you're against the thirty-minute stride. Come in the late afternoon. If the cliff face on your right is golden when you start out, it will turn pink as you watch it, and then grey. After that the owl comes out, a scops owl with a gentle `pioo pioo pioo' that echoes and is magnified against the cliff.

It cannot be one lone owl, but I had listened to it for five summers, nightly from the balcony and through the windows of the house I rented, and I always thought of it as singular. I also thought of it as mine. So was the air and almost the whole sky. That's not being greedy, for everyone who likes can think so, but I should not have been thinking of the house as mine. Built by the mayor of Aiyiali two generations earlier, it was my seven-pound home for two or three months of the summer, five hundred drachmas however long I stayed. I could not make myself believe that the owners of this mansion would return from Athens - but they would - to be the one couple in thousands who return to such a village for their retirement. It was an effort to persuade myself that if I wanted to stay in Langatha - and I did - I must have my own house. The signs and seasons were all indicating that I must go ahead with finding it, but I was down at heart and next to penniless.

Why Langatha? It's just another of those stone and whitewash villages built out of easy range of pirates, such as you may find throughout the Cyclades. They say it's the longest. There are over two hundred steps from the bottom to the top, and certainly that is plenty for three hundred inhabitants. The lower ones are a good two metres deep from front to back, but they close up with the gradient so that the newcomer is confronted with the strenuous part just as he thinks that he is getting there and giving out. And then, when he does get there, to the *platia*, where is that? A sleepy little village square, not square at all but rather narrow, open to the mountain on one side, with houses on the other and shops that shut at unexpected hours. Why Langatha? I walked in and it spoke.

By 'shops' I am translating the Greek *magazi* in village terms, a vague coverage of a grocery, a taverna and a café, allowing for a good deal of the more-or-less. Half-way down the village the bakery has become our seasonal taverna, there was none before the 1980s but either Mr N or Ioanna the grocer's wife or Evangelia would oblige. Evangelia's in the middle is mostly a café, with oddments such as rusks and paper napkins, while *Kyria* Mouska's at the far end is a butcher's now and then. Mr N's, the single building on the side toward the mountain, sold only what could be consumed at his own tables, except on Sundays when he is usually a butcher, but the definition still makes such a place his shop. The real grocer has three of varying kinds together, so you have to keep your wits about you there.

Ioanna, always tired and always willing, runs among them and her kitchen, which is almost on the public premises, rarely pauses, rarely sits down, carries a calor-gas drum without effort, and is thin. So is Mr N's wife, but exercise does not seem to have much to do with it, for every woman has plenty and almost all are stout. They are also cheerful, and most of them would deny that. Everyone is cheerful, and a little bit lugubrious. Their feet ache, their legs ache, their stomachs ache, if they did not have aches to complain of they would be deprived. They all say the same things every day and if it's funny they laugh every time.

Most special among this cheerful, aching lot is the widow *Kyria* Mouska. She's the prototype of the twinkling Greek-island café-keeper, so much the epitome of it all that she's unique. Her shop is huge, all creaking wood with its ancient pictures and its posters at drunken angles, and its ten tables round the walls as wobbly as the law of Greek café tables can demand. It serves a masculine society, though not the sort that makes a woman embarrassed to come in, and *Kyria* Mouska looks on cackling in delight. Widowhood changed her life. I can't imagine her without her black *mandili* round her head, wound in the fashion of all good island widows high over her chin, indoors and out, in heat and cold, perhaps in bed. She's a compulsive giver. Every time you order one thing something else comes free. She makes little packages to stuff into your bag with a surreptitious wink. Every time it's grapes, the grapes get squashed.

`All this giving!' I sometimes mutter.

`Huh! You buy your cigarettes from me don't you?'

Of course I do, I had thought there's nowhere else up here to buy them since it took me years to find out that I'd been walking daily past Langatha's second cigarette shop without recognising it as such. It's a house, and it's not my habit to stick my nose into people's houses in case they happen to sell cigarettes. Anyway, during the daytime the family are usually out. Before this discovery I had sat almost on its doorstep countless times, for it is on the way to the *platia* opposite Eleftheria's, a shop with barrelled wine which could be drunk on the spot. That was a good stop before the last lap to the top, but that summer I was beginning to be a regular at Mr N's.

That first evening when we rode up together he informed me that I would teach his Maria English - she was ten and it was time. I did not really want to add Maria to the small but steady trail of children who arrived with elementary books and bundles of home produce at my door, but there she was - for a short while. She was beautiful, with a thick, black waist-length plait, but she did not `take letters' as they say. After one summer she appeared no more. Yet the home eggs and the home cheese and all such precious items that in the harsh summer money cannot buy, and which had been the chief exchange for a few wasted words, continued to be stuffed into my bag. I found this perplexing. *Kyria* Mouska said: `He is poor but good.'

His shop was a new one, as large as hers in brick and concrete, but hers is not a wine shop - not often - and I was not allowed to pass his on my way home any evening without stopping for a glass. But I did not feel bullied. When I left quickly saying, `Evening is work-time in my factory,' I gained more respect than when I lingered, he would more nearly hurtle me from the shop than encourage me to stay. Yet I had to drink one glass and could not pay for it, because I had once given a few vain lessons to his Maria. As the village had never known me with more than a few spare drachmas, as nothing had yet suggested that I would one day be a house-owner, his behaviour was good reason for the confidence that grew in me for Mr N.

I had never sat round the shops much. I had in my time been boisterous on Mykonos and found my seamy haunts wherever I had stopped in Greece, but I like contrasts, Langatha was my ascetic corner to be a literary hermit in. It's a place where one's reserves are one's own business, which is what one is expected to get on with, and I did. The people are harmlessly narrow-minded and affably self-contained, they provide a buffer against loneliness, a background to be constructive in. When I first appeared among them, a lone young woman with a typewriter in a village that had never had a foreigner, my behaviour - or lack of it - was a mystery to them. Here daughters stay at home until they are married, and then they stay at home. I was glad that I had had my island breaking-in elsewhere, for we got to know each other slowly, and by the time that they had dropped the grand *kyria* and then the *thespinis* or `mademoiselle' and I became plain Carolina with a growing tendency to emerge, they were easy with me at tables where I would originally have surprised.

Mr N's shop might be a hard echoing hall with steel girders, but it was kind to me that summer when the world and I had fallen out and I had lost the zest to write. I stayed longer and grew anaesthetised. *Kyria* Mouska's shop was kind to me as well.

Some sailor relations on a jaunt to the old home were having a competition in places-I-have-been-to, rousing appropriate gasps and grunts from the audience. `Think of that!' *Kyria* Mouska was chortling in the wings. She had once been to Naxos, but that sole outing was rather an apology.

'Have you been to Chora, *Kyria* Mouska?'

'No, and I've never been to Katapola.' So she dealt with distant parts, and then came nearer home. 'I haven't been to Ormos for seven years.' There was silence for a moment. 'Why should I go to Ormos?' Everyone tried to think of a reason for her to go down to our port and no one could. Nikolakis her son owns an orchard down there, but that's a reason not to go. He lives in Langatha and brings fresh produce up. 'And,' she added, 'I've never been to Tholaria - ever.'

The sailors' competition had been exploded. If this was a round in one-upmanship, *Kyria* Mouska had won. Tholaria is not just a short hour round the mountain by foot or donkey, it's somewhere else. Why go there? Why go anywhere?

Why go anywhere? Out of the blue in the middle of July I had a cable from VANRGKOKSUV. Where in the world beyond us is VANRGKOKSUV, if it exists? There is great uncertainty in our little office about the Roman alphabet. CAN BOU MEET UT ATHENS ABOUST 15 AND ARRANGE FOUR DAYS ON NEARBY BEACH WRITING HENRY. Clonk me on the head, wherever this place may be, and somehow I deduced that it was likely to be in Thailand - for convenience sake let us call it Thailand - Brother, I love you dearly, but...

All I knew of the plans or whereabouts of my brother's family was that they were travelling the long way back to England from America where he had been teaching architecture in a university for several years, that they were aiming about now at Thailand, and that Greece had been said not to fit into the itinerary. Apparently it did now, and I was clamped to Mouska's wall. CAN BOU MEET UT ATHENS ABOUST 15? Frankly no.

`About 15' is no date for an external rendez-vous, and slowly it came to me that nobody could think it was. This must be `August 15', definite and serious. I was being given a month's warning and no opportunity to protest. I could hardly send a cable to somewhere possibly called VANRGKOKSUV, which might be in Thailand and which they would have left by now, answering SORRY IMPOSSIBLE, so I would have to go ahead and perform a miracle.

Sit down and think out that one. I have no indication of what they have to spend, but that's irrelevant. Being a millionaire is small help if you suddenly want accomodation for five on a beach near Athens in the middle of August. Every hole is booked, probably from the year before. A house to rent? You're joking. Hotel rooms? You're hysterical. Yet I love my brother and his family, I long to see them, and if it is assumed that I shall perform a miracle I don't like to fail.

Then I remembered an old friend in Chalkis, north of Athens, on the sea. And the whole disruption becomes another story in which the miracle turned into a simplicity. But Henry, Catherine and the boys are a part of the Langatha story, and so, as it turned out, was the nature of their telegram.

Henry was, in a manner of speaking, the only foreign owner of property in Aiyiali. Three years earlier he and Catherine, with one baby, had given me a fortnight's visit, liked what I had found and bought a plot of land above the beach, from *Kyria* Mouska's husband a few months before he died. A village contract was drawn up by the scribe, which is the only translation I can think of for 'the lettered one', the village's one civil servant, who deals with any paperwork that is not the business of the police. This paper has no legal value, except that Mouska's Nikolakis cannot evict Henry without refunding him twelve thousand drachmas, which would be a pity if he had built a house on it. By the early 1970s that was less than a hundred pounds.

Nikolakis is also the owner of the shop that Mr N was running, and had recently become the father of twin sons. He's hard-working, easy-going on appearance, though his disposition over half a kilo of retsina is admittedly irrelevant. Besides, the innocent twins of 1970 might one day modernise their view of the antique value of twelve thousand drachmas and their father's idea of the law. To him the land is Henry's. The scribe signed and stamped the agreement which is the only paper that the village can produce and therefore law unto the village.

Christos the scribe is small and awesome, he is so quiet and looks so wise, so unrevealing of emotions as he sits in Mouska's or makes appearance on his office balcony overlooking the platia and the inferior world. But this aspect too may be irrelevant to the twins in adulthood.

Henry felt that the matter should be considered further before he spent much money on his site, but before he left he had a thousand buckets of sand deposited, to be rained through in the winter and free of salt for building the next year. Everyone thought this a masterful idea from an architect, but he did not come back. Three years later the sand was still being washed through, and away. Gorse and wild flowers grew up, the roots helped to retain it, a good deal was dispersed in gales. How are Henry, Catherine, Jason and the sand? The villagers would often ask after all of them. By '71 the sand had settled into a natural feature of the mountainside, while the other three were turning into ghosts.

But ghosts do not own sand-pits, and here they were approaching the horizon by way of VAN-whatnot, with every intention of reaching Aiyiali the next year. When I came back from the happy reunion that took place in the great outside world, I came without a doubt of that. They would build their summer house `downstairs', as we said, with at least a long lease if that could be arranged, while `upstairs' in the village I would have my ruin, gradually to be transformed. Henry was to teach at a London Polytechnic, so there would always be real summer holidays. Upstairs and downstairs we would have a grand time. We would have to do it. Once he gets started on a project, Henry doesn't like delays.

By `ruin' I meant an abandoned house which - by my standards - could be occupied, a camping site with four walls, a roof, a view and some outside space, a place to play with, and that might cost two hundred pounds. Being next to penniless is not necessarily a stumbling-block if you are also feeling blithe and optimistic. You'll say then that it's riches for the future - what's two hundred pounds? If you're feeling blithe and optimistic you'll go ahead and find it, willy nilly you'll secure your ruin, but I was not. I was thinking that turning such a place into a home would depend on my going back to teaching, or writing a best-seller. The first course would deprive me of my plaything for nine months of the year, the second was a joke. I who had had summers of joyful, manic writing, had lost orientation, grown into the frame of mind where one asks to be defeated in one's purpose, and only out of what felt like a sense of duty I applied to Mr N to help me find my house.

Langatha is a deceptive village. It is so long that you feel it must be very thin. Yet there are enough side-streets to confuse, and at the upper end it widens out, streaming down the mountainside above the gorge, *langathi* in archaic language, and looking out over the plain down to the sea. As at Delphi, where it is the buildings on the outside edge, the lower ones, that have the grand scenic view, so it is here, and such a house he led me to, almost in the country, down the path from his. But on that stubborn Sunday I made the mistake of looking *at* this one instead of out from it. I did not attend to Mr N's eulogy of the underground cistern that would collect rain-water for a year. I looked at the house and saw a crumbling box, with two small upstairs rooms, and two downstairs which were dark and cavernous. I saw a rubbly hole beside them, which he called the kitchen, bearing a terrace that was much too cramped.

I would have peace and privacy down here, said Mr N. And where else in the village were there houses that were not more ruined, destined for a dowry or saddled with a problem of divided ownership? The owner was a widow in the village, I had only to say 'go ahead' and he would speak. He could make the contract in his name, but everyone was saying that the law would change, in a year or two it could be mine on paper, and it always would be in effect. Of course it needed fixing, but the purchase was the first and major thing. In that and afterwards, through all the stages, he would act as my commander, for how could I know how to find the hands and the materials, who provided what and who would carry it, how much each item ought to cost, or how to beat the prices down?

I agreed that I would not know, but the enormity of the decision still made me cringe. Perhaps, if I could find some money in the winter, I would write to him.

'Find' was vague. Even if I picked up the red pen that I had symbolically thrown away after my last class in an English Language Institute in Chalkis, it would not provide me with a lump sum to kick me off from starting-point.

The olive season was approaching. 'Stay and pick with us,' said Mr N. Now, that was real. That did not demand a grand decision. I could stay into October, I did not want to hurry back into the world. Let me go no further than the olive groves. I'll stay.

Then a strange thing happened. Before the olives ripened, at a moment when I thought that I was utterly in tune with *Kyria* Mouska, who had never been to Tholaria, I suddenly rose up and walked up to Chora and Katapola.

17

Perhaps it was a punishment for kicking heels - go and kick them at the mountain, there are stones enough for that, and certainly the four-hour walk in that direction - the uphill way - is fairly punitive. Four hours to Chora is arguable, but I had done it in a little less. Five is kinder. Mr N says three. In my book I likened the island to a dinosaur, and that is how I always think of it. The beast has an emaciated backbone, I have heard harrowing stories from those who have got lost around the ribs. In gales you really cannot make it. The postman does it, one way or the other, six times a week. I am always astonished at what a balanced character he is.

It was also from the mountain that I had my first view of Aiyiali. I had looked out and said yes. There, on my twenty-fifth island, is my place.

From Chora it's all downhill to Katapola, and there's a bus, but never when you want it, so I walked. It was two years since I had said hallo to either, and I really think there must have been some telepathy about the day and hour that I chose. There was little more than hallo to say to anyone until, walking round the harbour, I ran into the grand-daughter of my sister's godmother.

Amorgos is not the sort of island - is any? - where you expect to meet your sister's godmother's grand-daughter. You might not want to. I did not know I had one. If she had not recognised me I would have walked straight on. And assuming that the meeting happens, it is unlikely to be an influential circumstance. Yet Meriel had come from Paros especially to find me, on a whim roused by a nine-year-old memory of staying with me when I, not very wisely, was running a pension on Mykonos, and her journey turned out as important as it merited. She had found herself at the wrong port, been told that I lived at the other but had left, and had just decided to take the next boat back to Paros when I walked past the doorstep that she was standing on. We were ready-made friends, practically relations, and we took the boat together to Aiyiali. As soon as she had seen Langatha she offered me an indefinite loan of three hundred pounds, interest free, in exchange for staying rights.

It was just one of those Greek incidents that make one pay attention to the saints. After a few days of sparking a belief that a house would be our project she took the boat to Paros, and has not come back to Aiyiali once since that day.

How much would it cost to fix this ruin? Just to make it most simply habitable? The time had come to be dynamic. This was something to discuss with Mr N. Every evening I was at his table now, and all the talk in the shop was about olives.

I went out for a week with Mr N and a week with Eleftheria, while her Vassilis whose heart was weak kept shop. I forgot the world and all its problems, I ran out early every morning to groves in valleys and on hillsides where I had never been, and felt revivified. I was a child climbing trees from dawn to dusk and being thanked for that. I liked everything that fortnight except Mr N's tyranny in the trees.

I was astonished. Everyone was so cheerful, on the out-going and on the home-coming and in the trees, with greetings flung through screens of branches, `How are the olives?' and bursts of piercing conversation from track to track and grove to grove. On the way out our first morning, Mr N was chattily unwarning of any other mood. As soon as we laid hands on the first tree he turned into a dour maniac. `Shut up and get on with it,' was mild language to Maria, who was inclined to prattle. Beatings were threatened throughout the day. If I had not known how he adored her - he would tell me so, pronouncing her name in sacred tones - I might really have begun to wonder, and again when his six-year-old boy came down to join us after school. It was only with the baby Demosthenes that he betrayed himself. Demosthenes got dandles and proud daddy looks and kisses, but there was no baby in the trees.

I challenged him one evening on his treatment of Maria. He repeated that he loved her dearly, but fear of the father is an essential part of upbringing. She got that. One day she rode by while I was picking with Eleftheria, and the two of them began chatting on the subject of Papa. `He terrifies me,' announced Maria proudly. `Everyone is afraid of him. It came into my head last night, even the stones fear him.' She was sitting upright on her donkey looking thoroughly uncrushed, and I thought, though I do not like the paternal manner, it seems to do no harm and is not my business.

In the family there was little educational ambition, and since Maria had not `taken letters' at the village school she was one of the few children who had not left

Aiyiali to go on to Chora or elsewhere to *gymnasium*. The more ambitious scholars scuttle off to larger islands or to Athens, where they pick up city habits and afterwards never - for permanence - come back. Every time one stayed I applauded the decision. There are few enough young left to make one anxious for the future, if only to wonder about the destiny of olives and the oil.

Maria went about her first year's picking with the practical enthusiasm of one that has just been released. Nervous of climbing, she was the water-carrier, arranger of our midday picnic, gatherer of sawn-off branches, picker from the ground. Sometimes Mr N left us to it, going off on other business, and then we two novices worked with a frenzy of more eager than proficient fingers in an effort, with goals that were far beyond us, to impress the champion when he came back. We plotted with all the pleasure of companionship on how to reach what hardly could be reached. The branch I stood on bent down to her while I caught the ones above. `It's nice to talk among the olives,' said Maria, and we did not stop until the stones began to shake again as the man they feared approached.

Mr N was as much a tyrant to himself as to his daughter. Wedging himself into the branches he attacked them with growls and heavy breathing, when one was done there was no satisfied `that's that' about it, the next was a continuation of the first. `Eat,' he would say gruffly at midday, and while Maria and I did so with appetite and even dawdled over the remains, he, taking food fast and frugally himself, would be working out the next manoeuvre and getting on with that. As he could not give his foreigner the daughter's treatment, he almost entirely ignored me from the beginning of the day's work until the end. Once, suddenly, he said, 'Carolina, you don't talk.' I nearly answered, 'No, I daren't.'

Picking with Eleftheria was a party game compared. Every branch was conversational, we gossiped through our days. Then ruminatively we made tiny piles of those few olives which had escaped our sackcloth and companionably considered which of us could reach some spray of two or three remaining which we had spotted against the sky.

'Can you get at that twig? If not I might be able to pull it down this way. Careful, Carolina! You'll fall!'

'Shut up, Eleftheria. In Mr N's trees I climb and he never says a word.' Sometimes I added, 'And he doesn't tell me twenty times to eat.'

'Well, he's that sort of person. I can't help it, and if I ate what you eat I'd starve. Careful, Carolina! You're frightening me. I'll cut off that branch.' Eleftheria was rather vigorous with the saw.

'That finishes that one.' Ever cheerful, she praised the laden trees and thanked the Virgin when one or two were almost bare. She is a very religious woman, she would like to make a pilgrimage to Jerusalem. So we meandered through our topics and I would report to Mr N, 'Eleftheria and I talk all day long.'

'Ah! And tell me, how many sacks do you fill?' There was nothing formidable about him about the smiling, sleepy evenings, he was quietly paternal, he was teasing, he made his jokes and ate his supper and shut up at Athenian cocktail time. Maria is all right, I thought, the olives are all right, so are the evenings. Why then be upset if he is schizophrenic about oil?

`I had great appetite for work today,' he said once, grinning. `Did you notice that?'

`I did. You didn't say a word all day, and you didn't show much appetite for food.'

`My children eat, my mother and my wife eat, the animals eat, you're eating too. Everyone is eating. Where will the food come from if I eat as well?' But then, as he poured out the retsina, we both forked heartily into the supper dish. Evenings were evenings, a time for him to be the convivial master of his shop, a humorous tyrant at the most. Sometimes he fried meat or eggs up there himself, usually Maria brought a dish from home, and anyone around might get a forkful - there was great liberality with forks.

`Everyone is asking how you pick,' he told me.

`How do you answer?'

`Five star.' Whether or not I got a grunt all day, he was proud of having me. And everyone did ask. They were fascinated that their foreigner should stay and pick with them, they all wanted to know if a foreigner was able to pick olives - did I use a ladder? - did I climb? It meant far more than that I had written a book about them, for olives are not only to be respected but comprehensible, and I went out all day into the groves.

Suddenly there was a total reality about life - the trees, the air, the food we ate, and those faces round the walls. They took me a long time to distinguish, for the clothes are as uniform as the measures of retsina or the white coffee cups in front of them. The men wear baggy trousers, mostly faded blue, which would inevitably fall down without a belt. Their faded blue shirts when rolled up to the elbows give the impression that the bodies in them are as bronzed as any sun-bather's. A glimpse above the elbow-line, or below the V-neck, shows the skin as white as a baby's, while the crown of a bald man's head is as white as a priest's. But you rarely see that. The cap is there on every head, a part of the anatomy. Mr N's is khaki, pulled down rather low. There is tall Phanis the whitewasher, who is always jocular. He is not very tall, but his nose is long and he is taller than short Phanis who is wise. Short Phanis, pushing his cap about, sits observing and drinking his wine with a smile that is half for the company, and half for himself, and what he is thinking about is an acuter matter than what most people in Langatha are thinking.

This was a fortnight of identity. It was here, in olive-time, that I became decisive about the idea of a house. I had been hampered by a stickling attitude to ownership, but now I found the cure for that, the artistic answer to all the problems of the law, the paperwork, the future, how I felt. I would buy a ruin, make it beautiful, enjoy it, write in it and leave it to Langatha. More exactly, since you cannot leave a house to a whole village, it would eventually go to Maria - not the girl who had been whiny over foreign letters but my friend for this last fortnight in the olives. Her father was to sign the contract anyway, so I would not even have to put that in writing. If she did leave the island - which seemed unlikely - there was another daughter coming on. Mr N, who was poor, had two daughters and two sons.

Call that romanticism - it was. But the plan was also selfish, and that side made more sense. I was buying my attachment, though I would not have admitted it. There would be home-cheese for my lifetime without embarrassment. It was true that I had a brother with a family involved in this same island, but I had met them twice, briefly, in the last seven years, and the latest baby not at all. Langatha was my personal project, they lived their own life. Their faces, while these ones sharpened in my focus, shared half the unreality of VANRGKOKSUV. So I considered these things, made my decision and thought little more of it. I sat in Mr N's shop, at Eleftheria's and at Mouska's and answered that of course I climbed the trees - as high as anyone.

I was so airy that I did not even look closely at the house again, the house that Mr N had shown me, which circumstances were deciding should be mine. I kept meaning to, but had some block about it, I kept picking olives until the late afternoon before the evening when I had to leave. And during that last supper it was an effort for both Mr N and me to wrench ourselves from the subject of the season to another so conjectural.

All right, he said, he'd do his best. He'd get the owner of his chosen house to name a price. Fourteen thousand, he expected, fifteen at the most. Fine, but how much would it cost to make it habitable? As to that, he rolled his eyes. Fixing the ruin was Stage B. There was nothing more to say.

And so, since circumstances were doing what they were doing, it did not make much difference, when I got his letter some time afterwards in England, that I could not picture the house exactly or that it cost a few thousand drachmas more than Mr N had guessed. I was excited - as excited as I should be - that my `yes' could turn the dream into a fact. But in this now-or-never situation the word was there without the process of making a decision. The house was my project and I needed both.

Chapter Two

M r N was right. I stood on the tiny terrace of the house that he had chosen and looked out. Out is where you are up there, and outness is all about you. You have to lean over the wall to see the last layer of the village, two long houses in a straggle along a lower path. My path could be called the northern bypass, but I don't think that suggests a single-file line of trampling between multi-coloured banks in springtime, or a brown rib in the summer, curving out of sight at each end to meet street steps up to the platia, trodden by half a dozen villagers a day. Out here in the middle, where fields and ruins rise on the inside to the first houses that are inhabited above - all well back and not impinging - my house is solitary on the outside edge. I felt so rich in space that I thought I could be reconciled to not owing a patch of all this openness around. I would have sunrise over the mountains through my bedroom window, and sunset through my front door.

This is a panorama, real and ancient. This panorama is untaxed. Householders pay no rates in Langatha, this panorama is freely mine. Look at it - it is so well designed, you feel that the artist must in the beginning have set up this terrace for his easel while he mapped it out. Over the plain of olives the mountains need a white village on the skyline, so he put in Tholaria, wiping the brush a short way off to make a little outcrop, a tadpole's dislocated tail, and it is above the space between the two parts of the village that the mid-summer sun sets. But not behind our mountains. It sets behind Naxos, which rises slightly higher and according to the day is visible or not. And that is so with all the little islands on our horizon out beyond the bay, they loom in and fade out. Only Nikouria, the pike-backed island between us and Katapola, is always there - or almost always - and Nikouria is essential to the set. Without it our bay would be too wide-open and symmetrical, but there it is, rising off-centre from its own tail off the coastline to a jagged peak. In winter the sun sets to the left of that. Tholaria is way over to the right. I used to think that sunset was a static point.

Automatically you start looking seawards, but presently you start to swivel round, following the gorge as it rises to a meeting-point of plunging tracks at a favoured drinking-water spring. Above that, among prickly pears and boulders, the artist has placed Stroumbos, a deserted village with its few ghosts' houses - unwhitewashed stone on the rock it came from - looking as if it meant to be a message to the world. On again and upwards is the Panayia, the bright, blue-domed church of the Virgin Mary where our summer festival is held. There used to be an ancient city up above with a temple of Apollo at the top. I think that it would be excessive to have Apollo on top of my whole view.

When I arrived the hillside terraces, curling round the contours, were green with breezy corn, the poppies were being jaunty winners among the late spring flowers, and I had come to bring a ruin back to life.

It was not a total ruin, but could in times of necessity have been just habitable. We were about to turn it into one, but I did not realise that.

I had no other purpose. Everything else was given up. I had sold my car, I had renounced my typewriter and all its works. In place of those I had a house in need of renovation, I had un upstairs front door on a terrace with a panoramic view, but a small terrace, too small. `We'll fix that,' said Mr N.

Fix that? How? Its walls are a continuation of the kitchen walls beneath it. How can such a terrace be enlarged? `But Carolina, this whole old one has to go.'

But -. But what? Let's have it now. What am I committing myself to?

First things first. The shell of this house is built in stone and mud, with mud and straw plaster crumbling off the walls. The beams are juniper branches, no one knows how old, sagging beneath slabs of slate, as timeless and undatable. I like this ceiling. But Carolina, it won't do. It harbours insects, it's too low. And sooner or later the whole roof will fall in. It will have to come down to the lintels, we can leave the corners, corners are expensive in working hours and we're interested in economy - are we not? - but these old wormy wooden lintels will not do. They'll be replaced in concrete, and for the ceiling there'll be new beams - chestnut from Mount Athos - and new boards. We'll make a tour and see who has what and at what price.

So we're giving this house a new roof. And then, what next? Can we leave this nice bumpy mud-and-straw plaster floor? Bah! Besides, those old branch beams and slate slabs underneath are no better than above. You can't have a new ceiling without demolishing the upper floor. That goes for the kitchen too - another reason for pulling down the terrace. How can a floor be kept if there's no support below? And don't forget, this house is going to need a *cabiné* - with real modern lavatory seat, you hear? That will go in place of the old oven, we'll dig a pit, wall up the opening into the kitchen and give the *cabiné* an outside door. And when we've built that up, the new terrace can stretch over the full length of both.

I see, we're just going to pull this house to pieces and put it together again. And how much, tell me, will that cost?

No one did tell me that.

Mr N demonstrated his whole-heartedness about being my commander by walking me down to Ormos on May Day to talk to Nikolaras the president, chiefly about cement. `President' is the grand modern title for the headman of Aiyiali, who used, more appropriately perhaps, to be called mayor. It's his business to agitate with the powers that be in Athens, trying to persuade them that all the facilities of Katapola do not mean one whit to us, and that the people cannot confine their illnesses to seasons when there is a doctor stationed at Ormos. On the spot Nikolaras is noticeable as the owner of the one large shop in the port, a shop where you need courage to face what seems to be astonishment mixed with annoyance if you want to be a customer. But he's straight, Mr N was telling me. Business is business with him. And I, ignorant with the Who's Who of suppliers, did my sums along the path and followed in obedience.

I had three hundred pounds to last me and my building works until the autumn, when - obviously - I would have to earn some more. Even in 1972 that bordered on the ludicrous, but not so nearly in Aiyiali as elsewhere. Here I was accustomed to the sort of poverty that seems like richness, neither sponging nor deprived. Apart from the mayor's house with its palatial feeling and low rent, I had a room - a cottage almost, for it was detached - behind the beach in the fields of Laki, where the owner had discovered that he was growing his fruit and vegetables on potential tourist ground, and was planting rooms to let as well. A twelve-year-old daughter Irene, with four younger sisters coming along, provided without much discussion the happy exchange of English lessons for my midday room and a plate of food. I found so little reason for spending money on myself that most of my three hundred pounds would go into the wages and materials that nowadays, when we talk about the prices, make us hysterical. We do that often - it's a favourite conversation - boasting of our achievements, bewailing what we postponed.

The pound was having a low season at seventy two drachmas, but that bought two bags of cement with four dracs over for two drinks. A master builder's wage was two hundred and fifty, and a workman's one fifty, with no social security for the employer on Amorgos. Four-metre beams, from Mount Athos though they might be, were under two hundred, and so the list went - not totally derisive to my hopefulness.

Then we came to carriage. My optimism was running along like a fitful-fever chart. If you must situate your dream house in a village like Langatha, then you must pay for the reality. The cement and lime boats could dock at our old harbour, but it was wonderful to look about our shops and think that all the ordinary wares had been landed by caique, and that every single item not created in the village had come to it on mule- or donkey-back, or else by hand. Only if the laborious business of loading at the harbour and walking back uphill behind your burdens, sometimes all day long, should bring you to death's door, would you be so lucky as to get a helicopter ride.

Mr N was dinning into me the amount that I would spend on carriage, and making calculations of his own, the tightness of my budget inspiring him with economical ideas. There was plenty of work to be done before a master builder need be called and I could help with that, while he would hire himself as a workman at a reduced rate - he'd knock thirty drachmas off. And as we could not have the house-fund being squandered on my stomach, there was the matter of food to be considered too. A few days later he said to me, `Don't cook.' We needed every drachma - didn't we? - for the house. Then, having put his own affairs in order, he raised a pickaxe and demolished the roof.

I had been warned. I had given my assent, but when I approached by the steep path from above I stood riveted and rattling as though Mr N had never breathed a word of this. No warning can make you feel placid at the moment when you have an aerial view of a figure with a pickaxe on the roof of your own new possession hacking it to bits. One other workman was hired at this point, it did not take them long. Well, I had always talked of buying a ruin, now I had one. When they had hauled the lintels off, the walls - like the walls of all good ruins - were jagged and forlorn.

But I was not forlorn once I was heaving stones myself. Every morning I came down early to be workman's donkey, with all the enthusiasm of olive days again.

Something about the law of cubic capacity seemed to have gone wrong. How could one roof and four wall-tops produce so much stuff? The steps up to the terrace had been buried, and when you had clambered up and reached the opening for a door, you could only get inside by clambering on. Slate, stones, pads of seaweed, dried mud and broken branches, filled the two upper rooms, but 'room' was a euphemism now, and there was none left in the sense of space. The total length, eight metres, was cut through by a dividing wall as thick as the outside ones, nearly one full metre, making a sturdy obstacle between two crammed compartments of chaos.

But the ingredients of chaos can be useful. Even the dried mud, which covered everything in cakes and powder, was to be used again. The whole business became one huge game of patience, of clearing corners to pile materials in categories waiting to be built back into place. Few new houses are built in stone and mud these days, but old walls can only be built up in their old style. The second workman set up a great sieve across one corner to sieve the earth for new mud pies.

Only the old branch beams were lifted off and set apart, to be carried up to Mr N's yard opposite his house. He said, 'When you stay here in the winter you'll light a fire downstairs,' and there was a snug thought for some distant season - I owned a fireplace and a supply of wood. But these lower quarters, which corresponded exactly to the upper ones, had their own entrance and did not concern us that year except as a storehouse for cement and sand.

Their curly old wooden lintels were pronounced immortal - the master builder's word. And this was fortunate, since replacing those in concrete would have meant rebuilding the whole house. I often noticed that what was judged essential coincided with what was feasible.

`It's midday - come,' said Mr N after each morning's work. On the first day I was unenthusiastic as we walked up to his house. In my bewilderment I wanted to get back to the mayor's. I wanted to sit on the balcony and gasp and ponder privately on what was being done. And now, unless I caused offence, I was to be deprived. But when we had passed through his little courtyard asquawk with hens and children, where his aged mother sat motionless morning, afternoon and evening, I realised in the kitchen that I was to be handed the billy-can to carry on. His wife, who is bony-faced with a sweet smile, was ladling it half full with the day's fare. Mr N said, `Stop, you know Carolina won't eat more,' not grudgingly but being practical.

`What! Only so much?'

`It's all she'll eat. Cut her some cheese. You've got bread? Now get home. Back to work in a couple of hours, and tonight come to the shop.'

His wife thought it unfriendly to send me off with the billy-can alone, but it was his instruction that I should eat in peace. This was my first contact that I remember with this woman, who suffered much and seldom flinched. She was always working, with four children, a mother-in-law, hens, pigs and sometimes rabbits to look after, and a tyrant husband who sweated through a change or two of underwear a day. Yet, perhaps because he was so little of a home-lover, she found little incentive to present him with what looked like a home. Mr N's vegetable mother was revered, his baby was adored, so was his dog. His older children were given eulogies when they weren't listening, and only his wife - whom he had taken without a dowry - got neither kindness nor respect. It made me sad to see that, but there was nothing to be done except to take him as he was to me and be appreciative to her.

I carried the billy home and did my daily best with it in stipulated peace. It was always good. Broad beans were in season and we had those regularly, cooked in the pods with spring onion and fresh dill. Sometimes there was meat and sometimes fish. It was good, but in spite of Mr N's injunctions there was too much of it. I knew that I was depriving not his family but his pigs in throwing leftovers away, but I could not return the leftovers or eat them in the evening, for then I ate with Mr N. So I had a minor conflict with the billy every day, and that was a distraction from more formidable affairs. Imminently, we were going to employ two master builders. Immediately, we were to send a caique to fetch the notary public from Katapola.

Mr N had hoped that our local contract, drawn up by the scribe, would do until the notary happened to call in. But our policeman must have been having modern or high-handed notions, for he refused to give a building permit until the official contract had been signed. It was Maria's business to go down with the mule at eight o'clock one morning and wait for the caique until the middle of the afternoon. Patience is the greatest virtue in a child. She was not expected to need time-passing occupations to help her through those hours. She was also woken at four-thirty the next morning to lead the notary away. And yet it was considered as munificence deserving several exclamations that when I had parted with about two thousand drachmas for the contract, she got one hundred for her own day's wage as well. I was understanding about drops in oceans on the day when Mr N became the official owner of my house, free to order as many builders as he pleased.

But do we really need two master builders? Only for two days. We want to make a good start - don't we? - and it won't be more expensive in the end. Dimitris will stay with us, we're lucky to get him, but the point is that we have to sweeten Spiros, because we want to use his water for the building works. Yes, my well has water, but the bottom's full of muck and rubble, and anyway it's cracked. It will have to be cleaned out in the autumn and cemented round the sides. That's no problem, you wear your rubber boots, put down a ladder, and there you are. But do I realise what this well is - what it means to me? Why, to build another like it would cost the price of the whole house. With this one I could have half a dozen friends to stay and there'd be water for a year - so long, that is, as there hadn't been a drought. A dry winter is the householder's worst headache. After the olives, pray for the rain.

My terminology is sometimes questioned, but while a deep hole in the ground containing water may correctly be a cistern, my deep hole has always been a well. A cistern may be anywhere, it may be a metal box, but not on Amorgos, where bending and pulling up the buckets one is first of all aware of depth, though the roof is the aquaduct and the source is in the sky. A lucky housewife has the opening of her well, let us call it, in the kitchen. Mine was outside on the path. Everyone's is precious, no one casually gives or asks for water rights. This one of Spiros, which Mr N was after, was a bad-water well in a patch of wilderness a short scramble up from mine, in no way useful to his house. But for his favour we had to call him in for two days, for the compliment and to share the blessing feast.

You cannot build a house without having it blessed, and I would have been doubtful, without my master-in-command, about the etiquette. The second workman and I were set to clearing the way for the eighty-year-old priest, right through into what was optimistically called the bedroom, ten square metres still half full of rubble, where we were to hold the ceremony.

Mr N kept disappearing and coming back with the essential properties. He brought *loukoumi* - Turkish delight, but that's not a tactful name in Greece -, a bottle of ouzo, glasses, and a broken table which he propped up in the one flat space and covered with a piece of cloth. Its careful dressing was not due to the refreshments, but to turn it into an altar with an incense pot.

Mr N's wife and Maria, not missing the occasion, were bringing an early round of `*kalo riziko* - good destiny!' the greeting that is used for contracts, building works and christenings. Maria even let her hair loose - the only time that I ever saw it so spectacular - over a scarlet dress. The working gang assembled - Dimitris our long-term master builder, sturdy, ponderous and middle-aged,

39

Spiros and two other workmen besides Mr N. The priest was summoned and helped in, very nearly with applause. He came with the kindly smiles and grunts of the elderly who are hard of hearing, and with admiration of my view. Everyone, somehow, found standing room, and I was encouraged to perch above them and take photographs.

Photographs! I want them. But there is so much murk down there.

The upper, outer world around me was a dazzle from Tholaria to the Panayia, and I with my head in sunshine was looking down into a cell, where - to the chanting of an aged Christian priest in scarlet robes - the figures were about to enact a pagan ritual. Caps in hands, the working men looked unfamiliar, almost undressed, and a good deal of laughter mixed itself with head-bowing respect. Mr N's hair was a thick, dark stubble. Dimitris' was thin and grey. What I did not see was a live cock.

Why had the commander crowded us into this small cell? The first room is much bigger, four to five metres square - roughly speaking, for you cannot find a right-angle. Why did the commander not choose the larger room? There were nine of us with the baby, the altar took the space for two, and the priest had need of plenty, for swinging his incense-burner on its chain. Only years later it came flashing at me that this house has a door and window facing north, south, east and west, and that Dimitris stood at the one window that catches the rising sun. What ancient priest made sacrifice to any deity from any position in his temple but towards the east?

I was perching on a broken wall at the south-east corner having my house blessed. The priest was chanting my name into the liturgy with Mr N's. He was offering an icon round the circle, crossing Mr N's forehead with holy water, I was called down to make my kiss and kneel for my cross. Kneeling is outside the ritual, but the priest could not have reached my forehead otherwise. The walls were sprinkled, incense wafted, neighbours put their hands around the doorway, I climbed up to click again. Suddenly, at the climatic moment, Dimitris pulled something feathered from his jacket, raised a ferocious instrument, shaped like a pickaxe, hammer-sized, and all together there came a squawk, a bang and a flurry and a burst of *kalo riziko*! Dimitris crossed the window-sill with blood, took a trowel of mud from Mr N and embedded a twenty-drachma piece beneath our new foundation stone.

Then, without delaying over his ouzo and *loukoumi*, or the coffee that Mr N's wife had hurried off to make, Dimitris called for the workmen to be working and swung himself onto the wall.

Away from the windows there were a few beams left for scaffolding, he had no other aid. `You're an acrobat!' The swing-up took me by surprise. He smiled, not as if receiving a compliment but his due. From then on, watching him daily, I realised what a man we had. `I have more confidence in Dimitris,' said Mr N, `than in myself.'

The evening was for the cock-feast, and I, in a helpless way, was being lady munificent. The cock had turned into a succulent red stew, prepared under Mr N's supervision by his wife. He always said that he had taught her how to cook. My business was only to be present and to pay, but at cost price, for we were interested in economy - were we not? The dusty figures raised their glasses in endless rounds of *kalo riziko*, and Mr N - all jollity that night - received as many of them as I. I sat, beheld, laughed and drank for courage, totting up the day's wages and trying not to tot up the number of days there would be wages for.

But since I am responsible for this table, let me enjoy my evening of munificence. At all times in the glory and in the horror of what I am allowing to be done, let me remember that this is fun. Let me be grateful that at the yes-or-no moment in the winter I did not realise what I was embarking on. It is a great thing to be turning an old ruin into a house, giving a desolate area some whitewashed walls, and ultimately - since I am so relying on Mr N - leaving it to the first daughter, who ties her hair into one waist-length plait, does not 'take letters', and will always be an islander on Amorgos. That is the logical end to this whole enterprise.

Chapter Three

That night I was *afendikos*, the boss, but very often I was not. Who was who throughout the next stage might often have confused us if we had not exchanged our roles with such local adaptability. Sometimes as *afendikos* I was asked in formal language how I wanted this or that, and the next moment - `Carolina! A bucket of water!' - I was the bottom donkey. Sometimes Mr N was *afendikos*, not only as commander but as the official owner, with firm ideas about the reconstruction plan. He did not ask me if I wanted my walls raised fifteen or twenty centimetres - perhaps he was afraid I would say no - so up they went. But since he was also hiring himself as labourer, he would be shouted at as soon as he had finished shouting at Dimitris. And so we moved in our triangle, now and then confabulating on one level.

`I like niches. Don't fill in that niche.' - `I like irregularities. Don't worry that the lines aren't straight.' That's the nicest thing about rebuilding, the result is bound to be an old house in spite of the cement. Dimitris wondered what I could be up to. In my country was there a house like this? In my country did we carry water from a well, or make a trek through fields for drinking water from a public tap? Did we not have every facility that the Langathans lack? And yet I had come here to build my house.

The drinking water runs in a trickle when it needs repumping from the gorge, but it's a pleasant place for practising one's village patience, and I shared that chore with Maria, my equal or superior in the role of errand boy. I never minded being sent about the village - in my country I was never so completely exercised. 'Are you working with the builders, Carolina? How's it going?' In my country you can't have conversation in all directions through the streets, we're traffic-conscious, sticking to the right or left. And I would not welcome being sent off by my own workmen to buy their cigarettes. At Mouska's returning the daily answers to the daily questions, I think my errands fun.

'Are you working, Carolina? Are you working?' When Mouska asks a question it usually comes twice, and a favourite one will be repeated for its season as regularly as the ouzo or the coffee that it goes with, or the bundle stuffed into my bag. Am I working? You can see I am. It's not my habit in Langatha to run round in cut-off jeans - not because of any great decision, but it's not that sort of village, I never think of it. However, if I happen to be working with the building gang and one of them asks me for cigarettes, I do not - as perhaps I ought to - hastily change into a skirt. It's no good these people calling me a real *Langathiani* - I'm not. If I were I'd carry my trousers in the olive season to change into among the trees. Even teenage girls do that.

'Carolina! Where have you been dawdling?' These men could make me feel like a truant when I came back. I did not mind the workmen shouting at me, when that was balanced with *afendikos*, and anyway Greek shouting is not English shouting but a method of communication, between married couples, between children and their grandparents, among all alike. I would remind myself of that every time that Mr N's wife gave him a cup of coffee, and it was once or twice a day that she brought a tray down from the house. Greeks don't thank their wives for cups of coffee, as a rule. And in familiar circles Greeks make orders, not requests.

I had been prepared for working-hour surliness from Mr N, but there was none of that, he was the man that I knew every evening in his shop. When he seized a pickaxe and attacked the stones like a small tiger, he might growl as in the olive trees but in good humour, though he was earning the lowest wage of all. Perhaps it made him jaunty to be commander of the builder he was working for. I saw that he was my most dynamic workman while he was being one, and privately I totted up his daily losses for future recompense. Every now and then he made it his prerogative to be absent for some hours, at least it was either that - prerogative for time off - or for the mysterious demands of his commandership. I hardly knew of all the intricacies that were going on, I had not learned that gravel was gathered in the gorge, or who was beaten down and quarrelled with over the carriage of sand, which comes on an hour's journey from the second beach. Mr N did not care whom he offended, he fell out with his own brother, which did not bother him or me - I did not have to offend or quarrel with anyone. Then after absent time he would reappear with a roar and perhaps a cream cheese, calling us down from our walls for a round of drinks and joke-cracking, and equally suddenly charge at the next rock, demanding why we were all sitting about.

`Come on, Carolina, you're *afendikos*, tell me what to do.' Dimitris, a plainer, blunter man, would sit down in irritation whenever an irregularity prevented him from getting on with his work. Every day he would complain about the mess of rubble and dirt. 'When you build in brick you sing all day.' He was widely in demand, he could have gone elsewhere and built in brick, but every day he came to grumble in the mud again. Why then did he do it? 'I took it on,' he said. 'Besides, you treat us well.' He might have added that it was convenient, for his house was the one below mine, he could go in one minute for the midday meal, I could wave to him if he was standing on his roof. Later on I was invited there sometimes, and everything spread out between us - food and wine - came from his own land and animals. He was as much a farmer as a builder, which was one of our natural complications. Mr N was always emphasising that neither Dimitris nor he himself would be available for one day's work during the threshing in July, and both were out by daybreak, going to whatever goats or fields required them, making mid-morning of eight-o'clock building time.

My smallest workman, Stelios, was my oldest - nearly seventy - and it seemed as if the smallness and the oldness went together in a shrivelling of age. He had an apologetic smile, and arms dangling out of proportion to his trunk, he would have been a natural for the early silent films. One morning four of us walked to Vassilis for eight beams, and I was wondering if I could manage one on each shoulder like the rest - they were a solid weight. Stelios lined up in second place. Suddenly he had scooped up four and marched away, leaving the third man and me with one beam each. After that I always wanted Stelios on the site. 'It's the old ones,' Mr N said, 'who are tough.'

In Aiyiali you may wait a year or two for action, and then the happening comes all at once. Our walls were level above concrete lintels, the new patches recognisable by the pinkness of fresh mud. Dimitris was building the final layer around the beam ends, we had a whole, evenly-spaced skeleton along the top. Michalis the carpenter was issuing planks as from a factory, always in a harrassment of planing as we came up for the next batch, but always careful to incise a single groove of moulding on the inside of each edge. Gravel for the roof arrived from one direction, sand from the other, and every time I heard the hooves and heavy breathing and rushed out with the bottles I grew more doubtful about my three hundred pounds, scratching my mind to think of sources for a loan.

Sand and gravel are the price of carriage, paid for with the weekly wages. Timber and cement, like the lime that would be following, are bills allowed to mount. Mr N would say it was turning his hair grey getting all the materials assembled and the men to work. I would retaliate with my financial problems, which were not his business. It took me time to realise how justified he was whenever he spoke of his grey hairs. They are a natural threat to anyone in Aiyiali who undertakes to build a house. If you have every essential ingredient but one and the island has run out of that, you can do nothing until the unpredictable day when, say, Astypalaia has sent out its lime caique or Chalkis made a shipment of cement. By the time that that arrives, whatever else you had before may have dried up or blown away, or been begged by someone else, and when you have finally accumulated all your precious piles you have probably moved into a new season on the land and do not have the hands to work.

Yet under my commander in May 1972 we did not have one day's delay for lack of materials in the spot.

It was in the evenings that he talked about his grey hairs and the next step, and anyone who had been working might join in. So might anyone who had not. Those evenings gave completeness to the day and then I would rejoice that my commander, one might say, was the landlord of the local pub. At work few of the men wore watches, no one counted working hours, they stopped when a piece of work was done, or when dusk fell, often after longer than eight hours - with the exception of the youngest, who ate lunch twice a day. In the evenings it seemed as if our working progress could not stop. Dimitris, who was a Mouska man, changed his habits and dropped in. In olive season everyone talks about the olives, and so it was now, we were building and that was what we talked about.

Langatha had been my place for hermit summers, but I fell extremely easily into the new way of life. I liked being one of the boys, as near as could be - more nearly at any rate than one of the women. I knew that tall Phanis the whitewasher and short Phanis who was wise were adding their views to everyone else's on my walls and my roof, and that if I had not come one evening I would have been missed. Of course I liked having my place in Mr N's shop. He liked it as well. He had control of Langatha's only foreigner, who happened to be a young woman, with long legs and fair hair.

`My first daughter,' he would say. It was the only silly thing he ever said, though I daresay he was getting into practice at fourteen. It was just a cover for other inclinations, which became my life's new problem, but I suppose they were inevitable. Initially he had been so proper that I optimistically hoped that he - a sailor once - might prove the exception to the sailor's rule. In one way he was. He never molested me, he never made me afraid to be left alone with him at night, and it often happened that while he was making an enigma of the sand or the cement the others would gradually go off to bed, leaving us - late by Langatha time - alone over our wine. Then the licit discussion might carry us through until we followed, saying goodnight and parting ways right there in the *platia*, but sometimes he could not shut his shop without a round of the illicit argument.

Now I've had it. Now he'll be offended and walk out, and what shall I do without my commander on the site?

Keep things as they are. Keep things as they have been. Desperately I wanted to keep things as static as they never can be kept. I knew that I was too reliant on this villager, I knew that I should never allow the familiarity to grow beyond the point where it had grown, I had an abhorrence of its turning into anything but what it was - what it had been. One of the boys! I wanted my place at his table, but to keep apart. And so, refusing to give him what he asked for, I tried to play the fairy godmother, to buy my security by offering the only other thing I had to give eventually - a house. I was not altering my plan because of Mr N's approaches, but because of them I thrust it at him, I wanted him to know it and accept it, and shut up.

Nonsense, he said, he had no lack of houses, though I knew he had none habitable but the one he was living in. He had houses, he insisted. His hair was going grey, but he would not have it thought by anyone that he had an ulterior motive for letting it go grey. My house was mine, the law would change, it would be mine on paper too. Every drachma that I put into his hands was recorded and accounted for, he did not want one thing in compensation for more than workman's work. Not one thing? There was one thing he did want.

Hell hell hell - have a house. Won't you eventually accept a house? I want your commandership but not your bounty. Do not give me obligations. I want to be the fairy godmother.

`But Carolina -'

Here we go. `But' was another turn around the circle, and I did not walk out in the middle, it seemed better to let the words exhaust themselves. `Never mind,' he said then. `Everything else remains the same.' I wished there need not be an `else' about it, but it did not prevent me from being at that table the next evening, or from carrying on as if nothing had been said. And now we were approaching roof-day. Deviations do not go with roofs.

While the planks were being hammered into place across the beams, I had been having pleasant ponderings about seaweed. Seaweed is the traditional next layer for island roofs, so my pictures were not purely picturesque or fanciful. Was I to be sent down unaided to the beach? However many sacks were to be filled? Spring was turning into summer, workman's beach day would be fun. Then I got my instructions. The seaweed order was for as many cardboard boxes as I could scrounge - not as containers, but to take the place of seaweed, this was

1972. So I went all round the village begging cardboard boxes - each shop had a few. Tinned milk comes in the toughest. The flimsiest hold paper napkins, commercial rusks and loo paper. And I was jogging round Langatha being concerned with the quality of cardboard.

Above my flattened boxes we returned to ancient correctitude with a layer of earth. That was the remains of what came down with the old roof, carefully preserved to be laid back again, for I did not own a handful that was not precious to the little circle that Mr N had allotted to a future lemon tree. I was always trying to pretend that I did not mind not owning one small field or patch of hillside, but how could I not mind? Mr N would say, `Don't worry', he'd begin exerting pressure on a neighbour, but we both knew how people cling to their own plots and patches, whether of earth or gorse or rock.

Right now his head was buzzing. He'd got the materials for the roof, he had the men, a Sunday permit, and nothing more to do here but to hammer wooden bars for handles onto empty olive cans, or honey cans, for carrying wet concrete. He was exhausted, but don't think he could rest. He had his own life - didn't he? - with burdens in neglected heaps. On Saturday I could be a tourist, I could go swimming, I could sleep - not he. He'd be up and off at four, riding into the mountains to round up goats. It was fortunate that we had Saturday to wait.

Why Sunday for the roof? That's simple. You can't throw a roof in stages. It's a single operation needing six men - strong ones - and what other day would you find six strong men available? For did I realise how they would be working? Twenty five kilos of wet concrete go into those cans. And Sunday in Langatha is not overtime. Mind you, a roof is reckoned as a day's work, whether eight hours or six or four - no niggling either way. It begins at daybreak and goes straight on to the end. `Don't be late,' was Mr N's Saturday goodnight.

We gathered too early for the photographs the workers wanted with a round of ouzo and *loukoumi* - a mellow-sounding kick-off but the mixture seems to be a dose of stamina. Besides, it's etiquette. The stamina was needed - I kept our metal barrel full of water and that was tiring enough. What the men were doing might well lay out the average English labourer. The way up to the roof was a plank from Spiros' plot across the path, I tried it empty-handed and it gave me vertigo. The concrete was mixed, very wet, in the middle of the path, sloshed into the cans, slung onto the shoulders and erectly carried up. On top it is the master builder's business to do the ramming down, for he is also calculating how the rain water will drain. Dimitris found the continuous roof-work hot. The others thought he had the easy job.

Kalo riziko for the roof - at eleven o'clock, less than a fortnight after the first blow of the pickaxe. Automatically that meant another feast - goat for the roof and for a Sunday evening, roast on the spit. *Kalo riziko* for Mr N and *kalo riziko* for me. We toasted each other with an exchange of the same greeting, and which of us was presiding at the table was doubtful once again. I was thoroughly enjoying myself, but I was not enjoying my predicament. I had to go to Athens to raise funds and find myself a job. On the first of October I would have to be at work, a teacher with no more Maytime on the island for two years.

Now Mr N began digging out the old oven beside the kitchen to make a cess-pit for our *cabiné*. I said, `You need a donkey. That's my business.' I could not dig a whole cess-pit but I could clear the way. He said, `It's your business to get money. Go to Athens, we can do without you here.' We were talking as if money was to be found drifting in the streets.

Who would go to Athens? It's lovely here on Amorgos in May. Sometimes I go swimming - I'm *afendikos* and take this liberty - in the afternoons. Who would go to Athens and do unwholesome chores?

But I had asked for it, and this was a good time for a journey, before it got too hot and while the house was back to needing only workman's work. Mr N could dig a cess-pit and pull my terrace down, but I did not want to be absent while one stone or concrete block was going up.

Yes, concrete blocks - at the end of my stone house. I had been persuaded that we had to use them for the *cabiné*'s two new walls. The oven was a small one. Stone eats space. You might get your lavatory seat inside the old walls but you could hardly turn to sit on it. If we used concrete blocks we could put in a shower too. A shower? Yes, why not? All you need is a water tank on the terrace, just enough for several buckets, and a pipe-hole with a tap.

I hurried off to Athens, forbidding my commander to start on anything so revolutionary while I was away. At least I was able to stay with the deus-ex-machina sister's godmother's grand-daughter Meriel who had moved there with a spare bed in her flat.

I did not like to give the impression that I could simply go off, sweep up my pile and come back with a loaded purse, but though I did secure two hundred pounds and the promise of a job, that was not a breath-taking achievement during an absence of ten days. And I need not have been afraid of building development in excess. The time lapse was enough for island workers, in island fashion, to turn towards the land. When I cabled Mr N that I was coming, both he and Dimitris were harvesting their corn.

The cable was the beginning of a new tradition. Day or night or early hours, sleep or work regardless, Mr N, with a mule and donkey, was always at the port when I came in. He never joined the crowd around the landing stage, he would be lurking somewhere behind a pillar or round a corner to be hunted out. Then he would allow a quiet greeting and a quiet drink before the ride up, talking spasmodically at the bottom and non-stop towards the top. In those early days I answered by protesting - I could order Markos the muleteer, if not walk. He retorted that I could not. Carolina pay for a stranger to collect her? That would be neither correct nor economical. Besides, he was my man on Amorgos. The system was so pleasant that I shut up.

The area of my quarrel with Mr N was rarely enough opened that it never made me not want to be met.

Compared to many Greeks he was unusually forebearing, and he never needed fighting off except with words.

Now the first subject of his satisfaction was that he had set up our lime works, in a waste area a short way along the path. There was such a quantity of bubbling lime, being stirred by ancient Stelios with an oar far longer than himself, that for a moment my reaction was the wrong one - alarm coming out more strongly than delight. 'Don't be silly,' Mr N said. 'This house needs to be plastered, doesn't it? Don't talk about "later on". We could get to "later on" and have no lime. That's one weight off my back.' He had a habit of looking over his shoulder as if there ought to be a burden towering above.

I could not blame him. It was on the programme for me to be living in this house in August, when the owners of the mayor's wanted my old quarters for themselves. And now we were in June with harvesting, to be followed by the threshing, and our building - in no sense - had an end. The end was the *cabiné* with two walls missing, an open pit beside the path. The main part of the house was a shell with a front door you couldn't get to, for we were pulling down the terrace, and with no floor inside the front door, for that was going too. The kitchen was a walled but roofless rubble heap with two broken openings for doors, the far one leading onto a piece of hillside, where we needed to raise scaffolding, belonging to a neighbour who refused to sell.

If you do not own the land outside your door, may that door be opened? May you sit on your own doorstep dangling out your feet? I was having some natural optimism about our whole predicament, but - hang the scaffolding - this piece drove me crazy, I had to be able to walk out of my door, to own one patch of the outside - that strip right there with a wall along the bottom, not much to ask for, no longer than my house. I needed it, if only for a washing line. Mr N kept bullying the owner, but she was adamant. Her mother and forebears had owned that strip of land.

At the end of the first week of June, when the last poppies were wilting and the island was hastily turning brown, Dimitris began coming back to us. That is to say, he entered into a convenient coming-and-going way of life, prepared to alternate being a farmer with being a builder until threshing time. Mr N, who owned less land, was delighted, for we had exact need of a spasmodic builder. We did not, for instance, need one to bear the twisty branch beams of the lower ceiling, but no one else could be responsible for the major amputation that came next.

We had a heat wave on the way, but it was not heat inside our sun-resistent theatre that made the builder and the commander sweat in silence, and each tell me later how much sweat. Through hours of tension they knocked the stones surrounding each beam end away, and nothing that might have slipped did slip. I looked up at my new ceiling high above, thinking it a pity - if the house was going to fall down - that we had given it that pretty woodwork first. When it had not fallen down, when it stood as a six-metre trunk with holes round the midriff, Dimitris judged that it would take a six-force earthquake to make it budge. And after it had proved itself so enduring they used up every stone available to build two colossal buttresses outside.

The order of events might be eccentric, but I found it reassuring. I liked to know that my house was not upstanding only because of the strength of buttresses. Besides, we could not have built them in anticipation because it was almost on the day of the operation that my neighbour finally gave in and parted with the strip of hillside where they were to stand. I think that in the end she did so only to escape the pressure of being hounded by anyone so merciless as Mr N. *Kalo riziko* again! That was another seventeen hundred drachmas, which I have never been so glad to spend. It's peanuts now, but it was a chunk from my new fund.

Eating opens the appetite, I am always being told. I had enlarged my property on one side and now other itchy feelings were coming at me from the area of ruins across the path. Don't be silly, I kept saying, packing them away.

I was always on the path now, flaying dried bamboos. They arrived in rattling sheaves from orchards in the plain, where they grow as windbreaks in their lifetime and for ceilings afterwards. My downstairs rooms were to be low and homely, bamboos are homely, but the job of cleaning off the husky wrappings - a pleasant starter - is a winner for monotony as it goes on. To prevent your master builder shouting that he is idle-handed or your commander that he can do it three times faster, you must never let your knife slow into focus, but wielding it with a smooth wrist, like a drummer's, work down the joints until your bamboo shines, and seize another with no pause for admiration or calculation of how you're getting on.

Sometimes I raised my head to look out at the hazy sea below, and each long June day bleached my hair another shade before I left my station for a sundown swim. `How many bamboos did you clean today?' Mr N would ask at suppertime. My wrist ached and I had beaten everyone, not for how many but how few.

Another question, from another workman, was what colour I would paint my beautiful bamboo. He was told severely that it would have exactly the same treatment as the beams and boarded ceiling, which meant oil first and then matt varnish, and they would hardly change appearance, only glow. I was rebelling against tradition when it came to wood. Paint my beams and boards and bamboos green or blue? I would not so insult them. And I would have a wooden floor upstairs, wood that looked like wood.

This house would have to have some doors and windows sometime too. It would be a formidable order for Michalis the carpenter to carry out by August, and afterwards a formidable bill for a teacher to pay off.

Everything was happening fast again. The *cabiné* had a floor. We secured our concrete blocks and gave it walls. It had a concrete lintel, the kitchen had two more, the walls were level, the kitchen beams were going up, bamboos were being hammered, I was back to scrounging cardboard boxes - stop! I was an errand boy in danger of forgetting who was *afendikos*.

This is crazy. There are three steps down to the kitchen, but the *cabiné* is level with the path. If its walls aren't higher I won't be able to stand up inside.

Dimitris said, `But aren't you going to sit down?'

So we had a great palaver about the requirements for men and women inside a *cabiné*, and whether they minded bending their heads to take a shower. That was all very well, Dimitris said, but his aim was to keep the terrace flat.

`Why? Raise the *cabiné* and give the terrace a step up.'

`But Carolina -'

`The moment you have a step, someone will sit on it.' All the better, it would be a terrace with two decks. It didn't even matter that the snub end of my house would be an upsticking concrete box, for Mr N had promised me a lemon tree with a rounded wall in front of that.

The all-round dimensions of the terrace provoked the most intense of our three-cornered arguments. Mr N became impassioned about every centimetre we could gain - we were interested in economy but this was something I was doing once in my life. Dimitris was heavy about every problem because of the expense, in case I blamed him afterwards, and I insisted on a compromise because - fortunately - I liked it best. The lower deck was wide, the upper narrowed, my whole ship's prow eased off in the direction of the sea. Or else it could be said - and in due time it was said - that the terrace gave my pigeon wings, but a house needs to be whitewashed before it qualifies for pigeonship.

At the time of those discussions we were standing not so much on one part of a terrace as on the kitchen ceiling, with our feet placed carefully where there were beams, and with a downward view on the outside that could be a killer to anyone inclined to suicide or vertigo. The land beneath us fell so sharply that from across the gorge my house looked like a mansion, but on the village side it was a cottage on the path. And my terrace - aerial one way - was also on a level with the only house that might ever be impinging, an appealing piece of desolation that was giving me a daily turmoil.

The wall along the bottom of that property ran parallel to mine, and my terrace looked over into the courtyard of that house. Rather, it was two houses, a complex of crumbling buildings with three small fields beside, and one of the complications of my life was that the nearest room, which shared one wall with the main house but was blocked off from it with its own entrance on the path, was actually mine.

I did not need an annex across the way, but it had come in one lot with my house. It was a useless burden to me, and fairly useless by itself, one large room made prison-like behind a wall two metres from its door. From my terrace I saw that it had no business but to be opened up into the opposite estate. I also saw that whole area as a threat.

Suppose some bourgeois Athenian bought it, suppose almost anybody bought it, they would play their transistors, have parties and babies, I would be agonised. If that house was for sale, no one ought to buy it but me or mine. And it was infuriating that I had a brother who for once in a lifetime had a fund for such a project, who was planning this very summer to put that into a house, here in Aiyiali, but not beside me - down there, just above the beach. From my terrace I could just make out which line of hillside was covered with his sand. We could fire signals, we ought to open a funicular. Upstairs and downstairs was the summer life for us. How delightful. Damn.

But if this next-door house should be for sale, and if my brother were to buy it, then we would be joint owners of one complete estate. Of course, the chances were against it, since so few houses are for sale. I would do well to get Mr N to make inquiries, so that I could be told that it was not, or at least that it was owned by several sisters scattered round the world. Then I could get on with my own business, then I could stop being so obsessed.

But I could not. Mr N told me without asking that the house had a sole owner, one Katina whom I knew myself. Every year she brought her family from Athens to spend the summer with her mother, my neighbour on the far side of the next field, who had only to be asked if the daughter ever spoke of selling the lower property. And that same evening he reported that she had pronounced Katina willing - so specifically that she quoted twenty three thousand drachmas, just over three hundred pounds. We were both taken by surprise.

One fortnight after Dimitris had come back to work we celebrated the throwing of the terrace with our third feast. You can throw a pot, so why not roofs and terraces? Watching the workmen, you hardly think their idiom metaphorical. As soon as the concrete had hardened, just as I predicted, we all sat down on the step that raised the deck. We looked from Nikouria to Tholaria and to the Panayia, and we all wowed. Carolina, they said, we have made you the finest viewpoint in Langatha. And people have been saying that ever since. But I was not concentrating, my mind was full of desperate notions, I had entered into a piece of audacity which atoned for all my previous doubt and hesitation, all my shilly-shallying over the purchase of my house. My eyes were wandering from my outward view in all its splendour, over the wall and into the paved courtyard opposite.

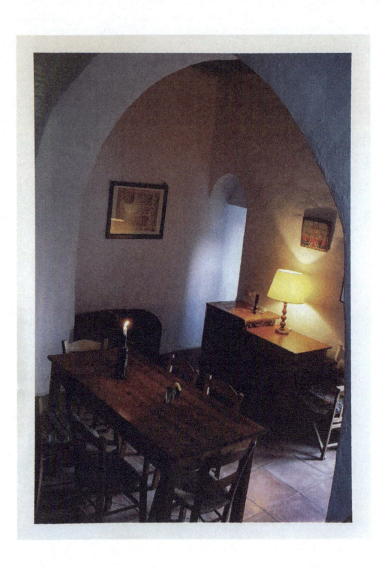

Chapter Four

Rainbow arches... How my brother would love these rainbow arches, the structural feature of every large room in the old stone houses, so simple in appearance and so solid that you might omit to wonder at the workmanship. But Henry is an architect with a special line in conservation. Interior design is Catherine's subject, and that does not mean wall-paper to her. They would see, appreciate, and say how satisfyingly the arch divides the room. It runs lengthwise down the centre, forming two recesses at each end, of one to two metres in depth, and there - in the deeper ones - you have your built-in platform beds. The old inhabitants slept with curtains hanging from carved frames. I think that Henry and Catherine would have claustrophobic nights in such a cell, but they could dispense with curtains, they would enjoy that platformed space.

There's an arch in the main room of Katina's house, and an arch in the lower room that goes with mine. One pair of the recesses in Katina's is deep enough to build in platforms. They could put the boys in one side, themselves on the other and the room would not appear to be a bedroom - they'd like that. They would? Or will.

I'll throw in my room as a present. They can use my *cabiné*. I know them, don't I? I can recognise their style. Didn't they agree with me about every visual choice I made on Mykonos? They spent the first days of their honeymoon in a house that I had chosen, and when they followed me to Aiyiali eight years later they said yes again, they went straight out and bought a plot of land...

...above the beach. They saw Langatha and chose another site.

Yes, but when they did that they didn't know about this house.

Catherine is no problem. She'll go along with me. She'll look at this house and tell me I am right. I'm sure of that, though we have met twice - briefly - in half a dozen years. We're such good friends that `sister-in-law' is a title we avoid. It seems too much of a cold mouthful to go with empathy.

And aren't Henry and I good friends as well? Of course we are. It's because I understand him that I'm doubtful now. I wouldn't have come to Greece without him, he was the ideal elder brother who drove me about Europe in our student days, who first suggested the pension on a Greek island - and so my life was changed. Then, when my landlady turned out to be a paragon of rumpus-making bitches, creating a drama that is still good conversation to the Mykoniots, Henry was with me, on the spot or telegraphically - he cared. And I care now. It was he who chose the site where all the sand is sitting, he was the one who spent his afternoons watching the changing light from every angle, and finally waived a difficulty of access in favour of an elevated view. The mules that brought the sand had a short journey from the next bay, but with a scramble at the top that mules don't like. They had to make it - he had found his site. I know that, but I also know how he would feel about Katina's house. The kitchen is carved back into the rock. The bakehouse has an oven large enough to roast a dozen goats. The well at the front door is roofed over with a terrace reminiscent of a threshing floor.

'It holds more water than yours,' said Mr N, 'and you could drink it - it comes clean off the roof. That would be a good place, on top, for making concrete blocks.'

Now really, that may be, but I am finding valid grounds to make my brother change his outlook, I am trying not to think how delightful this paved area would be for me, I am expelling thoughts like that. I cannot make him give up what he has chosen to provide me with a factory for concrete blocks.

Here's another thought. He might, for the rest of the summer, provide me with a roof.

'It will leak in winter,' Mr N said. 'It will have to be replaced, like yours. But you could live there now.'

We looked at each other. I could feel a lightness in my shoulders and almost see his raise themselves. Might the carpentry order be postponed? Might we not have to achieve the full catalogue of works to be completed in spite of threshing in the next few weeks? May all the saints protect my brother, I will light a candle if I can change his outlook, but let me keep a grasp on my priorities.

He will be fascinated by the complex, he will be the owner of a rosemary bush, an almond tree, a prickley pear. 'Onions and garlic,' Mr N was muttering. 'I could work the fields. He'd come in the summer and find his own tomatoes - and flowers of course.'

The strips along the sloping sides of Amorgos are far in character from English fields. Katina's were about ten strides in length and four in width, but they were terraced land, with earth.

On the evening of the day that Katina's property turned from my private turmoil into a valid proposition, Mr N seized on my idea as if it was his own and I the timid one. Henry's down-site had no materials except for the remains of a four-year-old delivery of sand. I found myself berated with its catalogue of disadvantages and held responsible.

But Katina's - now there was a house for an architect who honoured stone. On the down-site he'd have to build in brick. As for water, you could spend twenty three thousand just to build a cistern the same size as hers, or smaller, and - try to figure this out - it would need a roof to channel the water, and the water to make the concrete for the roof. Carriage? All right, let's talk of carriage - that's a subject. A right-minded muleteer would sooner deliver to Langatha than up Henry's track. Henry's down-site would give the mules heart-tremors every journey - and how many journeys, starting as he would from scratch? It would cost a fortune to build a single room there, let alone a house. Katina's was an offer to be snatched before the road came - everyone would be laughing at the old-world prices soon. Henry's down-site was in tourist country, an area waiting for development. Katina's had peace. Katina's was safe. The road, eventually, would reach Langatha right over on the far side, with not a lorry or a motorcycle to be seen or heard or smelt on our estate. And who would make the trek to that down-site in the winter, to see that gales weren't causing damage? Who would look after the land? Here at Katina's he would find his flowers watered, his string of garlic hanging in the kitchen, here we should grow vines. Of course, it was none of Mr N's business, but if he had this brother of mine - this Enrikos as we called him - at his table, and spoke his language, he could tell him that it would be insanity not to favour Katina's house.

`I've made you dizzy, Carolina.'

`You have not.' Why should I be dizzy when I'm being told exactly what I think myself? I must write to Henry and Mr N must phone Katina to confirm that she will sell. Hang on to this - however it may sound or feel we are on the same side in this argument. I only need a little breathing space.

It was not the content but the elusive metaphors and tangents that made me more dizzy than I would admit. It seemed that grand or dire decisions, however practical, had to be approached by way of verbal acrobatics that might have exhausted an Athenian, and we had not reached the dire decision yet. I was not allowed a gasp before it was presented, with a pose of angular elbows and a lecture on psychology.

Didn't I realise that as soon as the sale of a house is mentioned, that house, to all intents and purposes, had gone? Given the slightest time-lapse, the owner reconsiders, she doubles the price, she talks. The world discovers that there's a chance in a million on the market, the world decides that the chance must not be lost. Suddenly that house is the one that everyone has dreamed of, and meanwhile where's my letter to a brother in England? - Sitting on a caique for Naxos, waiting for a storm to drop. I wouldn't get an answer for a fortnight if it was telegraphed, and by that time what's happened to the house? Oh no, we couldn't phone Katina to make inquiries. An offer is the only thing to make.

There is a good Greek verb 'to unconfuse oneself'. At this moment, which was truly dizzy, I badly needed to unconfuse myself, but when you're talking to Mr N - or being talked to - you get no opportunity for that. I started to protest, but a sudden elation intercepted - Henry's decision could be made by proxy, and I was his representative on Amorgos.

'Carolina, I'll tell you what Katina will say - if she will sell. She'll ask for a deposit, seven thousand say, not more than eight, that's one third if her mother's right about the price. And when she's got that, then we've got the house.'

Seven thousand? I had seven thousand. I could put it on the table right away. And I could write to Henry saying, 'You've bought a house in Langatha. I hope you like it. *Kalo riziko.*'

Henry's decision, if left to Henry, just possibly might be the wrong one. If I made it we could skip that danger. I couldn't risk it. If he didn't want this house, I did. I could halt all building works indefinitely and have it as my camping ground. I could sell it with my own part at a profit. I could keep it as a safeguard of my peace. I would be crazy to refuse it, but really Henry had to have it, for where else were the second two instalments coming from?

But you can't do things like that.

Oh can't I? And can a brother send his sister a telegram from VANRGKOKSUV asking for a miracle?

Henry did that last year. A letter had gone before, he said, but I doubt if that could have been answered either, if it had arrived. Hearing nothing from me, he just sent a second cable with the flight number, knowing I'd be there. And how did he feel in Istanbul the day we were to meet, when that flight turned out to be double-booked? The family arrived at Airport B in Athens hours after I had watched the passengers come through from the scheduled plane at Airport A, and I do not know how long I would have remained stuck to the seat that I was stuck to when Henry finally appeared before me, but he swore that he had not for one moment lost perfect confidence. My car was parked outside, and when I drove them to a rent-free house on a secluded stretch of rocky coast they were as appreciative as could be, but not surprised. If sibling faith was being tested, that was its big day. Well, now it was my turn for trying sibling faith.

I might have said, `I'll let you know tomorrow.' But what's the point of thinking over anything when you know your own reactions once you get obsessed? Henry would commend me - stick to that.

And what of my commander? We would have need of him. When he had so often told me about the grey hairs my house had given him, would he move across the path and grow some more?

`I'll do it,' said Mr N.

`Then go ahead.'

The telegraph, telephone and post office of Langatha is the living-room of the scribe's house. His wife, who runs it with their daughter, has the convenience that she can simultaneously do the dusting and the cooking, with only three steps to the table and three more into the kitchen to be taken between sentences. The scribe habitually eats a light mid-morning meal, with two small glasses of retsina, which he achieves - like everything he does - in a private manner although he's sitting in a public place. After that you become increasingly aware of the main meal, usually in a simmering pot. Mrs Scribe has it very well arranged. As operator she has to operate, not at high speed but thoroughly. She presses buttons, turns a handle, conveys her customers' pleas to Chora, waits, and never loses her equanimity. Even the automatic phone, which like the road was on its way, could hardly change the aura of this kindly place. A single line of uncertain constitution would need constant overseeing, with the antique switches still in frequent use.

There's a pretty view from the scribe's terrace, and a fine display of family photographs inside. Once I had to make a call to England, and have been familiar with every whisker of the grandfathers ever since. And there's a diversion of conversations, for it's part of the procedure, whatever state the line is in, that you shout your tenderest and most confidential messages. After five hours in the audience my private language seemed unpublic-spirited - whenever I use it, good manners suggest that I explain whom I'm speaking to and why. In any case, when Mr N got through to Katina in Athens - he had been on the doorstep when the office opened - the permanently well-informed scribe's family, the operators on all the other island lines and anyone else gathering in waiting automatically became branches of a new grape vine.

Katina agreed to everything. She would sell the house for twenty three thousand, seven to clinch the deal and two further instalments 'before too long'. And that was very nearly that, but she also made the reservation that she would ring back the next day to confirm the confirmation, we were not to send the deposit until then.

Mr N believed that she meant what she was saying, though she might excruciate us first. The building works had stopped for threshing, and both of us were so intensely visualising my move from the mayor's house being into hers that we had lost our fighting spirit for my own. I wrote Henry a dissertation on the advantages of changing projects, adding on the last page that as soon as Katina phoned they would be changed, so would he please send a substantial sum of money by the speediest means possible.

No means can be speedy. When I had given Mr N the go-ahead from England, my bank had undertaken some method of conveying money to a post office on Amorgos, but it had taken two months to arrive. As Henry was in England and his island fund was in America, I could not expect twenty three thousand drachmas overnight, but the hoping for a phone call and waiting for his answer were enough to keep me jittering without worrying about that. Katina did not make her call, so Mr N started following his up. 'Yes,' he said, 'but I'll ring you tomorrow to say yes again.' June was disappearing with that conversation. It was repeated several times.

To phone someone in Aiyiali you have to send
warning through the office, `At such and such a time be
standing by,' only trusting that at such and such time you
will get through. Mr N was perpetually ready to leave
his threshing floor and stand by, but it began to look as
if Henry's answer would come first. The tension was
infecting the laid-off workmen and Dimitris, who still
joined us in the evenings wanting bulletins. He suspected
that I was dotty, and that made him curious.

I was slow to realise that Dimitris is as avid for a
piece of gossip as any villager, for he does so little of the
gossiping himself. Sitting aloofly, looking like a village
sage, he listens, gives very little, questions and obtains.
He was intrigued by what I was up to and amused, but his
humour is as quiet as his grumbling, he smiles more than
laughs as he mutters more than shouts. And now he kept
repeating, as if personally anxious, `Any news from your
brother yet?'

It did concern him, for like Mr N he took the attitude
that having taken on me and my house he would be taking
on my brother and his as well. That meant innumerable
mud pies and heaps of rubble. While he was saying `yes,
I'll do it' his face was shadowed with complaint. Thank
you, Dimitri. I would have been appalled to lose him, his
grumbles never got in the way of working hours, he was
solidly dependable. And quietly he kept a watchful eye on
Mr N's commandership.

Dimitris has one non-conformist habit, to wear
a straw hat for outdoor summer work - more logical, I
can't help feeling, than the cap for hours of exposure to
the sun. His threshing floor is in a field behind the beach

where, beating his mules and donkeys round their hot, dry, husky circles, he would wave to me as I passed by and there remain throughout my gentle hours of beach life and English lessons until I walked up at a kinder hour. Threshing demands the hottest weather, with only a light breeze for winnowing. It borders on a masochistic exercise, not for the sake of home-made bread, which is a side-treat, but for fodder for the animals.

'Come swimming, Dimitri.'

'There's no time.'

If we expanded on this for an evening's conversation, if I pointed out that one splash would not be one day's ruination, I knew that I was teasing, for there is one, unarguable answer for the working islander. He cannot go swimming because he is too tired, too sweaty and too hot.

Bad humour and anxiety would keep him from the sea as well. I was extremely anxious, but according to the summer timetable I swam in the morning and in the afternoon, I picked apricots and ate them too, I enjoyed the midday plate that one of my pupils carried to my door, and usually slept with summer soundness afterwards.

But not always. It was the sleep that was disturbed, with such a ticking of mental activity as was always going on. I had said - and I wanted to mean this - that I would if necessary halt all building works, that if the yes came from Katina but not from Henry I would go to any lengths of desperate action to hold on to her house. But building works cannot be halted. Once you have materials the best way of protecting what has been used is by sealing your house before the winter, which means putting on the doors and shutters that you may be hankering to postpone. My upstairs floor was earth on cardboard on bamboo and wooden beams, all vulnerable to damage from the winter rains. The door and window frames had to be in place before the plastering, the plastering included filling the gaps around the frames and had to be done in any case because we had an open trough of lime. Sand and cement were compulsively refilling my downstairs storeroom, and then there appeared a third ingredient called *savoura*, sifted from the gravel pits in the gorge, the finest grindings of ancient pebbles at the bottom of a dried-up river bed. The gorge is beautiful, with oleanders flourishing defiantly among rocks where nowadays no water flows, but it somehow shook me to discover that I was paying two men to make the expedition with a sieve. The whole subject of relentless progress was most habitually shaking in the middle of siesta time.

The rooms to let around the fields of my midday home, *Laki*, do not have the air of buildings erected for commercial purposes - it was a pleasant place for having brainstorms in. To reach my doorstep I had to push around a pear tree, collecting my salad from a crop of plum tomatoes as I went, and when I sat on that doorstep I was inside a private shrubbery, with a view above the branches of Langatha and the mountains all around. Henry's family would miss the glut of apricots that was happening beside me, but the pears would ripen for them - it was long agreed that I should book them rooms down here. Apart from all the brochure-filling attractions for a family, it fitted well with Henry's picture of continually running up to join the workers in progress on the site of his own sand-pit, while the boys played with their sand on the beach. He could watch them. He could almost call to them. Oh deary me.

And so back up the mule track to look into Katina's courtyard and be reassured again. One glance did the trick.

My mind was always obsessively pumping when I walked, but once on the way up I saw a sight which for some moment jammed the works. Ahead of me, making notably slow progress, was a procession of fifteen Langatha men, sodden-shirted, in two lines with some long, low object on a frame between them - what? They looked like pall-bearers at a Cyclops' funeral. I overtook them, saw and understood. Langatha's first private generator - that was it.

I could not blame Nikitas the *platia* grocer, who has all the stalwart island virtues, for being too impatient to wait for the public current that will come `after the road', but the selfish part of me was shocked. Nobody could say that the appearance of this monster meant any fundamental progress in Langatha, for there is no real refrigeration with twelve rumbling hours a day. The monster had to take a three-hour siesta, and anyway Nikitas would only be concerned with a few hours after dark. It would mean a noise around the *platia*. It would mean a television set.

I was shocked, but I could also feel triumphant that this was the summer for vacating the mayor's house. Thank God - or Mr N - for mine in its own isolation. Mine would not hear a murmur. Mine was safe in that respect. But this went to show the paramount importance of protecting one's own boundaries. Mine would be still

safer if Katina would only phone from Athens, and her
house became a part of one estate.

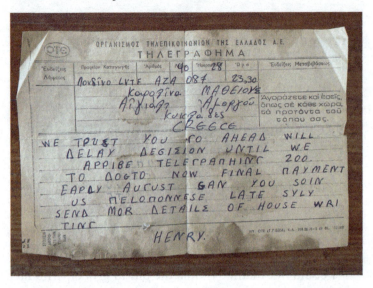

`Carolina! A telegram!' So Henry's reaction had come
first.

My confidence was not supposed to feel agitated at
that moment. My confidence, however, disintegrated into
a self-willed quivering.

There were forty words of Henry's cable, which was
tough on the scribe's daughter, but I quickly got the gist
of it. They trusted me to go ahead. They were deferring
their final decision until they came. There were a thousand
dollars on the way. Could I meet them at Delphi 22 July
for a fortnight in the Peloponnese?

The second sentence got minimal attention. It showed
a reservation unco-ordinating with the statements on each
side. If I was being trusted and sent a thousand dollars,
Henry was not going to have much further choice - unless

he sold the property at once. That sentence was not translated to the commander, who was full of admiration at the whole display of sibling faith. We drank a toast to Henry, but the raising of the one anxiety only made the other more uncomfortable. I wanted a house, and what I got in the first week of July was a lavatory seat and a *cabiné* door.

I suppose the old inhabitants of these two houses used the fields, for there was no sign of the standard hole in any outhouse, but so far as I was concerned it was the completed *cabiné* that made the estate - if we could have it - self-contained. When the lavatory seat had been borne up from Ormos, I stood our table an extra round of wine to say *kalo riziko* to that - 'Have you baptised it?' I was asked - and I could at any moment have moved house.

My own could more feasibly have been camped in before we started ripping it apart. In the unhaltable long-term policy of what must be achieved before the olive season, Michalis the carpenter had fixed the frames for the upstairs door and windows which would have to follow, but the moment had gone for herculean achievement before August, and anyway a house is not made habitable by window frames - it needs a floor. Anyone who entered this one had to drag round planks to step on, and I do not know what would have been devised for me if Mr N had not been sent a summons to the telephone.

But the summons came, a threshing morning was abandoned, Katina was saying the final yes to all her yesses, and doubtless the first *kalo riziko* at the triumphant moment came from Mrs Scribe. It was over three weeks since Mr N had made the first call, he deserved a little private glory after spending chunks of several mornings being patient by the telephone. A distant English brother, professor of architecture at a London Polytechnic, was barely a shadow to those who banded the greeting as the news was spread.

Anyone but Mr N would at that moment have hurried straight back to the fields and waited for me to come up in the evening, but Mr N's work was abandoned for the day. In the heaviest hour of siesta time he was saddling his donkey - he wanted seven thousand drachmas in his hand when the office opened in the afternoon.

It was Maria who was sent down to the beach to wake me up if need be, and she was cheerful about that as she was allowed a swim as well, before we squeezed onto the saddle to sweat into each other's dresses as we rode back up the hill. She had caught a sense of excitement from her father, who made a drama of whether to send our first instalment by post or telegraph. His inner debate about false economy at crucial moments was related to me several times. Was he going to concern himself with saving a few drachmas when we had a house at stake? Not he. He had me carried home at the unkindest hour to count out the seven notes, he was standing at the office door at five o'clock, he paid those extra drachmas - and do you realise what would have happened if he had not? He won that house by fifty minutes. At eight o'clock the following morning Katina had the money - at least, the official information - and at ten to nine some island Athenian who had been listening to the grape vine drove up in a taxi to offer her five thousand more. Very properly she answered that she was bound to us.

I was as impressed as Mr N could wish, until I started thinking about flaws. For two or three reasons the story did not work. After that I went on being impressed, by a piece of harmless verve. A half-hearted commander with no imagination would have been a poor fish in comparison.

But why the verve, and why the effort, when Mr N was being paid for muscle and had an extra mouth to feed? Nobody could be so ingenuous as to think that he was doing what he was doing simply for the heck of it. Nor did he make pretence of that, but saved me from a quandary by saying frankly that a field on that path would be convenient, so close to his house. He might park a goat in the bakehouse - let him, that seemed a fitting bonus for commandership. But that did not eliminate some element of heck. I would confidently say that for all his harrassed speeches Mr N enjoyed the kudos that went along with buying houses, getting permits, commanding teams of workmen, wielding the responsibility for foreigners - and why deny him that extra perquisite? In a village with almost no diversions my houses were sufficiently diverting that he did not even have to make a big deal of seducing me. Now that I was about to move house he could put his imagination into furniture.

Congratulations followed me through the *platia* as two donkey loads of my possessions were brought down. The mayor's house had been so solidly furnished that I was setting up my own with a camp bed, a folding chair and table, some kitchen equipment and a surprisingly large supply of sheets. Island sheets are striped so prettily that they had always been my weakness in the shops. Mr

N then scrounged his own back regions and his hen-house, bringing forth various battered and grimy objects to be nailed, scrubbed and painted up. The house also had a few pieces for this treatment, the moot point being whether they were of antique interest, functional or firewood.

Another moot point was whether or not I should sweep the dust of ages, when to touch the walls with a brush was like turning on a tap, and the floor itself was earth. Hooking the cobwebs of ages from the ceiling was another pastime as endless as any punishment of the ancient underworld. Each one that I freed from the old slates helped to tug another forth, at the same time encouraging a colony of spiders to keep doggedly at work. As neither chore could be completed I stopped when I had wearied, and set up my bed with great delight beneath the least sagging of the beams. By lamplight the irregularity of surfaces became extravagant; among those shadows I was taking possession of a friendly witch's house. Henry, Catherine and the boys would love it, for in the upstairs-downstairs life we would be leading, with them based in Laki, they would have their village nights. One of the old platforms still remained to bear someone's weight for one last season. I would not be defeated, for lack of ingenuity, in making the place hospitable.

As to meeting them at Delphi, I had dismissed that with the briefest thought. A fortnight with one's loved ones in their private van, among the ancient and scenic glories of the Peleponnese? Uncontemplatable. The habits of our boats give double weight to every reason for not leaving. The difficulties of timing a perfect rendez-vous make you clutch at every pretext not to try. I was reading

Treasure Island - a simplified version - with the baker's son and a friend of his, and could not abandon them. I had to lay on the family welcome, cooking till the final moment and arranging flowers.

The removal donkey had been Sunday transport. During the last few days of waiting the three-week threshing interval had ended, Dimitris was ready to turn back into a builder, and on the morning that I first woke in residence the enormous work of plastering began. Soon after five o'clock I heard a scraping spade outside, I looked out and discovered my most constant workman mixing the ingredients. It seemed to me that he was overdoing early workman's early hours, but he retorted, 'You can't have the builder coming if the materials aren't ready for them,' which made sense.

I think that workman had the most joyously-made cup of coffee ever drunk. It was a minor blessing ceremony for the house, the kitchen and - after years of cooking on a nasty paraffin gadget - a new three-ring gas stove. For years I had looked on life as a peripatetic business, in which possessions in any bulk were best avoided, money was for journeys, sheets were an uncharacteristic weakness that I could hardly justify. Now my adventure was turning me into a bourgeois householder, measuring my content in jampots and teaspoons.

'Carolina, where's the ouzo?' - 'Have you made the coffee yet?' I could not help with plastering, but I was joyful to be living my own domestic mornings while in communication with the three at work across the path. I greatly preferred to be distributing the coffee than receiving it from Mr N's house. We kept crossing over and looking at each other's progress. English lessons on the premises were treated with respect. The four or five village children who had returned to me at the beginning of the holidays entered the new classroom with shy curiosity at first, and easy acceptance of the wobbly nature of the furniture. The chairs they sat on were scraped of hen shit and after a few lessons looked so elegant in pale canary yellow that Mr N and I both stood in admiration at what a present he had given me. There were three of them with a small wooden settee, a veritable suite, which had come - I don't know why - from an Athenian dentist's waiting room. Their character was quite different from the standard Van Gogh style of island chairs, I enjoyed them - I was enjoying everything. All that was horrifying was the greedy consumption of materials by those old stone walls.

Mr N and Dimitris were slapping on the plaster without giving the mixing man a pause. Every time I felt lugubrious about the wages I had my hair raised by a panting and a snorting at the gate, which meant that one or other of our supplies had been brought a replenishment. I was so pinched for having parted with Katina's first instalment that I would have welcomed the postponement of any work postponable, but there was one more to begin. My terrace was an open slab of concrete, still perilously unwalled, with a five-metre drop on one side onto rocks and gorse. And I was shortly to be visited by three nephews, of two, three and four years old.

Mr N took up the point in a ferocious manner as if I was proposing not to protect them after all. He would pay for the wall himself rather than expose them to such danger, if Henry's thousand dollars did not arrive before they did. He was crazy about little children, and anyway if any of them was killed he would be held responsible. So we had a great palaver about how it could be managed, and soothed each other by talking about boys. The younger the better, he considered. He adored babies.

'In twenty three days Enrikos will be here.' Clearly this brother of mine was striking distant awe. Time measurements in Langatha are round approximations, and as I could not calculate which day the family would arrive, Mr N must have picked that number as a sign of deference. Anticipation was having a restfully benign effect, the menu for the first breakfast was recited before they started out on their long drive. It was to be a breakfast after a night which we plotted in endless detail, for we had decided to carry them directly from the boat to their own house.

Mr N could guarantee to get them up the hill as fast as the Laki family could get them to Laki - faster, on second thought. Tourists arriving in August for those rooms were flocks of sheep waiting to be sorted out. VIP treatment was required for Henry's family, and VIP treatment was what they'd get from him. They would see at once what house they had acquired, get over that impatience, eat fresh eggs for breakfast, have donkey transport down to Laki in the morning, and afterwards do what they pleased.

Suddenly I detached myself. Daily life in Aiyiali may be riveting, but really, you cannot be so off-hand as I was being about Delphi and the Peleponnese. I was as familiar with dirt roads as with the highways, and what was the point of that if I did not use my knowledge to guide my own people to shady riversides and almost secret ruins that they, on one tour, would not find? I did not have to be standing in welcome on this landing stage. The commander had such firm ideas about a suitable reception that he might be happier if left alone. I even had a friend in Laki who would gladly come up now and then for readings of *Treasure Island* with two bright boys. I was redundant here - not there. So I sent a cable to Brindisi and gambled on timing the perfect rendez-vous at Delphi. What's more, it worked. And more again, it led into a joyful fortnight without a moment of regret.

Somehow I had left the house with some sort of arrangement for a good many people to lie down when we came back. It was not five-star accomodation, but that was no great worry, I knew that what would move my brother was not bedding but the rock walls and rainbow arch.

Boats for Aiyiali often arrive at unkind hours. We were lucky, ours came in shortly after dark. On the quayside Mr N was formal in his greeting, we needed three small boys to break the ice. He brought his animals, arranged Catherine, boys and luggage on them, and then we were on the padding quiet of the mule track. After the great world outside I thought this night ride - a walk in Henry's case - the best possible way of introducing Henry to his house, a magic potion to wipe out hesitance. 'What does he say?' asked Mr N. - 'Wait till he gets there.' I spoke more cheerfully than I felt.

My confidence had had a fortnight's shaking. Henry and I had hardly been able to discuss the house. We had all talked animatedly on any other subject, everything to do with sight-seeing and camping and our togetherness was fine. But we had a tacit policy of evading the upstairs versus downstairs question, and when I mentioned as an encouragement that five thousand drachmas had been offered above the price - choosing to believe that -, Henry was more encouraged than I liked. I felt sensitive, I knew that he felt sensitive, Catherine was my private ally on the Langatha side, but he was not going to commit himself.

I had a sure feeling that the night ride up would help. It was the perfect prelude to the curtain-raising at the top. So I walked with Mr N, my fellow conspirator, who was telling me how my terrace had been walled, and this and that, leaving Henry to drink his prescribed dose of atmosphere.

Lamplight was glowing through the windows when we arrived. So I too was to be taken by surprise. In the kitchen Mr N's wife was shadowing about. 'It's them!' I heard Maria's voice. While Catherine was seized and kissed I looked about. There were flowers on the table, fresh cheese and bread. Quickly a whole boiled chicken was set down, and an enormous blackened saucepan with the broth. We stood gaping like bedazzled guests. 'Shall I serve them?' asked Maria. 'No, get home, leave them in peace.' And with an abrupt goodnight Mr N shooed his wife and daughter out.

The soup had the smoky taste of a brew cooked over wood, with rice, egg and lemon, a gentle welcome after long hours on a boat. We ate quietly. The boys were sleepy and the rest bemused. Henry had to speak first, and he was in a trance. He began walking round in circles, gazing at the ceiling and outside at the stars. The boys were laid down in their corner and he was still wandering round and round. I walked out and waited on the well-top, he was standing on the middle field. I kept my seat in silence until he joined me. `I think you have been very clever,' he said.

Chapter Five

Mr N and Henry did not like each other. There was little reason why they should. They did not speak the same language, in any sense. All they had in common was a question of ownership, which made Henry doubtful and Mr N hypersensitive. As Katina had arrived from Athens for her family holiday, the next step was a journey to Katapola to make the contract, when the house would become Mr N's on paper and Henry's only in good faith. And why should he have faith in this gaunt-nosed stranger, this weasle with the cadaverous cheeks? He did not say that, but I sensed something of the sort. I defended Mr N by emphasising his open-handedness in the days when there had been no hint that I should ever be a house-owner. Well and good, but Henry urged me to find out every detail about the legal aspect, whether or not the law might really change, or whether there were loopholes to the law. Meanwhile, could we not get something down on paper, a simple promise, a few sentences written by the scribe? I boggled. I made one of my silliest statements ever, that it might cause offence.

Henry is not a worrier, nor argumentative. But he combines firmness with forebearance, and on waiving the question of the scribe insisted that in Athens in the autumn I should somehow agitate. Aiyiali had its own society there - the president might help. I promised to be positive. Then we let the matter drop and concentrated on enjoying the next three weeks.

It seemed unkind that our only immediate problem was financial, when a thousand dollars had been sent a month before. That was my fault, I should have advised them to bring it with them, but I doubt if I shall ever get to the end of saying `I should have known better' in Aiyiali - perhaps in the optimist's future when a circular highway connects Ormos, Langatha and Tholaria. Mr N resented the embarrassment of explaining to Katina that she would have to wait for one instalment, but the Laki people, providing the family with meals as well as rooms, were unconcerned with lack of cash. Father, mother and daughters had been my good friends for six years, and as Henry said, they could keep me as a hostage if he left an unpaid bill.

No one can stay in Laki without being aware of daughters, though you need time to become proficient in all five names and characters. From Efdokia the afterthought to Irene the queenly eldest, who had passed the Lower Cambridge Certificate four years after her first sight of our alphabet, each has her own style. They have a flat in Athens where their parents, with a trust remarkable in any Greeks, allowed them to look after one another and take themselves to school, with not much supervision from Aunty up the road. And as the girls speak English, it is the girls who are in command of foreigners. Father seems glad to leave them to it, and Mother can seldom leave the kitchen, for Laki is their do-it-yourself business, which they had just expanded with a restaurant.

It was bound to be a success, for they have the monopoly of the quarter-mile beach. A Mykoniot could hardly believe what he would see - or not see - should he for some unlikely reason disembark at sleepy Ormos - not one commercial building in sight around the full sweep of the bay. Half-way along, Laki itself is hidden by a row of tamarisks along its boundary. It's a wonderfully safe beach for children, with a certain amount of donkey traffic as it's the highroad to Tholaria, and nothing to tantalise in the way of ice cream vendors or canoes for hire. The result, as near as may be, is rhapsodical content in what there is - and that is riches to a two- or three- or four-year-old.

Jason, Julian and Zachary did not need encouragement to make themselves known around Laki and Ormos, especially as no one could quite believe in the closeness of their age and contrast in appearance, even when the adoption of the first two was explained. If adopting two in quick succession can precipitate a pregnancy, that was the effect on Catherine who gave birth to Zachary after ten years of married life. For a few weeks she and Henry had three boys under two. As a variety of ethnic origins in Jason and Julian was emphasised by their brother's fair hair and Anglo-Saxon looks, and as the islanders have no inhibitions about asking questions, the emotional and factual history was thoroughly examined, but never thoroughly understood.

That was bound to become a village topic when they were seen about Langatha, but immediately they needed static time, and Henry had an up-night by himself. Mr N and I had often told each other that he should have his special supper to meet the working gang, and though the aura wrapped around an unknown brother had lost its warmth when he became substantial, the supper was lavishly laid on. Everyone was very well behaved, but I failed to translate ease along with words. I kept adding private messages about this shop's style of eating, and Henry - a natural linguist - would probably have communicated better by himself. Later on he became Enrikos in his own right. That year he was Carolina's Brother with a beard.

The beard, and hair beginning to recede, made him look like a professor - which he is - or, as my mother puts it, like Lord Tennyson in his prime. I thought the result distinguished, but Langatha has no poets or professors. Priests and mourners wear beards, and so do a few puzzling characters who live in tents behind the beach. Henry did not look remotely like a hippie or a beach bum, but Langatha needed a little while to get used to him.

There was nothing formidable about Catherine with her short dark hair and plain blue tunic, whether or not she was qualified to teach in universities and was taking on a high-powered job in publishing. I was the one who might have been unnerved by her achievements, but she is not that sort of person, she was my friend who was glad to be stolen from her family one evening for an up-night of her own.

We called it ladies' evening. Another inmate of Laki made three, we were a trio in a quandary. Three was too many to walk into a shop where we could not pay a bill, as if expecting to be fed. Our well-top terrace was much more beautiful in any case. We did not want to give offence. These points were debated, and for a compromise we made an omelette and a salad to be followed by a stroll for a glass of wine with Mr N. So we thought, but as we sat over the table Maria came charging through the gate, ran up onto the terrace and seized the plates. 'Daddy says you're to go straight up to your proper place.'

We went sheepishly, and from outside saw him at his empty table looking as miserable, Catherine said, as she had ever seen anyone. Then he jumped up to lay on everything that he had offered Henry, plus the benevolence that Henry could not have. That evening no language problem detracted from good feeling, which had little to do with Mr N's smattering of multi-lingual phrases or Catherine's smattering of Greek.

Building works had stopped, with only my lower quarters to be plastered at some later time, but Mr N still had one important manoeuvre to command. There was the contract to be signed. He had begun already with a day of sitting at the phone office, from eight to twelve and five to seven, trying to contact the notary public at Katapola and growing more grey hairs. Nowadays you couldn't do it. The modern world works shorter hours, Langatha is going ahead with the world's progress, the office never opens in the afternoons. There is also one automatic telephone at Ormos, but that is only available at certain hours and often out of order, and there is no longer a notary at Katapola.

There would not be one the next summer. Mr N went further, he told Katina that there would not be one the next week. He was in a hurry, he had to get that paper signed before the Panayia, which does not mean on the Eve. August the fifteenth is Panayia Day, the summer's great dividing line. Everything that happens afterwards drifts off into September - you might as well say 'before the olives' as 'after the Panayia'. Henry's family were leaving at the end of August and Mr N was playing safe. He had that notary and Katina lined up within a few days of our arrival, and a caique for the journey to Katapola.

It was reported that Katina, looking down on activity around her childhood home, was banging her head against a wall. To her credit she was most affable to us, awarding *Kyrios* Enrikos with particular respect, and disguising every emotion about setting off for Katapola on a rough day to sign over the dear house to Mr N. Only those two were obliged to go, but as Henry was paying for the caique we were determined to have our money's worth, and there was such a seizing of opportunity that we were seven adults and seven children gathering early in the morning on the waterfront.

Katina and her sister had a brother at the monastery, so the sister was taking three children on a pilgrimage, and Mr N threw in Maria for the ride. It looked like kiddies' outing, except that the Greek four of the seven were standing on the quayside terrified. Maria had never been out in a boat of any kind, the rest knew that they got sick. Katina's sister was on the verge of opting out with her lot, President Nikolaras our captain looked at the sky and grew impatient, our boys were jumped on deck. 'Make your cross and God will help you,' Katina bade the others. Afterwards we wondered how she kept her faith.

On a regular steamer the stretch between Katapola and Aiyiali is the worst part of the journey from Piraeus. It's cut out of the schedule in bad weather - passengers for both ports are thrown off at Katapola. The caique gets a respite in the middle, keeping to the channel in the inside of the islet Nikouria, but there can be exciting patches on both sides. The Greek party, except for Mr N, immediately disappeared into the cabin. We sat on the deck and sang. At every bounce and plunge we heard wails from below. Every now and then Mr N opened the hatch to look down on the scene that we preferred not to see, informing us with roars of laughter that it was pretty bad. At Katapola, nearly two hours later, when the bedraggled heads emerged, we saw that it had been worse than we imagined, and it was Katina who needed to be helped off and supported down the waterfront.

Hoping that she would recover to sign her name that morning, we crossed the centre of the island via Chora to go sightseeing.

The monastery is of eleventh-century foundation, a white patch of plaster on the cliff face a thousand feet above the sea. Only a hundred years ago it was the second richest in Greece, and it is still comparatively rich in land and treasure, but not in life. Katina's brother, a rare young monk in a new world, had only three aging fellows in his spartan fortress and may one day find himself alone. He does not seem to be at all morose about the situation, and likes being brought Langatha gossip. That day he had plenty from a great many visitors. While my party marvelled and took photographs, Katina raised herself and Mr N became the owner of another house.

When the contract and the pilgrimage had been completed, the Greek party went home over the mountain on hired mules, swearing that they would never again get into a caique. It was now too rough for any boat to leave. Mr N took off on foot, and Henry - who had to pay for Katina's mule as well as the caique and paperwork - was also obliged to put up his family at a hotel. It seemed tremendously hard work and expensive for him to buy the house he could not own, but he is not a complainer, he was the most cheerful of us all.

At five-thirty the next morning Nikolaras the captain banged on my bedroom door. The sea was still too rough, we could not go. He would come back to collect us as soon as the wind dropped, possibly in the afternoon. Come back? That meant that he was going. Yes, he was going, but we could not.

Then we three adults held a conference, and Henry - who is not often irate - became irate, saying that since we had paid for this caique we had the right to go on it. If Catherine and I could face it, would I please communicate the message. He did not want to miss time in Aiyiali, he had just bought a house and wanted to enjoy it, he was impatient to rebuild a courtyard wall. Those words were so joyful to me that I could not care what state the sea was in, though had I been alone I would have chosen the long walk.

We trouped along the quayside to the dour Nikolaras, and argued until he was persuaded into taking us, possibly because the children were wearing life-jackets. In fact a life-jacket would be of little help to an infant washed off in that sea against those rocks, especially when the manoeuvre most certain to capsize the boat would be turning round to pick an infant up. Island captains know exactly what they are doing in their own waters, as if intimate with every wave, and what Nikolaras really knew was that so long as we did not let a boy slip he would get us back.

If the engine breaks down, that's another matter. It had been known to happen, but one cannot go through island life expecting caique engines to break down.

Our fear was that he would insist on sealing us inside the cabin, but fortunately he started by filling that with goats. We were secondary business, financing petrol for the main piece, which was butchery for the Panayia. He instructed us to sit with our feet against the side and our backs against the cabin wall, clutching an infant each. When we hit the first wave outside the harbour we were all wedged tight.

Riding those waves depends on timing. The speeding up and slowing down is as important as the precision of the steering, and Nikolaras, like all proficient captains, was obviously enjoying it, synchronising the two operations with his own two eyes and hands. He also awarded us one good grin on each side of Nikouria as we took our shower-bath. Perhaps it is worth smiling so rarely as he does, his smiles make such an impact when they come. And all that time the wailing from the cabin was indistinguishable from the wailing of the day before. Otherwise, if goats don't wail, the women and children had bleated on the way.

I was holding Julian, who lay in a coma with his almond eyes unopening from Katapola to Ormos and was speechless for several hours afterwards. I had no idea if he knew whose lap he had been attached to, but in the evening he came trotting up to me to say, `I like you, Carolina,' so I suppose he did. That was Julian behaviour, I liked him too, I liked all three, and the moment was sharply relevant to the whole summer business of houses, families and ownership. I had dragged my brother into my own project, to make an area of confusion into one complete estate, and I had arranged that in the future it should be split up again. My beautiful idea of giving a village girl my house had not allowed my own family one thought.

They had not been in my life. Nor had Katina's house. I had had no inkling of such developments.

I could not say that I wanted to retract my promise, but I was in a conflict where the familiarity of my three nephews pricked deep doubts. Zachary, whom I had met for the first time that summer, seemed to know me as easily as the other two had seemed to know me when I met them for five days the year before. 'We talk of you so much,' Catherine explained. 'We make a point of that.' It was like bringing up one's children to be bilingual, a thoughtfulness.

'If ever you need children,' she said, 'these are yours.' The words came out with an intensity which made an impact, though I did not appreciate their meaning at that time. I appreciated her for saying it. She was talking, as mothers may talk to their relations, about her sons, and suddenly, flashingly, she added, 'These are yours.'

Coals of fire, that's called. But I had promised my house away and nothing could be done.

We were greeted with generous admiration from the mule party when we met, and in Laki admiration was mixed with curiosity about the reason for our voyage. 'Lucky man!' exclaimed Kaliope, the mother of the family. She meant Mr N, and she was opening a conversation on a pattern that I did not like.

Lucky man? What do you mean, lucky man? Henry's house will be transferred to his name by some means or other. Mr N himself is encouraging me to get that arranged, and everyone says the law will change. The question of mine is different. That's my business.

And what about the money, all those thousands of drachmas passing through his hands?

What about it? He is scrupulous in the way he goes through the accounts. He's always finding ways of being economical. I couldn't have done without him, we need a commander, we'll be away for months on end, we're foreigners.

Kaliope made doubtful faces. Someone else...

Someone else? Who? Why? He was the one who looked after me when I did not have a spare drachma to my name. No one else showed me a house. But for him I wouldn't have one now.

That summer I was always on the defensive, because I also had to defend what I was doing convincingly enough to satisfy myself. The festival came upon us, knitting families in cliques, and I - having my own to be knit with - became less eccentric in village eyes, even more respectable, for the same reason that made my policy less defensible.

Second in feasting, third in fasting, the Panayia is Langatha's most festive festival, falling in the season for family reunions and celebrating all night out of doors, and wherever in Greece there is a church of the Virgin that is likely to be so. It must be unendurable on Tinos, where upwards of thirty thousand pilgrims are landed off a shuttle service of packed boats, but fortunately the church outside Langatha does not offer annual miracles. There is no jostling on its doorstep of souvenir vendors among the halt, the maim and the blind.

Our church, in the person of tall Phanis the whitewasher, who is master-in-command, offers a fasting feast of chick peas and a barley porridge on the Eve, and a two-course meat feast after the morning service on the Day, when a lonely path becomes the gayest trail on the island and any child is allowed to ring the bells. Anyone can come. If there are five hundred they will all be fed. Gifts in kind or money - a sack of potatoes, a thousand drachmas, a cow or sheep or goat, from farmers on the spot or islanders in Athens, are made out of patriotic spirit or as bargains with the healing Panayia. And there's no stinting. In the feast house next door to the church, quantities are enormous in deep bowls. Many are defeated, many ask for seconds, and the only person who will not sit down at those long, laden marble tables is Mr N.

Once I met him at the festival of the two doctor saints Anargyri, which happens in Tholaria and offers the same fare. He ordered grilled meat at a shop, and drank beer until going off to work at dawn. But as his normal habits are comparatively abstemious, as the bill for such a night is heavy for him, and as he also keeps away from churches, there is not much lure for him at festivals.

Going to church is a fine thing, he says, but your mind needs to be rested and his never is.

I have mixed feelings about these celebrations, but I thought his attitude plain snooty, just because he had not been the cook himself. The first course is a light and tasty soup, the second a rich and tasty stew, and he could not possibly have shared the horror of some foreigners at identifying the frilly pieces in the broth. That soup is delicious if you are mentally prepared for it, and I was always glad to go along on the Eve with my best knife to help chop the nameless wodges up, gladder by far than to stand about in my best clothes exclaiming, `How beautiful!' the lengthy duty of the Day.

That seemed a lighter business in a family unit with three small boys of our own being beautiful and admired in Thai shirts. One of our annual habits in formation was decking ourselves and boys in a manner befitting village residents, though Catherine and I could never produce hair-dos or high heels. The footwear of the village ladies on Langatha paving is their triumph, one which they even carry with them on the wildest, most rugged trek a rugged island offers to the crazy festival of the Holy Cross on September the fourteenth. Then the meat is cooked with rice because it is a hell of a way for mules to carry so many kilos of potatoes, but a real *Langathiani* knows what is what, and high-heeled shoes are light.

Another of our habits was to keep faith, not with any shop that dancing night in the *platia*, but with one pair of musicians. Music means lute and violin, there's no question about that, but who plays with whom and at which shop is a sensitive piece of village politics. Partnerships are formed, the *platia* is divided by a strict territorial line, however the chairs may overlap and bulge, and if you are sitting in the middle you have overlapping songs as well. When Stephanakis the cobbler played with Michalis the carpenter we sat well over to their side.

Stephanakis, the violonist of this pair, was an old friend for Catherine and Henry. He had made them almost the only sandals he had ever made for foreigners, and was the subject of one of Henry's *Mule Track* photographs, which hangs on his shop wall. Michalis, the lute-player, was a new friend, and an important one, but none of us knew how important yet.

He is also the godfather of Stephanakis' boy, which makes them as close as blood relations. They like to play and sing together, and are equally prepared to do so from early evening until morning, as long as dancers dance. Afterwards Michalis will take a nap and go straight back to work, and even Stephanakis - a wilting cobbler for days and weeks at Panayia time - will rouse himself and a sorry stomach if work means bringing out his violin again. This is lucrative season for musicians, and splurging season for the rest. Holidaying relations like throwing notes around - that's what the cardboard box at the musicians' feet is for, a fee for every dance. They may toss five hundred, or a thousand if they're drinking well. One hundred is standard. Coins are unacceptable.

Dancing on Panayia night is cramped until the small hours, but if you have arrived in time to find a place you may need stamina to stay so long. Our favourite evenings were the Sundays following, when everyone was a member of an open party and the *platia* was more than ever a public sitting room, with its spectators grouped around. Then there was scope for leaping leaders and acrobatic twosomes, as well as for circles of any diameter in which the women, along with patient male relations, unwearyingly and properly performed. I had casual dancing rights as I taught English to Stephanakis' boy, but Henry waived those if we made a family circle to swing the boys around. He preferred to toss his note like anyone else.

Our steps were not like anyone else's, but nobody was critical about that. Who was concerned with footwork when the joy of Jason, Julian and Zachary was joy for all, and the whole performance a public compliment? 'Langatha, we like you,' was our dance, and that was understood by all. Stephanakis and Michalis sang the impromptu words for us.

'Did you dance?' asked *Kyria* Mouska, who had been watching from her end of the *platia*. 'The musicians were playing - did you dance?' If I was alone she would go on to ask me if the boys had equal shares of love. Otherwise, since she only asked the question because she liked the answer, she would pass the marvellous information on. Everyone was approving of adoption, and no couple would adopt a child themselves. They sat back telling me and one another what good people Henry and Catherine and all such parents were.

And so when Langatha's first foreign family came up the mule track, the greetings at the top were not only friendly but appreciative. The boys were given rides on the way, sweets - too many - when they got there, and more kisses and caresses than they liked, melting hearts with their Greek syllables. Dimitris would walk in with bottles or baskets of home produce, saying 'Eat this,' or 'Drink that,' or - when he brought eggs - 'Boil these.' *Kyria* Mouska discovered how much Henry liked her best black grapes, and only Mr N remained equivocal.

He was enchanted with the boys. Zachary was the same age as his own Demosthenes, whom he encouraged to stop and play with them. He sat them on his knee or on his donkey, calling them 'my friend' in English until 'My Friend' became their name for him. He had devoted awe from them and open friendliness from Catherine, whom he called Kat-er-i-ni, reverendly drawing out the syllables. But I was more convinced by the way he spoke the word 'Enrikos' than I was by Henry's toleration of him as our commander.

Sometimes Henry visited his down-site and looked out saying rather wistfully, 'How beautiful!' It was also very comfortable with so much sand. But he never regretted what I had done to him and would come charging up the mule track in the early afternoon, when others consider it too hot to go down, to wield a pickaxe, knock down courtyard walls for air and view, and build steps to his middle field. Foreign methods arouse every possible suspicion, Dimitris made a point of looking puzzled, but Henry is capable of achieving great feats quickly and all observers were impressed. So was Mr N, but Mr N did not want Henry to see that. Whenever he showed off Henry's work to others I had to report that to my brother privately. Complaints were muttered that every time Enrikos raised a pickaxe he was raising a question of a foreigner working without a work permit. The responsibility was his - Mr N's - and it was turning his hair grey. Yet I am sure that our policeman would not have queried Henry's having a pickaxe in his hand on what everyone considered his own property.

Any other islander would have been a waving passer-by or casual dropper-in on the family's up-days. Any other islander would have accepted a cup of coffee or shouted, 'Where's the ouzo?' being brief about it, but at least walking through the gate. For Mr N there could be ouzo and coffee only in his shop, and then he would usually insist on treating but would seldom sit with us. If he walked along the path between our houses he would go with eyes set, bee-lining ahead. Why don't you come in sometimes? - 'I cannot.'

He made two exceptions. If Henry was seen lingering after an up-night, being perhaps a mason in the midday sun, a lunch plate was likely to arrive, sometimes delivered in the commander's hands - swiftly if so, and with not more than one word. Once it was whitebait with green beans and garlic sauce. Considering the amount of words that might accompany a lunch plate, it was extraordinary that a foreigner's complaint could be the studied way in which he was left in his own peace, hankering for a little friendly chat. Mr N's garlic sauce beat everyone's - he knew it - and afterwards, off the premises, he would accept a compliment. That was the happier exception. The other was that he came here to slaughter goats.

Gateways are the perfect place for butcher's work, and as there were two in Henry's wall along our path Mr

N had doubtless worked out that he was neither in our way nor encroaching on Henry's property, for he stood on the outside. The goats, having had their throats cut a little further - but not far - off, were hung up, disembowelled, cleaned and flayed with skilful speed, and with a smile for the boys which he achieved even while holding the knife between his teeth. For the boys, hardly able to approach, could not hold back, pushing one another forward they did approach. Hardly able to look, they looked. And Zachary nearly became a lifelong vegetarian.

Henry showed notable restraint about this use of his portal, if largely because these operations did not happen often, and before they came back to live in this house the next summer the portal was to be blocked up. He and Catherine knew that you cannot logically come and be enchanted with the animal traffic, antique threshing, lamplight, goat's cheese, gifts from Mouska, and then be revolted by the sight of entrails, but these ones were a little too close, too attractive to the flies. The flies on windless days were very bad.

Butchery could not continue without that second gateway, but livestock needed a long-term policy, especially as Jason was allergic to any kind of bite. If the bakehouse had been a henhouse until the day that they arrived, or if a goat was parked there overnight, the retinue of insects would linger for a while, and however forebearing Mr N might be about his greetings, he found the bakehouse extremely useful for his hens and goats. We had a constant battle to make our old houses unalluring to all forms of biting life.

I was a middle person. So long as home base for my family was in Laki I lived upstairs and downstairs in two camps. Devoted to them I grew edgy. Joyful to have them there, I would not spend an evening with them unless they came up. Fond as I was of the Laki family, I could not be persuaded - if one of the girls told me what good *mousaka* or meatballs had been made - to stay and eat the *mousaka* or meatballs, however many nephews might be sharing them. Laki belonged to the midday and afternoon, the evening was Langatha's, I wanted to go home. I wanted to go to Mr N's shop, to be one of the boys again. Festivals and Sundays were a disconnection, I had to get back into my place, to drink wine with my commander who had looked so miserable on Catherine's evening and reassure myself.

All the islanders are tired at the end of August. Winter is the time for sleep. Now that the days were shortening, Mr N was glad to make his evenings earlier, to potter round his shop and bring out what he could find to go with half a kilo of retsina in a quiet and undemanding way. Nothing that I swallowed made much difference to his economy, I had worked that out, and there would be a time for recompense. His table was liberal, but not extravagant, he did not like excess. When someone else might have refilled the wine jug he would pass his hand decisively across the top. '*Domani*,' he would say, and that was fine, for I was wary of long sessions when the others left, yet I wanted to come back. A Greek 'tomorrow' is not nearly so exact as Mr N's *domani*. That was a date, when ease would be balancing to any tension there had been, and he my conspiratorial friend.

Henry's last days were full of mathematics. His dollars had not come, the contract had scraped out his wallet and he was making a precedent of leaving bills behind. He drew up a building programme and left me with instructions for distributing the money, assuming that it came before I left, including two thousand drachmas as commander's fee for Mr N, which I commended, and the same for me, which I did not.

I needed it, but that was another matter, and I boggled at the way this list continued with all sorts of pretexts for bounty more than I thought he could afford. This brother of mine was paying me for organising work on the house that I had forced on him, buying the room that I had meant to give him, and adding an extra fee for lavatory rights. It seemed to me that the state of sisterliness had fallen pretty low.

It had not occurred to me in June that having a brother's funds to borrow or embezzle was another good reason for making my brother buy that house, but as I pocketed five thousand more as soon as it came into my hands, it obviously was. The punishment would come in Athens when my accumulated debts, including everything, such as the galling lavatory rights, that I chose to call a debt, were to be paid off from a salary of six and a half thousand drachmas, less than a hundred pounds a month.

In 1972 that did not seem too low. I had applied for my position at the headquarters of the most highly organised, above-board language school I knew of, where treatment of teachers might be dictatorial but was also fair and square. I could give private lessons too. What horrified me, now that I saw October looming, was not how tough my sentence had to be in working hours, but the setting and the metamorphosis. A teacher in Athens? I was a workman's donkey, an island goat. I hardly knew what I looked like after these four months, and soon I would have to be standing at a blackboard, discoursing on gerunds and infinitives, being quick-witted with chalk. For the sake of my Langatha house, still uninhabitable, I would have to search for some flat or cell or hovel in the city fumes and grimy streets, and live in it for nine months of two years. Well, I had asked for it.

Catherine boldly gave Mr N a goodbye kiss until next summer, and the boys showed more than usual readiness to follow her example, for there was only one 'Mr Friend'. He and Henry put cordiality into their handshakes, and everyone said, 'What good people!' a great many more times. One week later their money arrived.

A thousand dollars was exactly thirty thousand drachmas, more than the postman was allowed to carry. I had to go to Chora to collect it, just at the worst moment for my sandals, which were in an end-of-summer state of wreck. I did not want to waste money on a boat, so Mr N lent me his donkey, bringing it at daybreak with a pot of provisions and instructions to tie my hair up because it's always windy round the mountaintop. That day's ride became a joke which kept him laughing for a week. 'What time,' he would repeat, 'did you get back?' I had just beaten the dark. There had been plenty of friendly interest at the monastery and in Chora, both in the donkey and the dollars, but I had not lingered there, I had been on the mountain for ten hours. Greek donkeys, I have often noticed, are expert at recognising foreigners.

On the way back, dawdling round the ridges, I was struck by an incongruous thought. It was well known in Aiyiali, in Chora and the monastery, that I was up here with a thousand dollars. Where are the brigands? On Amorgos the only answer is a laugh.

This would be good brigand country for the cinema. For much of the way there is hardly any path, and I have seldom been so sorry for anyone as for the Athenian postman who was sent in as a substitute for a few months when our own postman was ill. Having no mule of his own, he had to walk - one day to Aiyiali and round its villages, the next day back to Chora, and back again, and back, with a bag weighing up to thirty kilos, so he claimed. He looked as if he thought forced labour in a prison camp would be preferable to such punishment. 'What have they done to me?' he cried out in a passion when I met him somewhere in the wilds, and it seemed to me that the almighty 'they' could have no inkling of what they had done to this poor man.

So I was in possession of thirty thousand drachmas, which felt good for a brief while. Mr N immediately began mustering the wherewithal for the roof of Henry's lower room, the one which came with my house and was most likely to fall in. Fixing that before the winter meant fixing it before the olives, so he was feeling pressed. I just felt melancholy, because I could not stay to pick.

On the ninth of September the same cast of characters assembled as for the blessing of my house in May, only without the cock - I suppose there was no cock available.

The rest of the ritual was thoroughly performed, though the priest's interpretation of who this house belonged to was chanted out as Mr N, Carolina and Carolina's Brother, in that order, which I did not include in my report. Henry was missing all his own feasts as well as his own blessing, so my selection was for happy details. I made the most of Mr N's enthusiastic seizure of a set of handmade wooden Thai bowls for the meat and potatoes that the working gang sat down to on the well-top, after the priest had left at half-past-ten.

That morning feast was a move to the right and proper in procedure, we had not had the place or the equipment for eating on the spot before. Eight days later, when the new roof was thrown, the stew-pot was brought down again, and this time Mr N - always decisive about details

of stage-management - had me prepare the table on my side. There on my terrace, working through the wine flagon, we all surveyed the view for one last triumphant time. The water tank

for the shower was the best seat for the panorama - no one could work out how to make the water run, but I had my orgy of looking out from it, thinking about Easter when this would be the terrace of a lived-in house. Would it? That seemed as hypothetical that day as seven months seemed long.

`Stay and pick with us.' How I wanted to. I had to go and be a teacher, and my fingernails were ingrained with orange paint.

Island blue would be our final colour, the orange is a lead preservative. I had started on the frames, but there was no hope for the blue coat, or for my nails, as Michalis brought the door and shutters the day before I left. If optimism is a fault, it's the only one I know of in Michalis, but in the end he never lets you down. He makes you fret and flutter, and then asks why you're fluttering - and why indeed? He's right, you should not doubt him, for he will set aside a year-old order to give precedence to a customer in a state of urgency.

Michalis was promising a floor of interlocking Swedish pinewood, to be found on Naxos in the winter, which seemed beyond belief, and Mr N was promising a thoroughness with the varnish I would send from Athens, for the ceilings too. Please don't be too thorough - but do be thorough, please. It is not easy to leave anything to anyone's commandership. Mix paraffin with linseed oil for the undercoat - that's for insect proofing. Be careful about drips.

Henry's own prescription for the treatment of the beams was to soak the ends in paraffin before they were built into the walls. I officiated over this innovation for his lower rooms, and all the workmen, sloshing paraffin about, exclaimed, 'What a good idea!' and would never do such a thing again. It's no good overdoing the instructions. If you must be absent, keep them island-like, and remember that anything upsetting or unsatisfying - because of your absence - will be your own fault.

At dusk the day after that new roof was thrown, I found Dimitris watering the concrete, which is essential to prevent it from cracking in the heat. 'It's none of my business,' he muttered, 'but I saw that it hadn't been done so I came and watered it.' He paused, glancing about, and added that my lime was not his business either, but once or twice he had seen that it was drying and had also watered that.

If you must be absent, that is your own fault.

What I could not stomach was people giving their opinions simply for the pleasure of being critical. But there was one who had no business with our houses except giving his opinion, who did not irritate. Short Phanis who is wise turned a chat over a drink at Ormos into a lecture over supper while I was patient about hearing, though not agreeing, that I was putting too much trust in Mr N. I thought I was familiar with that topic, and he went through the familiar part, but then his message took a different turn. Look after your own people was his theme. He had been watching me with my nephews and it seemed very wrong to him that I should have promised my house to a family of no blood relationship. 'We don't do things like that,' said wise Phanis.

`We don't do things like that.' I had never claimed to be an islander, but this was rather like a punch below the belt.

What could be my answer? There was no easy one, except that when I had launched what I thought to be a single, unambitious project I had not been much concerned with my last will and testament. And it was not my inclination now to be concerned, but this was the price of ownership, I was having the subject foisted on me, and Phanis was talking sense. The Greeks, most praiseworthy in the way they look after their own grannies, are far too clannish to make a virtue of give and take between the clans, or much like public spirit. I could not confess to all the selfish reasons why it suited me to look after a child of my commander's family. I could not confess that the idea had evolved from a wish to resurrect a ruin and leave it, not so much to one particular Maria as a daughter of the village.

We don't do things like that.

`One day,' said wise Phanis, `you will remember this evening at this table, and you will say to me, "Phani, you were right."'

His words were as dispiriting as the autumn feeling of those late September days, when olive season was approaching and I did not want to go. On my last Sunday evening I wandered up to the *platia* where Stephanakis and Michalis were playing in an end-of-season way - for enjoyment without expecting wads of notes - when a doleful occurrence put an end to song. Nikitas - grocer Nikitas who three months before had brought his little generator up the hill - turned a switch and after weeks of fiddling the televison worked. Instantly, at whatever shop they had been sitting, one and all picked up their chairs and swooped. The whole *platia* was empty except for two startled musicians and one foreign woman calling for consoling drinks. There was not even a chair left.

Stephanakis said, `That's the first time.' Michalis said, `Of course they want to watch it now.' I said, `They'll get used to it.' Or something of the sort. Then, in rotation, we said such sentences again. And all the while their fingers were quietly playing with the strings.

No one joined us. Perhaps it was as well. Someone else might have said, `*Finito la musica*,' which is one of the phrases that Mr N's customers enjoy. They were saying, `*Finito la musica*' with rather too much repetition on the night I left them to walk down to Ormos and get onto a boat.

Chapter Six

❯ T eachers are to be on the premises at least ten minutes before their lessons. Otherwise they will arrive panting, which is undignified and not to be tolerated.'

Rules for teachers covered nearly half a dozen pages. Aiyiali was a distant country. *Finito la musica.*

When I had read my circular and decided not to start life by being offended, I took a bus to the café of the Amorgots in Athens and drank a bottle of retsina with Mr N's eldest brother. It was the first time that I had met him and I found it as uncanny as looking into a mirror and seeing the difference between a workman's donkey and a tidy figure on a teacher's dais. Appearance at the school with a coat or other garment merely slung around one's shoulders was another item on the blacklist. Clearly the donkey would have to be incarcerated for a while.

Most of the faces around the café tables were more or less familiar. If I did not know them or their brothers they had an island air about them, and at first I thought it might be cheering to live somewhere in this colony, for islanders - like Greeks abroad - are gregarious in their own areas. I thought so for a day or two and changed my mind. This was a dismal place, and grimy, with its crowded café on a street of non-stop one-way traffic and the volume of the television being suitably competitive. Here they sat murmuring and shouting fondly about an island where they would like to spend their Easter, but where few would happily go back to live. Only Stephanakis, who has moved into this lost souls' limbo for most of the year while his son goes to gymnasium, miserably and laudably admits, `I don't do here.' Athens is loaded with country ex-patriots who don't do.

It takes forty minutes to walk to this area from the city centre, and the cottage that I found was slightly further, in Kypseli directly on the other side. It really was a cottage, up a flight of steps and a country path, which no one would believe, but there - for barely over ten pounds a month - it stood. A non-flush loo and one cold water-tap explained the rent, and they could not deter me after island time. It had a terrace larger than its floor space, a clear view to the Lykabettos and almost to the sea. That was what I looked at, the reward of my habit of going straight up hills.

Regular flats do not have one stick of furniture, and sticks would have been the word for what I could have bought. A large, solid table, a wardrobe and a kitchen cupboard went with this house, and then the saint of timing, who had produced the sister's godmother's grand-daughter at the moment when I was baffled by the lack of three hundred pounds to buy a house, went back to work. Meriel had made her long-term base in Athens, but now on sudden whim decided to throw up all and go back to an English home. That meant hurriedly disposing of a load of furniture and household objects, including a chest of drawers, a chair, a bed, and boxfuls of kitchen utensils of far higher quality than I would have looked at in a shop - all the essentials for an unpretentious cottage except the three that mine already had. She named a small sum to be paid by English cheque, and left. I was sorry to see her go but could not have asked for her to do so, if she must, at a more convenient hour.

About a year later she needed her three hundred pounds back, and after being such a fortuitously good friend on two occasions went out of my life.

Once I had moved into my house, I seldom went into Amorgos country except on business. Then I liked to do so. I did not want to linger, but I liked having business there. The Aiyiali Society was not a grimy place at all, it looked strangely like an airway terminal. From there various bun-fights, meetings, dances and excursions are arranged, partly for joy and partly to raise money for the island cause. President Adonis, a dapper architect, nephew of my neighbour from whom I had bought a patch of land, was perpetually on the telephone. He spoke too rapidly and too long for me to follow, but his tone of voice was the tone an orator would use to plead for a city postman doomed to walk between Chora and Aiyiali six days a week. There are so many causes for a president to agitate about that I had to keep alert between the conversations to push in mine. Was there any way of changing the ownership of our houses to our name?

Adonis thought there might be, and he had time for this question, for he approved of us - we were resurrecting our houses to look like island houses, with plain wooden doors. Real islanders today, he pointed out, would go for wrought iron and frosted glass. Our response to that was that we had never known an Amorgot so much in tune with how we feel, which he later verified by teasing me because I did not fill my house with plastic flowers. He was such an agitator for tradition that he even gave a slideshow one summer in Aiyiali, displaying frosted glass and knick-knacks to the very people who had installed them, with a commentary that was merciless.

Adonis knew of no particular reason for everyone to be saying that the law would change, but thought that he would be able to pull some strings for us. My book, if not our doors, might be grounds for a special dispensation, he would talk to some bigwig about that. Somehow, by some means or other, with patience, we would change the ownership. I was quiet about the future of my own house, for I did not want to complicate the issue with a local promise that he would not approve of any more than wise Phanis. As patience was so strongly emphasised, I could let that be.

My other dealings were at the café with the island errand boys. I don't know what else to call them, they are not boys but in Greek they share the title 'postman' with the man who delivers letters, which they were not supposed to do. They do business and shopping for the islanders, carry gifts and orders between Athens and Aiyiali, spending weeks and fortnights alternately in each. I sent varnish, money, and various oddments that Mr N wanted for my house or for himself. His personal orders were tacitly regarded as presents, which strengthened my position, so I was glad of that. They were not many, and I in turn received a box of sixteen eggs, hard-baked island bread, a clump of prickly pears still thriving on their leaves, and a pot of casseroled rabbit which had been sent with a flagon of red wine. That errand boy drank the wine on board and abandoned the flagon, which Mr N had taken from my house. I think the casserole was rabbit, but it had sat in the café for a fortnight before I happened to run into it.

It would have been a moot point which of the two most frequently-appearing errand boys to choose, had there been a choice to make, but their comings and goings were too unpredictable for that. One was always drunk and forgot his orders, but clung to payments in advance. He was not the one who drank my red wine. That was the one who could only read by tilting his head backwards, an attitude which led to pride and on to laziness. The third had a sick wife. He was the reliable one and was sometimes off for months.

I took one leaf of prickly pears to school and distributed them around the teachers' room. Some of the Greek teachers asked, 'What are those?' That was like my students denying that threshing, anywhere in Greece, is still performed on threshing floors. They may have wondered why my tones grew ardent, but I regarded revelations about my private life as being a form of extra-mural friendliness, so I did not quote my sources when our set topics were agricultural. Extra-mural friendliness, like panting, was undesirable.

At first I asked those teachers to help me decipher Mr N's letters, which were surprisingly prolific for an islander who had been through two classes of primary school, and also rather like the foreign-language telegrams that come through the Langatha office, with the plaster running without a comma into the varnish and the prickly pears. I gave that up because the teachers often could not help me, and what was worse they always howled with snooty laughter, tempting me to make retorts about the salt of the earth versus middle-class Athenians. He could have taught them endless mysteries of their homeland that they had no idea about. The biggest threat to that homeland, I wanted to say, was the extinction of his kind.

Amorgos cropped up all over Athens, going about its business and being tired, as I was. I taught a thirty-hour week beginning at eight-thirty on Monday mornings and finishing on Saturday nights at ten. At that moment the teachers said to one another, 'Have a nice weekend.' A nice weekend? Three years before, in Chalkis, I had been free from nine on Friday evenings until four on Monday afternoons. In those days you could run a car on a salary of five thousand, which I did with verve for what seemed like half the week. Now there was no car, no time, no adventure, and this worked very well. I was living a mathematical game, amusing in its own way, of how little I could survive on and how much I could put by for Amorgos. Careering had no more appeal. I ate lunch with the same friend on Sundays, and went to the cinema.

I walked up and down my hill with my mind on English grammar and mental arithmetic. On alternate days I was free at six o'clock, which was a hazard for my budget but a private lesson solved that. Two hundred drachmas for an hour and a half, three times a week, that makes six. That was enough to live on and consumed potential spending time.

My student was a rich, fat sixteen-year-old slob who had to have his supplementary lessons because the Lower Cambridge Certificate was a necessity of life. He believed that he could learn enough to pass by doing exercises so fast that I could not chip in to ask a question, correct him, or explain 'the unknown words'. His flesh bulged out between the buttons of his outsize shirt, he would alternately be stroking that and biting his nails to the quick, and he developed a surreptitious habit of cancelling the Friday lesson because his private school was closed on Saturdays. I could hear his voice lowered on the telephone, for he had learnt what moment he could catch me coming out of class, but Mother was bound to find out afterwards. She told me to pay no attention, but I could not see the point of going if he was at a discoteque. I should have, but I was thinking like an islander. Truancy is not a valid reason for lost fees.

Sometimes I had to go round just to be paid for the last lesson, sensitively aware that the two hundred-drachma notes, my own weekend, were peanuts to the well-coiffeured lady who usually made some difficulty about finding them. She did not end her months with ten drachmas at the most, or leave herself with one thousand on the first day. That was what I did. I sent at least three-quarters of my salary to Mr N, walked to save three-drachma bus fares, and lived off a fat slob who cancelled me on Fridays.

I began by sending what I owed to Henry, and he sent more, so the errand boys were carrying wads to Mr N, to put into his pocket as the doubting Amorgos community liked to suggest. Not into his pocket, I retorted, into his hands. He was my commander, he sent detailed accounts, at Easter I would see results, to which they answered, 'Yes, but...' and went back over their arguments. I always reacted ferociously to that 'yes, but...'

In fact I found the financial statements rather too mysterious. It was difficult to tell whether they always started from the beginning, or from the point where they left off before. And if I had been pushed for details I could not have explained the distribution of all the days' labour and cement.

From the New Year until Easter the weeks seem to contain an interminable amount of days for a teacher to be dignified - through flu season as well. But at least we were allowed to have the flu here, which my directress in Chalkis had begged me not to do. There too on the last day of the month she had sometimes come into my classroom to beg the students for their fees, collected as much as they would part with and placed a pile on my desk, audibly asking, 'Will that do until next week?' Here our tidy pay-packets were correct to the last drachma on the penultimate day of every month, with bonuses at Christmas and Easter according to the law. For a full-time worker the total of the year's bonuses is equal to two months' salary. I was employed for nine months, but even so my pascal envelope felt fat and real and good.

But what was Easter? Our school beat every other in the country for the shortness of its holidays - another part of the director's pride. We had one week's freedom, so abruptly ending that I would have to be severed from the island on Easter Monday night. It did not really matter that there was more fasting than feasting on my schedule, but this was an occasion for a severe reminder that one reason why I liked this silly island was that getting to it was such a business. Aiyiali would not be Aiyiali if out of my precious week I did not have to deduct a day's journey at each end.

Once you have got to your boat and it has set off, fourteen sea-hours is good time. Eighteen is not bad. I have once been on a freak express that made Katapola in eight. I have been on another boat for fifty two, and only twelve of those were spent sheltering in a storm. It all depends on so many elements to do with ports of call and weather and the disposition of the engine that by the time you think you've mastered it the programme changes and you start again. The subject is so unfathomable that even my director, whose first aim was to run the school like a computer, came to make humane allowances for the boats of Amorgos. I was given a day's leave to get me to Aiyiali before the end of Holy Week.

When Mr N rode me up the mule track in the small hours of an April morning, and we rounded the last corner on the north side of Langatha, I saw a gleam ahead. He grunted at my exclamation, 'You don't expect to come to a dark house?'

A lighted house that you come to occupy for the first time cannot really - or can it? - be your own. Mr N opened the door. We stepped onto a warm, matt-varnished, wooden floor, so pretty that I could not care about the minimal camp furniture. The walls were whitewashed - what did I expect? On the table were eggs, cream cheese and bread, a bottle and a few implements. He moved round, turning up the lamps. 'Come, you must be hungry, sit here. Welcome to your house.' He poured out wine and cracked an egg - he should not have been doing that in Holy Week. I felt like an elated shadow, but not too shadowy to say how good that tasted, how delicious that fresh island cheese. `And there'll be more. Don't think of shortages in spring. In the morning you will see - flowers.' A great whoosh came out with the word.

He should have left the house right then. It would have been the perfect moment. But he said, `And what about the real welcome now?'

That's the tax for so much magic. I really cannot blame him, for he is only making a suggestion, but it takes the joy out of these whitewashed walls and glowing floor. He doesn't get his tax and mine is only the necessity of going into argument, so it's all thoroughly pointless after more than half a year's hard work. I grasp the subject and give it one great shove around the corner. I will not have my Easter spoilt. My Easter does not need this bonus, Mr N. I can forget the subject, for it will not arise again during the few days that I can stay. I can forget it while next facing him, the commander who is often good company and whom I need, for somehow or other he has become as much a part of my Langatha as my house.

`Until tomorrow, then.' When Mr N, reproachful but not belligerent, went out, I had an illogical feeling that he might have locked the door. I opened it as soon as he was safely up the path and breathed in the meaning of his `whoosh'. That's air. That's flowers. I don't need daylight to tell me that. Until tomorrow then - today he means - two or three hours to the transformation scene.

When I opened the door to that tomorrow it rushed in upon me with a scramble of what could hit first, the sun, the flower competition beneath the sun, the poppies which believe themselves apart from competitions, the spring wheat that knows all about dancing, my white-pigeon walls. There is so much of it all in April. There are so many flowers, so many colours, primary and rainbow, pushing and shoving, and - slapped over the landscape - that wheat green declaring itself a primary colour too. I gasped, and all the dazzle and the pollen burred around. I gasped for five days. It was an exhausting experience, to gasp so much.

There were not only wild flowers to bombard the senses of an Athenian teacher. I had my own petunias and carnations in a long bed sheltered beneath one terrace wall. Perhaps I had sent seeds, but Mr N was otherwise responsible. I gasped at that and promised to take over the watering from Maria, who would be busy through these Easter days. It was strange how it felt like an act of obedience to be watering my own petunias.

When he first found me on my terrace staring at my flower-bed, Mr N stood watching me with a half smile waiting for my approval to be turned into a grin. After his first proposition he was very nice that Easter, which is an unlikely statement to make of Mr N. The trouble is that people are more interesting to write about when they are being extraordinary, but I did not aim at having an extraordinary commander. Niceness was much more of an achievement.

There was another grin waiting, a more anxious one for a far larger subject than a flower-bed. He had turned my strip of hillside into a long thin terrace four steps down from the kitchen, and a neat little field below.

`We couldn't have left it as it was,' he argued, as I stood dumbfounded. No, I suppose not. I hadn't told him not to do it. He hadn't specifically asked. He may have suspected that I would have silly feelings about that hillside patch, and I was glad that they had not been given occasion to assert themselves, for here was the best kitchen terrace and neat little field that could have been designed. You could pass the plates out and eat in mid-June in the shade. If I lived here permanently I could have a kitchen garden. He had planted two peach trees already. Thank you, Mr N.

I had not been paying off my debts to Henry after all. I had been reshaping my own field. That accounted for the mysterious element in winter letters and was certainly a set-back, but I could not wish the work undone. Here too was one in the eye for anyone who told me not to trust this man. Look at my house. I'm living in it. It has a floor, it's plastered, it has a kitchen terrace and a flower-bed. And look at Henry's. His main room and his kitchen have new roofs. We're moving. And every drachma is materially explained.

I might have had one blotch less on my floor if I had varnished it myself, but so many months of absence could not end without one small complaint. My floor needed to be walked on, and a little titivation, that was all. It was our triumph, it cost five thousand drachmas, including the work of laying it. One front door, two kitchen doors, four upstairs windows with their shutters cost a fraction more. As near as no matter the total was one hundred and fifty pounds. Then, with shelves and tables to be ordered, and debts about me, the bill seemed outsize for my lean teacher's purse. Now it almost makes me weep to think how low it was. It almost makes Michalis weep as well.

The front door was in three leaves, and the kitchen doors in two, like stable doors with a top leaf and a bottom, as Adonis in Athens thought all island doors should be. You can keep the wind out at the lower level. You can leave the top open, meaning `back soon' and go shopping without fear of stray donkeys, dogs or hens. A neighbour can lean over the bottom leaf for a chat. I was delighted with them, but now I had to spend my holiday with paint. Only one coat on all the windows meant one hundred and twelve straight lines around the panes. I don't know how that got done with the distraction of flowers and the people to greet and Mr N teasing. I don't believe I could have done two coats. He said, `Hold a piece of cardboard over the glass and make a quick sweep down.' I tried. It doesn't work. All right, I retorted, I was beating records for hours spent on painting windows and they would be the cleanest-edged on Amorgos.

At midday I trampled through flowers - there was no other way of moving - down to Ormos for a plate of Holy Week lettuce leaves, some olives and a glass of wine. The landscape was bespattered with blue, and so was I. The best blue is of wild lupins, which like the mauve-pink gladioli grow in a display of territorial consciousness, while the yellow clover and the poppies have none of that, and all the island's species of convolvulus twine themselves without respect on other people's backs. The daytime sparkled with a sunshine busier with visual effect than heat. Evenings came early with a chill, and a damp rushing straight into the sheets.

During evensong, when all the shops officially were shut, Mouska's Nikolakis, Mr N and I sat in a lone huddle over plates which more or less accorded with the fast, and chatted for my absent months. For the owner and the proprietor to eat supper with a visitor in semi-darkness was not, they reckoned, opening the shop. It was only on Good Friday that the policeman came to shut us up.

I might arrive here panting without offending anyone. No one cared if my arms were inside my sleeves or out. I flung myself into this shop. And then the taste of everything in front of us made the taste of Athens bland. Islanders won't eat eggs when their hens stop laying, you can see the difference in the watery imported yoke. If our barrels run dry they won't drink bottled wine, one reason why there's so much beer drunk at summer festivals. In the spring there's plenty, as tangy as the air.

I wished that Henry could have shared so amicable a supper, and relaxed with these two, Mr N and Nikolakis, who could by law have shooed him out of his village house and his down-site. Nikolakis would have to refund twelve thousand drachmas, and Mr N not one. Yet I could not feel the need for much impatience about the manoeuvring of names on a contract in our lifetime, and I was also going along with not regretting that I had promised my island house to an island girl. At this murky table that made sense.

The days were so invigorating and so enervating, both together, that we were yawning over our early suppers before I was normally preparing for my last class. How was I to keep awake on Easter Saturday for an evening beginning, on a fasting stomach, with the resurrection service after eleven o'clock? Even Mr N, who never went to church, was fasting. No lettuce leaf in Aiyiali had a drop of oil. And island sleepiness was baby-like.

That's no problem. Paint shutters by lamplight.

I did not know that my invitation from the Stephanakises for the fast-breaking gut-soup, delicious *margaritsa*, was for half-past-two. When Christ had risen, with the lighting of candles, the bell-ringing and the fire-crackers, the rockets and the cracking of eggs and the hand-shaking, all the excitement of a climax that needs the next thing to happen, I did not know that the next thing for the faithful was a two-hour mass. I rather thought it ought to be a bowl of soup. The faithful in Langatha must be as many in proportion to the community as in any secular community in Greece, and they have the required stamina. I don't. By the time we reached the boiled meats and cheese and eggs, as well as *margaritsa*, they seemed to be too much.

'Next year I'll come to you,' I promised Mr N's wife in the morning - or rather a little later the same morning after a short sleep that felt more like a siesta than belonging to the night. She had taken her children home half an hour after the resurrection, which was late enough for me and left a better gap before the Sunday feast. I was glad that I had agreed to eat that with the Laki family, whose home is in Tholaria at the end of a good walk, but I could not leave Langatha without taking a forkful with Mr N in his shop and a forkful with his wife at home. He was adamant on both points. I ran around the contours through the dazzle and the flowers in bright yellow trousers and a white shirt and a little blue paint, and my bright yellow trousers were tight.

On Amorgos the Easter goat is stuffed with rice, spring herbs and bits of guts and roast whole in the baker's oven overnight. It's a winner for succulence and tenderness with crackly edges, while the juicy stuffing provokes an annual discussion about which part who likes best. Every family is proud of their own stuffing, and it's equally good in every house. An annual invitation to one table in Tholaria does not stop me from being fairly sure of that. It is so well cooked that it will keep for half a week, and every housewife is anxious for it all to be consumed. Wherever you walk you may be caught by someone running out with a chunk on a fork.

My heart was broken that Easter. There had been a suspicious amount of activity around a ramshackle hut on the path that leads straight up into the village from the side of Henry's house, and one evening while I was watering my flowers, which is a special, almost sacred hour, I discovered in one blasting revelation what it was all about. A neighbour's generator began to work.

No - no - no! I must have shouted aloud, for several women, known to me and unknown, came running down. They stood with me on my terrace and we went through all the tearing of hair and gnashing of teeth that our heart-ache and that monster deserved. Mary, Mother of God, not here.

I always find it irritating when tourists out of their romantic fancies want to condemn good village housewives to endless years of filling irons with charcoal, cleaning smoky lamp-glasses, doing without refrigeration, washing nappies in all weathers by their wells. That's all very picturesque, and I would happily forgo the iced drink that I sometimes yearn for if there was no electricity at all, but I don't wash nappies, I know this is the attitude of selfishness. Unhappily I say that 'unspoilt' means 'neglected' nowadays in this respect. Now that the mini-generator has become a feature of Aiyiali it rumbles that harsh message out into the public air.

Vassilis had one too. There was another in Laki. On the stillest nights I could faintly hear a chug-chug from Tholaria. I told myself that at least the generating shop-keepers were providing some sort of public service. Langathans could choose their telly programmes - bless them - from two shops, and that did not prevent the dancing world from coming out to dance on special nights. But this man above me, this piece of grit among the scum, had brought his generator so that he could watch his own telly with his wife at home.

'He's a sailor,' they were saying. 'He'll be away for months. He won't run it in the mornings. He won't run it late, or every evening, the petrol costs too much. The public electricity will come soon and that will be the end of these machines. Don't worry. That's life.' But I stood there bawling at that hut, which had neither a proper door nor window to contain the sound. Go to the police station and you'll be offered a soothing cigarette, so yell into the air, there's no place else, for this is Greece. It's no good protesting that the man who owns the land that the noise and the fumes come from does not own the air that the noise and the fumes fill.

Then I shut up. For a while I pretended that it - that thing - did not exist. It was much more difficult to shove away than my arguments with Mr N. I did my best. On my lower terrace - thanks be for my lower terrace - I could hardly hear it. I could hardly hear it in my lower rooms, but they were a dank and earthy storehouse still. Turning these into homely quarters would be my next project, with a new incentive - I was growing doubtful about Athens being two years' work.

Athens was demanding, but it did not give me shocks.

Upstairs the generator was worse, but not overwhelming, so long as I could calm myself. When it stopped I banned it from my mind. When it ran I shut my ears and used my eyes. I loved the way my two rooms had turned out as one and an extension, for I refused to put a door between them, and the floor ran smoothly through to the far end. In the thickness of the dividing wall there had been cupboards on both sides, but I had got Dimitris to unblock one, making a vista that is the most unGreek feature of my house. The next year when I had a Greek teacher for a tenant, he pinned up a plastic curtain as if it was as indecent as the see-through dresses that - quite rightly - were not tolerated in my Athens institute.

There would be paint in my teacher's fingernails again, on the Wednesday after Easter, and I wondered where my head would be. As for my stomach, I felt like a camel before going back to court a lean existence until the end of June. On Easter Monday, while everyone was still working hard at family goat, we had a wedding in the village, and a wedding feast.

I could skip the whole occasion, one happy composition of local colour, except that I made a discovery about the bride's father, Christos the scribe. For years I had been misled by his aloofness and his parchment face, and it turned out to be fortunate that I got the matter straight. The courteous way in which he brought his personal invitation to the service and the feast demolished my fixed ideas that he disapproved of me, while the magnanimous way in which he gave his daughter a proper village wedding, instead of packing her off to Athens, dispelled my suspicion that he disapproved of the world. As his daughter was marrying a Tholaria man and the best man was from the third village, Potamos above the port, our scribe had chosen to act host to half Aiyiali, with no stinting at all.

The shop where three of us had made our huddles by one lamp was shining that evening with all the light that the next-door grocer could provide. The *platia* was nearly as crowded and quite as festive as for the Panayia. The bride was exquisite in her second outfit. The bride's mother looked ready to walk into the Grande Bretagne on Constitution Square. But Christos, neatly open-necked, did not sit back, look like a bride's father, grow talkative, or dance. I did not see him change expression at the beginning, in the middle or at the end. At eleven o'clock he was being a waiter from table to table, and I realised that the parchment had nothing to do with misanthropy or xenophobia, but simply belonged to the scribe's face.

It seemed crazy that I had to watch the hour, sitting with a suitcase at my side. `What a pity!' exclaimed Markos the muleteer, taking an interval from the festivities to ride me down. `All the schools are shut, all over the country, you ought to have fifteen days.' Everyone said so, but I had also realised that the middle of a wedding feast is a good time to leave a place if you are being a visitor.

`Lean well forwards,' Markos called all the way down to Ormos. He had been lurching with my suitcase at the top, but lurching was the minor problem, there was nothing to balance it but a kilo or so of roast goat and stuffing from various households, and twenty four baked and fresh eggs. `Forwards' means `outwards' to islanders, sitting side-saddle, and leaning outwards from a down-hill mule right after Easter and a wedding feast demands a concentration of sobering muscle-work. My legs did not ache from the mule track when I arrived at my house in Kypseli. My shoulders did.

Aches and blue paint and stuffed goat in the kitchen were proof that my island Easter had been real. But it was outrageous that I should so enjoy that Easter in the satisfaction of being back in my safe hole, relishing the week in retrospect. I went about washing myself and my clothes in a suburban manner which was shaming for the pleasure that it gave. I flung open my terrace doors and marvelled at the convenience of not having to run up and down stairs every time I needed a tea-spoon. Here it was three or four strides from the tea-spoon to the cushion in the sun. This house was self-contained, and so was I.

Chapter Seven

You live in Athens. Mr B is staying at a hotel. You are permanent residents, "live" with the simple present. Mr B is a tourist, use "stay" with the present continuous - unless you say, for instance, "He stays there every year." He stays, he is staying, repeated and temporary actions. Can we use "live" with the present continuous? No? Think again. You could ask me, "Where are you living?" - I am living in Kypseli. I am not a permanent resident and I'm not a tourist, I'm somewhere between.'

I am a teacher. I am living in Kypseli. From time to time I stay on Amorgos. That's getting personal, let Amorgos remain mysterious. Teachers' circulars, I must say, are extraneous to my enjoyment of the English tenses, and little in them is unreasonable. I don't know why the items cannot go without saying, that is all. Sitting down through the class-hour is bad. Vitality is good. Of course. I almost never sit. Come to think of it, I don't like to come panting into class. The English language is my subject. The director, who doesn't know the English language, treats me well. I really do not mind that I shall have to stay here for three years.

There was no more doubt of that. My projects and my debts were elongated, and meanwhile inflation had hit Greece. After a creeping up that had been barely noticeable, it happened almost overnight. I left Athens at the beginning of the summer when retsina was eight drachmas a kilo from the barrel, and when I came back it was eighteen. Simultaneously my landlady installed a flushing loo and bathroom basin - an improvement, I could not deny - which swallowed half my salary-rise with a suitably embellished rent. The rise was a standard thousand, less than fifteen percent.

There was almost no subject of conversation but the rising prices. You couldn't walk up a street without hearing a snippet of housewife's outrage at how much she had paid for her sugar or her beans. I had one private pupil who told me that as everything else was so expensive she would have to have cut-rate lessons by the standard of the year before. I was in such straits I took her on.

Mercifully I also got onto a richer vein. One family leads to another. I discovered that it's the ones who pay most who add the best treatment and the taxi fares. It's a slow process to get going, but I had incentives. First of all were floor tiles.

I made a bargain with a factory which produced large pink-brown tiles, like a faint attempt at terra-cotta, nine thousand drachmas for a hundred square metres, for Henry's house throughout and mine downstairs, with a good many to spare. There were nine to a square metre, so we must have had nine hundred of them, weighing eight and a half kilos each. It was Mr N who weighed them, I had not worked out that he would be receiving more than an eight-ton delivery. Nor had I realised how many items there would be to add to carriage costs. One, loading onto the lorry. Two, lorry to the port of Perama. Three, unloading onto the caique. Four, carriage to Amorgos. Five, tax on carriage to Amorgos. Six, unloading at Ormos. Seven, slow process of mule rides up the hill.

Nine thousand drachmas turned into fifteen. Heaven knows what it would be today.

Apart from being shocked by what I was doing to my brother, I was afraid that he would be disappointed by the faded-looking tiles. He must have spent his first Langatha summer with an earth floor, for it was the next Easter that I was preparing myself to be agonised on seeing them in place. There was altogether too much agony about that Easter, which began and ended with quayside treachery. I missed the boat to Amorgos, and fell into the harbour when I left.

I had always thought that someone, one dark night, would fall into the harbour clambering from the caique to the gangway. I did it stepping from the landing-stage onto the caique, very neatly with my suitcase in my right hand, so that my left arm, with my watch, shot up in balance, and that was seized before I was submerged. I also did it so vertically in the half-metre gap that I did not wound an elbow or a knee, and was hoisted out so quickly that the baker's son, who was standing in the scrum, asked me on board, 'Did you really fall into the harbour?' and I felt surprised to answer yes. There was no doubt about that when all the absorbant woollen clothes that I was wearing on that chilly April night began pouring sea around the ship's reception hall, but the purser, rather than protesting, handed me a glass of whisky, which was kind.

Missing the first boat was far more melancholy - unendurable, except that it had to be endured. I arrived fifty five minutes early, and that was five minutes too late. I saw it, almost within yelling distance, in its over-enthusiastic Easter spirits steaming off to Amorgos, and there was not another in two days. My boss' idea of a holiday and the boat's idea of Easter behaviour left me with four days in Langatha, at the end of which it seemed like an appropriate comment to fall into the harbour.

Henry's best vine had been three-quarters eaten by a donkey.

Mr N had quarrelled with Dimitris.

Mr N had quarrelled with Nikolakis.

Our fifteen-thousand-drachma tiles were spattered and stained with everything available for spattering and staining tiles.

I had made a miscalculation of fourteen thousand drachmas.

Mary, Mother of God, I have only four days for my island Easter, and I am tired, tiredness is ingrown. I have a little lump of it, a small walnut on my right cheek, and that needs more than one night's sleep to cure. When time is too precious for much sleeping you can relax without that, but not when problems take precedence of flowers.

It was not exactly my fault and not exactly Mr N's that I was greeted with an issue of fourteen thousand drachmas that I did not know about. It was just that his accounts had been going on from the last item instead of starting from the beginning as before. They were perfectly comprehensible when they were laid out between us, showing that tile-laying was more days' labour than I had thought, and all the prices had gone up. Or maybe the total figure was fourteen thousand and I had expected part of it, but I do remember that this was a bad moment and that he made sense of every drachma he had spent.

When Mr N saw my face as we worked out the figures, his reaction was entirely concerned with self-defence. He frightened me out of making a big scene by making one himself. 'This business has turned my hair grey,' he was shouting. 'I'm stopping. You can finish by yourself. I don't know what you're going to do, or how you're going to do it. That's not my business. I'm getting out of this.'

How could I finish by myself? Didn't I rely on him, and hadn't he promised to see us through, on both sides, to the end? Did I know where the materials came from or who should carry them? I was learning, but he had never made it necessary for me to understand the intricacies. Anyway I lived in Athens, I wasn't here to operate.

He shrugged again. That was not his business. I wished he would not keep repeating that, when we had sat at the same table so many times, sharing everything but two glasses and two forks. Now he was battering his knuckles on the table. 'All I'm afraid of that you'll say I'm embezzling your money. That's what I can't stand. Every drachma that you've sent me is written down in my notebook in the shop. I can show you how everyone has gone.'

So that's the problem. Why be so difficult? Of course I trust him. I have no reason not to, I just don't know where this sum is coming from. Perhaps I could borrow from the school. I've borrowed smaller sums.

Mr N looked at the ceiling. I knew what was coming. It was not his business how I found the money, and that was true, however tough. Don't try to shift your burdens onto other backs. `Carolina, I simply want to be informed - stop or go on.'

All my house needed was furniture, two downstairs windows and a door, so the immediate issue must have been on Henry's side. But caretaking was another matter, and that had to be included in commandership. I had a sudden yen to run down the hill and dive into the icy sea. `Go on,' I said. `Go on.'

Mr N leapt up. `That's fortunate. Because you see how the prices have risen, and they'll all go up again. Your wooden floor - could you have that today? You couldn't start, you couldn't buy the house. Cement - how much was that last year? Thirty five - and now it's seventy five. And we've got a really good builder, Lefteris' - that was last year's bridegroom, who spent half his time being a ship's cook round the world. `He'll be leaving again soon. Do you know how much he earns at sea? Twenty five thousand a month, with no expenses - no wonder he's away so much. We're lucky to have him. When he places a stone - it's in place.'

`What's wrong with Dimitris? You said you have more confidence in him than in yourself.' This was bold, but I was not going to have Dimitris, whom I liked and respected, so lightly thrown away. The quarrel was not, as I had feared, about our houses, but some goatskins, and was clearly as serious as goatskins could make any argument. Dimitris had turned from white to black. I found this fundamentally upsetting, perhaps I attached too much importance to people being nice to one another, but part of the building pleasure had been in the humour of our triangular relationships.

Mr N looked at me scornfully. 'Come.' He hurried me into my lower quarters, a real cellar as he was housing two retsina barrels here. 'I know you're complaining about the cement around these tiles - don't worry about that, it's easily cleaned off. This is Dimitris'. Now -' we ran in the middle of a sentence across to Henry's side - 'here's Lefteris'. See the difference?'

The cement, which does not clean off easily, seemed fairly distributed between us. The chief difference was that Henry's tiles lacked the splodges of blue paint and spots of wine that decorated mine. Four-year-old Demosthenes had got hold of the paint tin, admittedly in an unobtrusive corner, and as Mr N said, children will be children, though I did not really know why they should be being children in my absence in my house. The wine spots toned in better. There was a wide sprinkling of those, but I felt disinclined to object to wine barrels, especially as he encouraged me to help myself. The next year he moved them onto Henry's side, and when he tapped the first one he found himself in the possession of four hundred kilos of vinegar. He decanted most of that into two great earthenware vats, one of which leaked, and the vinegar seeped into the earth. Henry's best vine, which had just recovered from being eaten by a donkey, drank, sickened and shriveled back to ground level. It was like a cannibal getting indigestion, but very sad. Mr N's natural reaction, apart from sorrow on losing four hundred kilos of retsina, was to prickle - exactly as he was doing now.

Quarrelsome behaviour had its compensation. Falling out with cheerful Nikolakis also meant falling out of Nikolakis' concrete shop, with its harsh floor, its steel girders and, since the last summer, its television set. Nikolakis tapped his electricity from the *platia* generator and our evenings had collapsed. There were the village lads and cronies still sitting round their tables, still sharing their half-kilo wine jugs, staring at the box. These were my workmen, the Phanises, Mr N, all saying how much better life had been without it, but not turning it off when the picture was lost and the sound track American. 'When you've seen televison,' they would say, 'you've seen it. Well - what are we to do!' and they goggled on.

Mr N's replacement to that shop was a step back into old Langatha, small with an arch and creaky floor, and a fire-place looking like a wall-cupboard with a little blue door. There was not room for a quarter of the customers at Nikolakis'. 'So much the better,' said Mr N. 'Here we can drink our wine in peace.'

Thank God for that. Let us have some drinking of our wine in peace these few sharp days which make the Athens institute seem like a sanatorium. For can none of you critical people understand that every time my commander is fractious and impossible it is from him that I need ointment afterwards? No one else precipitated the purchase of a house which today I could neither buy, rebuild, nor give a wooden floor to - he's dead right. So since I have Mr N I am having Mr N, except in one place, and he's keeping out of that.

This new shop was an all-round improvement, for now when he met me off a boat he would bring me straight round here instead of having refreshments at the house. It offered all the welcome that I wanted, and none that I did not. Here I felt relaxed. Here after the confrontation of our different styles of sensitivity we sat quietly and unconfused ourselves. The only bonus he was offered was a thousand drachmas from my pay packet.

Fortunately I handed that to him before the financial revelation, which might have made me waver and him less able - with a slight protest and an 'Oh well!' - to pocket it. I think it was my boss' reaction to inflation to start adding 'the present of the present' to our obligatory bonuses, an extra thousand for every teaching year to fatten the Christmas and Easter envelope. In my second year I could lightly say to Mr N, 'There's one for me and one for you,' and afterwards moved on to sending him a thousand for a Christmas present through the post, more satisfactory because it was also more impersonal. I did not have to call this a negative form of prostitution. I owed it to him because I was never able to come to his shop as a customer.

Christ rose, bells rang, and I did not have to stand in the ranks of the supremely faithful until half-past-two. The chanting and the incense and the candle-light create their mystery most beautifully and impressively for those who share the atmosphere for half an hour. Then, for Mr N's wife, it is time to go. I don't know where the lord and master had been lurking, but this was the only occasion when I have ever seen him eat like a family man at home. In honour of two pairs of Athenian relations he sat benignly at the head of his own table, which was spread with the best of Easter-Saturday-night fare. Surely, I decided, this fast-breaking midnight scene was worth a day or two of anguish, when the feeling and the flavours were so good. What else was I to do - refuse enjoyment because anguish had preceded it?

Mr N thought it a pity that Henry and his family should never see the Easter scene or taste the Easter goat. We often talked of that, and though we could not lay on the multi-coloured, lush spring landscape in the summer holiday, we decided to reproduce the feast. We would have to adjust the stuffing to the season, but a mature onion is an onion and fennel can take the place of dill. As a proverbially English style of coldness was Henry's chief complaint of Mr N, my brother was delighted that Mr N should take this attitude, and he was also eager to have his oven used. That summer was the obvious occasion. It was the year of the great family gathering, with fourteen of us on the estate.

Fifteen might have been too many, but fourteen fitted pretty well, so long as everyone put the joys of togetherness on a Greek island - which we had - before the joys of five-star accomodation, which we did not. On my side I had my sister's family, with the parents in the upper bedroom and four children, aged ten to sixteen, below. It was floor-level sleeping for almost all of them, which was no hardship upstairs as the floor was wooden and I had a large foam-rubber mattress waiting for a platform but the downstairs tiles were less hospitable. Eleftheria did good business replacing broken lamp-glasses, for which no one could be blamed. One camp bed was about the only piece of furniture above that floor, and the children had a choice of darkness with the ancient shutters closed, or the full force of the notorious north wind.

It seemed to be a happy camping ground, and I was not inordinately apologetic, as I was the one who could only be accommodated on the lower terrace, with a mattress which I pulled into the kitchen on cold nights. I was inclined to do that more often when the wall beneath my *cabiné* began to seap. Obviously a run on it of fourteen was excessive for the pit, which needed time to settle, but I was far more occupied with delight at being surrounded by so many of my family than with worry about that. However, it was then that I told Henry that he would have to build his own *cabiné* for his own house.

Henry's main room had two platform beds, with space enough for his whole family, though there was more successful sleeping with one boy on one camp bed. That left his lower room free for the two who brought up the numbers to fourteen, a real Norland nanny and nanny's friend.

As Catherine was in charge of a publishing department, they really had to have a full-time nanny. We were all impressed. She was not, as she should have been, in bowler hat and gloves and bow-tie, but was a plump jolly girl whom we all called Cubby in cut-off jeans. Her name was Anna, but until she turned - with style - into the well-proportioned person she became, Cubby suited her extremely well. The boys adored her, she loved everything about our houses, Langatha and Aiyiali, and so did the friend who shared her nanny hours, so everything was satisfactory.

The village looked, exclaimed, and thoroughly approved, one and all. My sister's name, which is Imogen, was not attempted, but everyone was able to tell me from the first moment that she was very good. She was good-looking, a good mother, even a good housewife, which is true - but how did *Kyria* Mouska know? Jack turned into Yannis, and he was not only a good father, with a great many other virtues, he had a haircut at Michalis, the carpenter-barber, and brought his boys for haircuts too. With Henry as their contrast, that was widely noticed, and was compensation for Michalis who got itchy fingers whenever he looked at Henry's beard.

There were plenty of people to talk when the generator went on, which was not very often or for very long. That's making light of it, but there was nothing else to do, unless to take the attitude of Julian who swore he could not get to sleep without the rumbling lullaby. There were plenty of people to walk about the tiled floors, which was the treatment that Henry considered best for wearing off cement. They mellowed in a month, and President Adonis on holiday from Athens thought the tiles most appropriate for village houses, removing my last doubts. He spent a cocktail hour on my terrace talking about village history, telling us - as no one else could - that these houses might be five or six hundred years old, but unable to add that progress had been made about their ownership. It was not his fault that at this moment we had reached the downfall of the dictatorship. The bigwigs whom he had been working on, out of necessity, had just been put out of office, or imprisoned.

As the ownership question would have to go back to the beginning, and for such a cheerful reason as the resurrection of democracy, there was nothing to do but enjoy what we had now. Everyone was enthusiastic about a feast from Henry's oven, and Henry was fascinated to find out how the oven worked. He wondered about the old beams, which had been removed with mine to Mr N's yard - might they be used for fuel now? No, it was promised that they were being stored for us, but they were not the right wood for this sort of fire. Mr N had everything in hand. On the day that he selected he arrived with two donkey-loads of holly-oak, the proper fuel to make a tremendous blaze and leave a tremendous heat, daylong or overnight. Then with an exceptional display of zest and affability, he presided over the preparation of the goat, measuring the rice and water, sending Demosthenes for herbs, sewing the stomach, raking cinders, poised to the last moment, and in the evening taking off. He ate his portion with Yorgos the new policeman, in his shop.

A horde of his family were left with us, for he had chosen an evening when his Athenian relations had come back, and even his fairly immobile mother, who had not walked out of his courtyard gate for years, was brought along. There were over twenty of us being hungry and appreciative on the top of Henry's well.

The trouble about 'little did we know' occasions is that you never do know at the time. You cannot appreciate the way the plot you're living in is building up. What we did not know that summer Easter night was that the most important person present, the key figure in our island story, was Jason's, Julian's and Zachary's young Norland nanny.

Chapter Eight

T here were too many aeroplanes that summer. The people of Aiyiali, living headlines, walked about with their transistors staring at the noisy sky. War had broken out in Cyprus, Greece was on the verge of war with Turkey, foreign tourists cancelled reservations or fled the country, the Colonels had fallen and Karamanlis was prime-minister of a new democracy.

There was no noticeable rejoicing here about the end of the dictatorship, for life had gone on in its dissociated manner for seven years of that régime in comparatively unquestioning calm. It was the rallying of military forces that affected islanders. Every able-bodied man under forty had to go. One dismal day in a gale with squatting-room only on the boat, the flower of the island rose up and left. For a few days the island faces were suitably lugubrious, then most of the flower - with slightly sheepish smiles - came back. It had all been a big mistake. They had had white cards instead of yellow, or green instead of blue, and life went on again, with a financial loss. The foreigners who had squashed themselves aboard on the day of the great exodus did not come back.

Imogen and her family had been packing their suitcases in England when they heard the news and warnings, and while most others in the same predicament thought twice and did not come, they thought twice and came. Henry and Catherine, who had been driving down through Jugoslavia, noticed that most of the traffic was going in the opposite direction, and did not turn back. An American family who had come annually since reading *At the Top of the Mule Track*, to rent rooms behind the beach, were among the few who did not leave. In proportion to the total of the season's foreigners they were giving the impression that my book drew crowds. That was as untrue as I wished, but grocer Nikitas had good reason for his speech, 'We love you, Carolina, because you bring all the foreigners and we do good business.'

The Laki family, who had just seen ninety percent of their customers desert them in one swoop, could love me in the same frank style. I could not in normal circumstances, in high-season, have hoped for the open arms that welcomed my own people, the attentive service and the smiles. We pitied the deserters their unnecessary ordeal. The beach was empty. We had a marvellous time.

It was only Mr N who could not echo the speech of the grateful shopkeepers. Bringing foreign business to his tables would have been an obvious means of balancing indebtedness, but I had given that up in the early days because he only put himself out and left me more indebted than before. For 'a friend of Carolina's' there would be flowers on the table, home cheese on the house, and a main dish at cost price. Now I did not try to do so because his new style in his new shop was to be too busy for the tourist trade. He had seen foreigners. Foreigners were no longer such a rarity that proverbial Greek hospitality had to be turned on for each one. Sunday-evening spit-roast goat was the standard offer for a limited number of customers. On other evenings he wanted his shop to be his home.

I rather liked that, but Michalis pointed out that a poor man with two maturing daughters really had no business to 'behave like a pasha'.

Mr N made it his prerogative to deliver eleven members of my family and two nannies to our doorsteps, and thereafter concentrated on leaving us in peace. Fourteen was a large number, no one could deny, for more to be expected than Sunday-evening affability or some avuncular unbending with the boys, and after all he did arrange the Easter feast, though he did not eat with us. We were such a numerous fourteen that it would be a teasing questionaire that demanded detailed information on each one, though there is plenty to be said of all. Some of us sometimes suggested that it might be simpler for the two houses to eat their suppers separately, but the children went on moving chairs and tables from Henry's side to mine and vice versa on alternate evenings to the end. Scratching around my mind I cannot haul out from this setting a single memory of Anna, who was our Cubby, though I remember Henry spending a day at home to make her twenty-first-birthday cake, which was consumed as desert to a celebration dinner at the shop. Mr N accepted a piece, commended it and called for more to pass around, and one of the inside customers calling the appropriate greetings was Michalis, but that did not seem notable at the time.

I can reconstruct the occasion, but Anna - not a shadowy person in the least - is still a shadow. I only know that she was there, so ecstatic about Langatha and Aiyiali, that presently she was planning to come back with her friend Helen in the spring for a few months. And when that time came, at half-past-three in the morning of the next year's Easter Saturday, she walked thoroughly into my life.

In the meantime Catherine had resigned from her high-powered office and was at home with part-time help. Anna had thought in any case that nannies, however devoted, should move on, but it was not her aspiration to be earning a fat salary in a foreign embassy in gloves and a bow-tie. She and Helen were being Norland losses on the April night that they walked up the mule track to Langatha, with their knapsacks on their backs and enough savings in their purses to eke out into the joys of frugal living for a few rugged months.

That was the year when my house was rented by a teacher, so I, on my third Easter holiday, was asleep in Henry's house when they walked in at half-past-three. In a healthy manner they swallowed whatever I could find to offer them, climbed onto a platform and went to sleep. Five hours later they were out with a spade and a pickaxe in Henry's middle field. That is my first daylight memory of the stalwart English nannies. They had brought aubergine and green-pepper seedlings, and were planting them.

There had been no particular design about the Easter timing, I had not known exactly which day they would come. But in spite of their independence, since I was there and it was Easter, it was assumed by the villagers that I was responsible for them. And I must admit to feeling jealous of my esoteric island Easters round tables where I was a guest. 'Bring people in the summer,' Mrs Stephanakis said, 'and at Easter come by yourself.' I could not know that in the near future I would be saying that nothing was too good for Anna, I hardly knew this admirable nanny planting aubergines. But everything turned out as well as she deserved, thanks to Mr N.

He talked to me that morning like the man I had first known, who sent Maria home for titbits every time he saw a foreigner. Here were two girls sent - as he saw it - from Enrikos' house in England to Enrikos' house in Greece, and he was the commander of this estate. I did not have an Easter table - he did. It was his business to give them hospitality. After the resurrection, according to a mutual promise, I should go home with his wife, to break the fast there with the children, while Anna and Helen joined him and the policeman in the shop. The next day, rightly and properly, I should go as always to Tholaria to join the Laki family, while the girls came back to him for their due portion of stuffed goat. On these two occasions he would look after them. After that they could look after themselves.

There was no question of his eating his Saturday-night soup in his own home, when he shared all his evening meals by special arrangement with policeman Yorgos at the shop. Apart from the financial profit, Mr N was rich in pleasure when this new companion, who bore four stripes at twenty-five, was posted in Langatha, simultaneously with a teacher needing furnished accomodation for nine months. They were both good customers and he had a snob reverence for their kind. To the latter Mr N was less of a landlord than a host. `It's good for the house to be lived in,' he explained to me. `We can't charge him more than one hundred a month.' The happy teacher must have been away that Easter or I would have heard him singing. I had come at Christmas that year and he was singing the whole time. Once I was woken by the volume, blaring with the tape-recorder, and found him having a party with a joyful Mr N. If Langatha had had a doctor, unless he had resisted, he would have been in the same hands.

Mr N's wife was not expected to have parties in her life, which was one reason why I particularly wanted to go home with her. And it really was a party that we had together. She loaded the table, tucked in and clinked my glass, with glee in every moment and each word. Unlike most village women she is as bony as her husband, and more wrinkled, which gives a different style to her eating, she is feeding something more needful than the portly stomachs of most Langatha wives. So we kept our alliance, while the girls were having their introduction to a real Greek Easter with so much merriment that they came home with bellies aching, not - they said - from the amount that they had eaten but from how much they had laughed. They fell on their bed gasping, '*Nostimo,*' which means 'delicious' and was an acquisition of the feast to head their new vocabulary. If they had disappeared for ever they would not have forgotten it, and yet Anna has always been disgusted by gut-soup.

I always had to leave for Athens so soon after Easter that there must have been some fast work between my next two memories. The first is of a little festival at the bottom of the village where the girls and I were crushed in a corner next to Stephanakis and Michalis, and Anna was wound in what looked like a carpet - their clothes were curious that season because somewhere on the route they had lost their suitcases. The other is of the grin on Mr N's face when he told me that Michalis was badly in need of a wife, and that Anna would do very well.

I passed that on to her. She smiled and did not answer, `How ridiculous!' - or else she did not do so with enough conviction for me to remember it.

There had been no groundwork. When I tell Anna that I cannot remember her in her first summer, she answers that she cannot remember Michalis, it was at the little festival that she became aware of him. And if looks were exchanged I don't know how they could have come to Mr N's attention, for Michalis was not a regular customer of his. He had little time to kill in any of the sitting shops, for he was not only carpenter and lute-player, but also grocer, barber and first singer in church.

Langatha has two carpenters, and it was Mr N's business that we had switched in early days from the man in the *platia* to Michalis, but having no difference with the rejected one myself, I was happy to be in the hands of anyone so versatile. The grocery part of his achievement took me by surprise the day I discovered that while talking about windows I could buy salami too. No other shop had that. Michalis had ideas. He started life as a goatherd and by his middle thirties had set up his diverse business through clear thinking and hard work, making himself, I would have said, Langatha's most constantly eligible bachelor. He still had goats, as well as pigs and hens and olives, and only a mother in her seventies to look after them and help him pick. Various crude reasons for why he did not marry were a part of village gossip, but

I thought the real reason was his being, in some obscure way, different from the others.

He is almost different in looks, but that may only be because he seldom wears a cap. An unusual amount of wide forehead is exposed, with nothing to shadow the humour in his eyes. He is fairly short, not thin or fat, there is not a feature that you could point out as typical. Struggling to think why, I realise that he may wear a cap more often than I visualise, but you do not notice it so much because what you see first in Michalis is the way he looks around as if everything in sight is interesting.

Anna, with her thick fair wavy hair, her health and vigour, was extremely interesting. She looked back and both were pleased. It did not seem to matter that *nostimo* was an isolated word on a one-page vocabulary. *Nostimo* made a good beginning in the circumstances.

Throughout May and June her letters were full of exultation. She and Helen were climbing mountains, swimming, painting, making baskets and evening potages. `Oh so happy!' was the chorus line. Meanwhile in Athens I had added private lessons on Sundays to my programme and it seemed symptomatic of my life's condition rather than incidental that one of the visitors to my house had a miscarriage. Bearing burdens had become a habit, and I had no mental conflict about informing the director that I would be staying on for a fourth year.

But why was I so numb that I could not even manage a little healthy jealousy when I read of the island doings that I would have liked to do myself? When I had a pang it was at realising how in my nest in Athens I was not sufficiently regretful of the island life I did not lead. I wanted to want it, but kept evading it. I went to England to see my mother in September, and in Langatha was a two-month summer visitor with Easter bonuses. I looked at my house, thought, 'How pretty!' and did not quite know what to do with it.

Anna and Helen had no doubt what to do with Henry's house - enjoy it. They were not perpetually going round in circles, they just went, or otherwise sat still. They were absorbed in creative occupations. They could spend an evening reading as soon as being entertained by Mr N. And then it became apparant to me that there was no offer of entertainment from that quarter anymore. Mr N's shop had closed its doors to them. Clearly they were worried by some breakdown in the friendly mechanism since Easter, not so much on their own account as because of a diplomatic problem that might confront me, and then Henry, when we came. All this was lightly thrown into the general ecstasy, in which Michalis was playing an important role. They lacked nothing, except perhaps a child.

I wrote to England, ordering one. On the day that my school closed at the end of June, seven-year-old Jason was put on a plane for Athens at Heathrow. Demand and supply were happening fast, and I felt taken by surprise, though I was responsible.

It was good to have a nephew, and good to have a home to bring him to. Sometimes I thought that I would have to keep this job on just for the sake of a base in Athens for occasions such as this. Jason stayed with me in Kypseli for two nights, and on our in-between day we went up the Lykabettos on the funicular. At eleven o'clock on his first evening he asked me, 'Shall we walk up your path - now?' I had told him that you could see the Akropolis from the top. Yes, let's go. If I did not agree I would have an over-excited boy who could never get to sleep. Then he said, 'Shall we walk up there in bare feet? I ought to get my soles tough for the mule track.'

Aiyiali was very real to my three nephews, and they were becoming real people in Aiyiali - Yasonas, Julios and Zacharias, though there was always confusion over which of them was which. Mr N was the only one who had that straight. They enjoyed using those names, at home as well as outside, just as they enjoyed Greek greetings, shopping, and ordering refreshments more difficult than *lemonada*. Zachary was the one who had to be most careful, but fortunately he thought it funny that his English name was the Greek for sugar.

It was about midnight when Jason and I reached Ormos. As soon as the caique drew up he leapt into Anna's arms, while I looked round for Mr N. But we were not being met by Mr N and the girls. Mr N was meeting us with his animals, and the girls were meeting us by themselves.

After we had unloaded at our houses, I for one side and Jason for the other with the nannies, I went in with them and realised presently that Mr N had disappeared. He was squatting on my terrace smoking and looking at the stars. 'Are you staying with them?' he asked, 'or coming with me?' I went to the shop with him.

Mr N told his story from the point of view of a proper villager who does not like to see unseemly goings-on. There were goings-on between Anna and Michalis of which he - with two teenage daughters to protect - could not approve. He had come to my house that night because it was his business to deliver me, but it was not his practice to stop there. What's more, he could no longer use that path, and he did not wish his daughters to use it either while that girl was living there.

Inconvenient for him, I was thinking. That path was the direct route from his house to his shop. I also thought that whatever the romantic situation between Anna and Michalis, she was not a girl to upset the villagers with unseemly goings-on. I said so, rather mildly, still swaying from the journey and very ready to move my attention to another item of romantic news. One of those tender daughters, Maria who had celebrated her maturity by cutting off her plait and looking ordinary, was engaged to be married at Christmas to a fisherman.

`What's wrong with that? She's turned sixteen. She's a complete woman, isn't she?'

Nothing is wrong except for the shock of what is happening to our little ones. Dazed, I listen to the details, fascinated by each one but hardly able to believe the central fact. The fisherman, it seems, is a tremendous fellow. He isn't even asking for a dowry - this is a love match, do you hear? He has a house at Ormos, one of the finest, and Mr N will only be responsible for a few minor repairs. `I always told you, Carolina, we're all right for houses. Oh yes, I'm delighted. Maria deserves the best, she's got it, this is a good match.'

It was a pity, when I left him so gleeful at the thought of babies, that I had to revert to anger on the first day that I woke up in my house. Anna's story removed any mystery about his version. She had been too *nostimo* for Mr N. He had made advances and had been rebuffed. The Greek male was offended. Damn his guts, he was jealous of the carpenter.

What made me really angry was his prudish speeches, but it would have done no good to tell him so. I stated my opinion about Anna and talked about Jason or Maria, or the cooking at the Laki restaurant. Quarrelling with the commander was not in our interests, and anyway I had no inclination whatsoever to start quarrelling with him or anyone.

Play it quiet. Be an ostrich. See how things go when Henry comes. The Amorgots are not the people of the Mani, renowned by their length and ferocity of their feuds. Two years' hostility is serious. After that the coffee or the wine is drunk at the same table with the same outward appearance as before. The population is too small for no reconciliations. If that were not so, no one would be on speaking terms with anyone outside each clan. Perhaps Maria's wedding will have a mellowing effect on Mr N.

During our first building season he had spent the evenings, with reservations, commending the men who worked for us. Now, since that quarrelsome Easter, everyone was crooked or lazy, or out for his own ends. This was not only wearisome, antagonism was getting in our way. One dreadful day when Dimitris had promised to do one piece of work for Henry, I had such a damaging experience with Mr N that the work was never done and Dimitris would never put a foot inside the gate, or pause outside, again. I cannot remember which summer that was or any of the details because I purposefully expelled such matters from my mind, but I can feel the feeling of the day, and that was bad.

I could not believe that there was guile in Dimitris, who had watered Henry's roof when it was not his business, just because it needed watering, and looked after our lime. He was always mumbling to me about how this or that had been neglected, the trees and vines that we tried to grow in Henry's field, and he knew all about growing trees and vines. But apart from that, you could not look into his face and speak of guile. He is so much the epitome of what the true Cycladic type is said to be that it is hard not to compose idyllic sentences for him, to say that he has the grey-blue eyes and wrinkles of sea, mountain, fields and old times. Never mind, the time will pass and there will be no more of his kind for fine writing. I really do not know if Dimitris' eyes are blue or grey or brown.

Arrival from England always meant whisky and Senior Service for Mr N. He looked forward to that with smiling confidence. `Katerini will bring me the whisky when she comes, I know' - `When Katerini comes she won't forget the Senior Service.' It was always put like that, as if Enrikos had no part in it. Even duty-free, these gifts were more expensive than ordering a muleteer to the boat, but they were a tradition and they came. If Henry had been one to make small calculations about the give and take of things, he might have argued that since the building works had finished, commandership meant caretaking, and there was no call for Senior Service when caretaking had become a matter of making use of his bakehouse and his well, and growing garlic in his lower field. But Henry was not that sort of person, he preferred to be pleased with his own string of garlic than to tot up how much Mr N had grown out of his soil. However, he could not be bland about the situation when Mr N started insulting his friends and being an impediment.

If Henry wanted a piece of work done, he ought to be able to call in a builder and get it done. If he wanted to lend his house to a friend, that friend should be respectfully received. This was our Anna, our own Cubby, who had spent July being a mother to his first son, while I with all my swivelling circles, was merely the presiding aunt. Really, Mr N's behaviour was intolerable. What would the situation be if Anna wanted to come back next year, at a time when I was absent and he held the keys?

Anna did want to get back, more than anything. She was to leave for England towards the end of August, England meant remote Northumberland to her, and though tragedy is not her style she spent her last days looking as though prepared to try a tragic role if circumstances should keep her away for longer than six months. All that was clear to report of a discrete romance was that she sometimes left us for a while, that when she reappeared there was a glow about her, that a happy hum went with her, and that infatuation was not the word for it. She would go nannying in the north of England, temporarily, a nanny saving funds for the return.

But Mr N was equally decided. If that girl came back, he would not give her the keys to Henry's house.

Very likely I did not pass that on to Henry. Defending Mr N had always been an irksome occupation, and now the man was indefensible. The whole business made me as prickly as when Henry's best vine was eaten by a donkey and drank an overdose of vinegar. Henry, Imogen and I had been extraordinary as children for never quarrelling. Nobody believes the 'never' of that statement, but so we all remember it and my mother says it's true. It was on our lovely island that I started bickering with my brother, which was my biggest disappointment in the whole affair of buying two houses side by side. And yet there was an English nanny in our midst, who - innocent as she might be - was causing an upheaval in a sensitive area, a fair-haired, twenty-two-year-old reconstruction of myself when I set out for Mykonos, living the island life that I was supposed to lead, managing her life-style far better than I had, and I at a fractious thirty-seven could not even feel irritated with the girl. I can't claim any credit. That has to be hers. She is one of those people who instinctively say the right thing at the right moment, and know exactly where and how to place each foot.

Privately I warned her of Mr N's attitude about the keys, and we had some days of distress. I also told her that I thought he should be made to hand them over, but as we could not think of any means of making him do anything he did not want to, I was relieved when she decided to take a proud and independent line. Surely there must be some other place where she could stay. Attached as she was to Henry's house, she would not beg the keys from Mr N. Besides, her hopes were high that if looking after herself proved troublesome Michalis would look after her. 'No problem,' he said. That was one of his first English expressions, and he did not need to give more detailed illumination, for when Michalis says `no problem' you feel confident.

Naturally her Greek words were multiplying faster than his English ones, and she was doing well with getting the hang of simple sentences, but that did not solve the problem of months of severance. She worked that out and came to me with a significant request. If she wrote to Michalis in English and he wrote to her in Greek, could they send their letters to me, to be translated and sent on? I often felt as if I ran a freak's agency in Athens, but I could not think that this rare duty would be burdensome.

Anna's attitude towards Henry's house and its commander saved us from the sort of confrontation we were trying to avoid, for while `intolerable' was a word that could be spoken, there was a marked disinclination for anyone to practise it. For one thing, this was to be the year of our grand party, a party that was promised when all the major building works were finished, for every man who had done a hand's turn in the houses, and all their families, with dancing and another Easter-style feast. And it seemed extremely problematic that the master-of-ceremonies was not on speaking terms with one of the musicians, or a good many of the guests, and had sworn - though he did not always manage this - never to use our path.

The answer is simple in Langatha. Bring out the white flag. The ability to do so is one of the village's best qualities, and is usually performed without a word. In this case a few mild words were spoken, and Mr N assured me that Dimitris was the most important guest. We weighed the meat together, two lambs and a goat, cost price was the figure named, and he would not take a day's wages for his work. At midday he was working at the oven, and though Anna had gone down to the beach he would not come inside to eat with us, but when Henry carried out a plate of stuffed tomatoes he took a forkful, looked surprised and gobbled up the lot. Gastronomy had a corner where he and Henry, with no effort of self-consciousness, found a friendly meeting-point.

Dimitris did not come to our party. At the time it seemed as sad as a defeat. But when I delivered a hunk of meat to his house quite early the next morning, he called his wife to bring out the home-brewed retsina and insisted on my sitting down with him for a cheering off-beat orgy there and then. He said he had been tired. Saturday would have been a better evening than Sunday. I don't know. Perhaps that was the valid reason for some other absentees. Certainly there had been no lack of party spirits among the forty or so who did come to make the most of piled plates and free dancing on the well. Our thank-you celebration for the workmen was talked about for years.

Henry and Mr N had carved the meat together. Ostentatiously Mr N heaped up one giant's portion, bellowed, 'Camby!' - which was the village way of pronouncing Anna's nickname - and stood waiting for her to approach and take the plate. 'Give that to Michalis,' he bade her, and she was one who had a memorable night. A few days later a very subdued nanny stepped onto the caique to be borne out to the steamer and away from the island where all her hopes were set.

The best-behaved boats come in the early morning, or at the end of a fish lunch at Ormos, hooting with the final glass of wine. Anna had the fish lunch and perfect timing, but also a noticeable lack of appetite and a need for a nice cuddle with Zachary. Hoping for the best, as we were left, was hoping for something that strained the laws of nature and nationalities. Only Henry was bold enough to say that Anna ought to marry her Michalis, and that if she did so it would not only be a joy to all of us but would also mean that we could have our houses in her name.

Ought she? Could we? Romances between islanders and foreign girls do not turn out like that, or - on the rare occasions that they do - they are notorious for disastrous results. And Mr N was not a man to sign away his name in favour of a girl who had wounded his male pride and caused him an embarrassment, in spite of any truce, about the route he took from his own shop to his own house.

So we said, but Anna was so single-minded that I had at least another reason for warding off the weary question about ownership. Apart from Henry's problems, which seemed insoluble, I was more than ever dubious about the future of my own house since Maria had been wooed and won by so affluent a fisherman. I had a triumphant retort to all those busy-bodies who liked to tell me that as soon as Maria found a husband I would lose a house, but now that she had done so I had to face the flaw in my old scheme. Houses are supposed to be for dowries, and I had never aimed at dying on anybody's wedding day. Maria was provided for without my doing that, and I was certainly not going to die for the sake of her little sister, who neither had Maria's style nor was a person in my life. 'We're all right for houses,' Mr N had said. Given the opportunity, if he wasn't very careful, I would think of my nephews and take him at his word. And yet again, I could not confront him with the paper that Henry wanted to confront him with. For myself I would have been glad for the warding-off to remain indefinite.

It was Henry's house that had a quarrel with him. Mine had none. I was cool with Henry's commander, but I would not fall out with my own. That made life complicated, but it was hard to spoil my private island pleasure because of the complaints next door, even though my neighbour was my brother and I was responsible for his being there. My own commander and I were doing very well, rather better since the appearance of Yorgos on the scene, our voluble four-stripe policeman whose presence explained and satisfied a need in Mr N. The former sailor had been stranded with a craving for a supplement to village life, and whether or not he succeeded in seducing me, whether or not I brought in foreign goodies to be enjoyed about the shop, I had been a supplement. Now Yorgos took first place.

This was truly a masculine society, and Yorgos was not only entertaining in his way, and a profitable customer, but good for the proprietor's ego. My own place, being secondary, was safer than before. Yorgos' evenings for lingering at his table were mine for leaving quickly, but often when I came in he had already left, and whether we were fourteen on the estate or whether I was by myself, I could not feel the day completed without dropping in - however briefly - at the little creaky shop. My sudden sorties were not clandestine, and yet they had that sort of feeling, and Mr N would greet me with a look of triumph that was, as ever, conspiratorial.

Sixteen-year-old Maria still waited on her father and his customers, the daytime errand boy and evening serving girl. Every time I looked at her I thought I might see something of the amazement that I felt myself, but she was betraying nothing of the sort. She had lost a plait, which all my family lamented, and gained a little self-assertion, but sitting between orders on her upright chair she still seemed to be a child demonstrating why waiters are called waiters, nothing more mysterious. Passing from her father's hands into her husband's was not to be the greatest change imaginable, but the route and the method gave rise to questions which should have filled her eyes with awe. What was she thinking of? What did she know? Maria, who had never left Aiyiali except on one day's outing with my family to Katapola, when she had had to come back over the mountain because the caique was so horrible, was to be put alone onto a steamer, shipped off to Piraeus to her Athenian relations, and turned into a bride. This little girl, who had seen two cars before that day, and had a ride to Chora in one of them, but had never seen a bicycle or traffic light, was to be tossed into the seething city for three weeks of matrimonial preparations, shopping, hitting hot spots with her new lord and master, three weeks for growing up. And then she would come back to Ormos to have babies and mend fishing nets, and rather soon be middle-aged.

`It's the only way to do it.' Mr N was gloating in the satisfaction of having a fine band of her aunts and uncles to rally at the other end. He could never have afforded to lay on the village wedding that the scribe's daughter had been given, and all that was irregular was that the bridegroom seemed to be prepared to put down more than is customary for the furniture. The proud father was getting a light deal, but even so he lacked the funds to pay the bills for house repairs. It was embarrassing, when he already owed a little money to Michalis and was not on speaking terms with him, to ask for more, but for want of any other source he sent his wife, with tears in her eyes, to appeal to the kindness of Michalis' heart. This was an inconvenient moment for the carpenter, who took four percent on loans and could make more than that out of his money faster than Mr N could pay it back. However, in spite of the businessman in him - and he is a businessman - the tears prevailed and kindness won.

But which of the fond parents should go to Athens for the wedding? This was the first daughter being married, one of them would have to be there, both could not. Mr N was gnawing at the question and could not make up his mind. He longed to go himself, not only for the wedding. He had not left the island for four years, and then only for a week, he hankered for a sniff of city life. But the trouble was that he'd spend money. If his wife went, it would be far more economical. What should she do but sit with her sister-in-law at home? He'd spend five hundred drachmas every evening - more. He wanted to go. Perhaps she should. He did not know.

So I left him, but in late December, a fortnight after Maria had been put onto her boat, it was Mr N who was preparing to set out. As he told me, he rode down to Ormos with his luggage and his expectations, in a rising gale. The boat was delayed. The boat set out. It was held up at another port. By the time the wind dropped, it was so far behind schedule that it cut out Amorgos, and Maria was married in Athens without either parent at her side.

Mr N was making 'that's life' remarks good-humouredly enough when I next saw him, but Yorgos the policeman said that the disappointment had left a large kink in his moral frame.

Chapter Nine

Maria was married at six in the evening, and I was in her aunt's house from midday, so there were hours in which to see how practical the bride was being, how cheerful and composed. She seemed to have taken her great stride into the city in the way that island girls take strides, with perhaps too much aplomb, so it was some relief to hear that the traffic was indeed overwhelming and that she did find sleeping troublesome. 'It's terrible,' she cried, but laughing. She was doing well.

A hair-dresser came in to take control of the entire afternoon. Maria ate up her midday meal and took first turn, followed by Aunty and two or three girl cousins, and I needed all my resistance not to find myself arrayed among them in the inexhaustible supply of hair-curlers. It was no good weeping about gales. The good relations had taken Maria on, they decked her, led her out and married her. She was a happy, pretty bride, and very small. The bridegroom's burly hand that had been hauling nets for years seemed to be something of another species as it enveloped hers.

The young are a moving people. About one month later a letter from Michalis was delivered at the translator's door. 'Anna, you know that I have a lot of work to do and I need someone to help me. Do you want to live in Langatha for ever?' - 'Yes,' came the answer by return. If the question wasn't a proposal of marriage, I thought with a large smile, it certainly ought to be.

The young are moving. I walk up my hill and walk down my hill thinking about grammar, Maria and Anna, doing my arithmetic. `You live in Athens. I am living in Athens. Mr B is staying at a hotel. He stays there every year.' And if I stay for a fifth year, perhaps I shall say, `I live in Athens too.'

Anna is coming to Greece. She will be living in Langatha. She will live on Amorgos for ever. She wants to. Michalis says she shall.

Langatha is a village. Amorgos is an island. Greece is a country. It's not a dictatorship. It's a democracy.

The only outward difference for a foreign resident was that under the dictatorship there were no strikes or demonstrations, the children were brought up not to shout. Now our Polytechnic students, who had kept their mouths shut through all their teenage years, were having a grand time yelling and causing traffic jams, while the rate of inflation rose daily with their cries. A year before the loyalists had been proclaiming, `Long live Papadopoulos and democracy!' And now the Greeks, who invented the word, seem to think its meaning is `not monarchy'.

Is it a sign of growing old and jaded to be cynical about what you approve of whole-heartedly in principle?

Anna would stay with me on her way through Athens, before catching the boat to Amorgos. She was coming as quickly as a nanny could leave a job with respect to her employers and not much need for preparations. She would put a few possessions on her back and get onto a bus. It would be good to see her, a gust of healthy air.

Soon the circulars would be appearing in our school registers, asking our intentions for next year. It was the first time that it depressed me to be signing on again, but Greek life could no longer be lived royally on shoe-strings and I had only just opened a bank account. I had been at this school long enough to feel the perquisites, the extra bonus at the time of bonuses, the knowledge that the boss' answer would be yes to reasonable requests. There was no reason not to leave, but I did not think that the best one for staying on.

On the twentieth of February Anna came. I had various visitors in transit to whom I could not truthfully say, 'It's lovely to have you,' but I could do so to her. She did not leave me feeling like a trampled doormat, she even managed to behave - in what she did not show to be impatience - as if three nights and two days of waiting in Kypseli were a pleasure in themselves. My little house was island-like in any case, which helped. Like all my guests she was abandoned for long hours, but I would find her reading or drawing unfretfully when I came home. Afterwards she said she managed her feat of self-control by forbidding her imagination to get working on the next thing, the known and the unknown - and that, for an imaginative person, had been difficult.

The next thing - the what and how of it - was something that we hardly dared to broach. Only waiting for her first letter would be bad enough for me, but her mental discipline was given the severest test. When, belatedly, her boat left in the worst weather since Maria's wedding, it was held up at Syros for two days. She went for long walks making snowballs - on an Aegean island approaching March. And as part of the next thing was turning into the real Anna, whose name as yet we had not used, there may be still a Cubby who appears at the half-way port of Syros in late February, playing in the snow.

`Carolina, I can't believe it - I'm living with Sophia and Michalis.'

I could believe it. It seemed to me a logical conclusion, but my imagination had not been so restrained.

Sophia is Michalis' mother, seventy three years old that year. Charging downhill on a donkey she is the best witch on a broomstick that the village has. Everything amuses her. Nothing makes her tired. In the shop she is the most generous weigher of whatever you are buying and the slowest adder-up. She's a bony Mouska, more laughing, covering much more ground. Anna adored her in those early days when she couldn't understand what she was saying. They waved their hands and laughed instead. I always think it might be more convenient for the laughter if she did not wear her *mandili* wound quite so high around her mouth.

Michalis' house and shops are alternate with Eleftheria's, on one of the two street stairways leading up to the *platia*. First is the carpenter's workshop, then his house almost immediately opposite Eleftheria's shop. Outside the courtyard wall a narrow staircase leads up to a separate room, a proper place to put a foreign girl who has suddenly turned a son-and-mother couple into a family of three. Immediately above Eleftheria's a four-metre alley, full of scales and boxes, is the centre of Michalis' public premises. The barber's shop is on the right. More carpentry is on the left. The grocery is straight ahead, and the name of that shop, on a board over the door, is Love. Greek groceries have as much of a right to names as English pubs. The next house up is Eleftheria's, with her second shop a little higher, so it is important with all this overlapping that part of a growing rivalry should be remaining on good terms.

When I first came to Langatha, Michalis' grocery was hardly in evidence at all. Building that up was a major project, involving structural alternations, in the year that Anna came. Being carpenter's mate had a thorough meaning for her, but she made it clear from the beginning that it was not her vocation to be a full-time shopkeeper.

`Carolina, of course I'm going to marry Michalis.'

Had I lacked faith, I wonder, to ask a question needing an answer in those words? I was glad that I had asked it, to provoke that vehemence. Of course! Of course! But I did not like to tell my friends in Athens that my nephews' English nanny was marrying an island carpenter. It was so boring to hear the inevitable response, `Give that six months.' All right, in six months after the wedding I'll have my proof in happiness that Anna and Michalis have defied a natural law. You see, it makes an enormous difference that she looked first at Langatha, and at Michalis afterwards.

But there could be no wedding until they had their own house and had dealt with all the red tape, which in Greece is muddy-coloured, resolving her status as an alien and a protestant. The decisions and the preparations would take more than a year; all that could be resolved immediately - and Michalis was firm about this - was her name. He could not marry a girl outlandishly called Cubby, or Camby in the local style, which means caterpillar in Greek. Henceforth that name was banned. Symbolically speaking, it was the appropriate moment. Cubby had been someone else. And as she was also visually transformed there was to be no difficulty, even for the boys when they next came, in calling their friend and erstwhile nanny Anna. They would look at her and speak the name with pride.

Anna was certainly not under-nourished by her future mother-in-law or husband, who grew anxious as her skirts and trousers began to flap about her, it was more as if a teenage plumpness had got the message that it was no longer covering a teenager. Besides, she was living an islander's life on a rugged island, up the mountains to the goats, down the mule track to the caiques, across the gorge for haymaking, taking a man's dose of physical exertion all day long. `Oh so happy - oh so tired!' were the chorus lines. She went milking two or three times with Sophia, then she knew how to milk goats and went alone. She took the donkeys down to Ormos, the donkeys listened to her instructions and did not take her for a foreigner. She picked up sacks of cement, potatoes, onions, and loaded them, needing help with ropes at first but not for long. She took a sickle and knew how to cut hay, which really means not fainting from continuous hours of bending in the sun. She wore a good village skirt and went to church. She spoke Greek, not in isolated words but very soon in sentences, with an island accent, like English spoken by the Welsh, lilting and grammatical. The villagers, goggling, gaggling, watched her, and they did not say what a lucky girl she was to have been taken by Michalis, they said what a lucky man.

'Our girls don't work like that.' They told me at Easter and they told me in the summer of all the feats performed by Anna, how she never wearied, how willing she was and how well-spoken, while short Phanis asked me to bring another one like her. As for Michalis, he looked astounded - more so than all of them. He had expected something good from Cubby, but how could he have known that Anna would be a paragon? And the man who had had the vision and the boldness to find himself a wife in such an unlikely and unusual manner was not going to make a chattel of his prize. Little Maria down in Ormos appeared like a pathetic fish-wife, with no relations among the one hundred inhabitants of an unlively port, no resources of her own to fill the days when she was left alone, and lordly behaviour from her fisherman husband whenever he came home. Life for Anna would not be like that.

If Michalis went out in the evenings, he went out with Anna. He was companionable inside the house and out. Occasionally they were Sunday-evening customers of Mr N's, but it was always a moot point whether they were on speaking terms or not. Being in Michalis' debt was not a softening circumstance for Mr N, but Langatha only has one barber, so sometimes he had - however gruffly - to be on speaking terms. Neither Anna nor Michalis was going to break a heart on that account, and nor was I, for now that she was living under his wing the atmosphere was easy when Henry's family arrived.

The boys rushed off and pulled her, like a bride already, to the house, calling to their parents to see what they had found. Michalis had completed the transformation by turning into a successful ladies' hair-cutter. Catherine and Henry took a look and gasped, 'How elegant!' But however much that 'elegant' was repeated in stunned tones, privately we always had a Cubby in our lives.

That was the last summer that Mr N was brought his whisky and his Senior Service. And yet, while it was happening, it seemed more propitious than the one before. That had been full of visitors and troubles, this one was quiet and constructive, it was the year of the temple and the loo.

Henry had continued to feel wistful about his down-site, and always longed to use the sand, which had been sitting there for seven years. He would raise wooden columns on a concrete base with a roof of bamboo, and it would be a lovely midday-shelter, a sanctuary for afternoon reading and gazing at the view. There was no discussion about calling it 'the temple'. That was what it came to be, but first of all he had promised me that he would build his house a *cabiné*, and he began with that. It was a necessity - apart from my loo being over-used - for his house was now in rentable condition, and renting it would pay for some improvements and cover items such as annual whitewashing.

He didn't need a builder. He could lay the bricks himself and only needed Mr N to find a man to dig the pit.

`What man?' asked Mr N. `I'll do it. I'm responsible.' And he came in such determination to impress Enrikos, and with such a growling - always his sign of concentration - that there was grinning and congratulations afterwards exceeding any that had yet been exchanged.

This was the perfect moment to get Mr N inside the house, sit him at the table, give him a cup of coffee and talk business. I cannot remember any other time when that manoeuvre, with the coffee, was achieved, and when he had settled in that position it seemed such a natural one that everything said became coherent and symphonious. `*Symphono*,' he kept repeating in agreement to the end.

Henry had borrowed twelve thousand bricks from Michalis, which Mr N would replace when the next shipment came. Henry would build the *cabiné* walls and put in a lavatory seat, Mr N would add a roof and plastering at his convenience - probably before the olives - and he made an estimate for that. He would also concrete some metres of the path where damp came through the walls of Henry's house. Another estimate was made and a total of six thousand five hundred drachmas was put into his hands. Then we came to the more delicate matter of renting out the house - delicate because we wanted Anna to be involved in that, but even then the symphony was not spoilt. `Anna,' he said, `is good.' It was more than a year since he had fallen out with her.

The only thing he would not agree to was to take a commission - not one drachma - from tenants whom he put into the house. He would certainly cooperate with Anna and let her have the keys if foreigners came house-hunting. There had been a few already, including a brave

Norwegian couple in February when some would say the house is uninhabitable, and communication was always difficult. There are so many things to be explained. Don't throw loo paper down the loo. Burn combustible rubbish, give compost to the field, throw the remainder down the gorge. Yes, that is the only method. There's a public hurling place, it all goes down in one heap - what else are we to do? Don't leave dirty sheets, please, don't let dirty water drip into the well. Oh yes, you can write instructions but there are so many, such doubtful details, so much to be shown. Where do they get drinking water? How do they buy vegetables? Having Anna in the middle was much more satisfactory for everyone. `*Symphono,*' said Mr N. The only thing that Henry did not ask me to translate was a hope that when Anna was married to Michalis the contract might be changed.

Feeling encouraged, Henry went out to build his temple. It made him light-hearted not to have to wonder what the commander's whim or mood would be, for the down-site had no entanglement with Mr N. I, on the other hand, mustering the men and the materials, had an experience fraught with revelations about commandership. Gravel, water, a water barrel, beams, cement all came from different sources, all to be carried by whoever would agree to beat their mules up Henry's path. If we had needed sand as well, I think I would have failed. Mr N's brother took offence and didn't bring the gravel when he promised, because Markos the muleteer had brought up four sacks of cement that had been part of his - the gravel bearer's contract - and I began to feel that Mr N had been rather mild about grey hairs. And then at eight o'clock one morning Henry and I were on the site with all the materials assembled, and Dimitris too, Dimitris grumbling that the mound of sand was exactly where we wanted a platform to be built and the workmen had not come. That was one Manolis, who had an orchard right below us at our end of the beach. And he was standing in his field, digging, waving at us in a chummy manner as if to say, `Good morning, how are you?'

`Come on, Carolina,' said Dimitris. `Go and get Manolis, and tell me what to do.' I had a fever that day. It was too hot on the mountainside for me, I would get Manolis and go home. `Oh no, you won't,' Dimitris said. `You'll stay right here and tell me what Enrikos wants. How are we to understand each other if you go?' But I knew that Henry's Greek vocabulary was half composed of building terms, and also that nothing could make him happier than to be left on that unsheltered patch of stone and prickle with his pickaxe and his spade and his Dimitris, part dour and part good-humoured, to sweat and burn and build. He would come home in the evening with a sore top to his head, with aching shoulders and a happy heart, telling me that they had conveyed their meanings perfectly and achieved tremendous feats. I left them to it and gave myself a ride with Markos up the hill.

That summer I had cicadas buzzing in my head, though I was surprised that they had given me a fever on the thermometer. For the last month in Athens I had been repulsed by food, now I was thin, slightly hysterical and extremely difficult. My family - in a kindly way - complained that I was less able than ever to sit still for two minutes or finish sentences. I did not mind leaving Aiyiali to go to England in September, but I longed more than ever to come back and pick the olives afterwards. If I envied Anna anything, I envied her those days. Teaching for a fifth year because there was no reason not to, turned out to be a big mistake. It was only in the olives that the buzzing could be cured.

It is undignified and not to be tolerated to come panting in the class. I was in danger, daily, of doing something far more undignified than that. But the island message reached me just in time for me to save myself. I had to pick up my belongings and go and live in my own house. At the end of October, with great compassion for one whose aim is to resemble a computer, the director released me from a new contract on grounds of ill-health.

Chapter Ten

We're having a battle with the olives, Carolina,' muttered Mr N at two a.m., turning over in his bed and falling back to sleep again. His wife had woken fully to my knocking, found my keys and whispered the right welcoming things, but there was nothing more or different that I wanted Mr N to say. He was having a battle with the olives. I was here.

The here-ness of that moment was too real to be miraculous, and yet I marvelled as one does at miracles. My guiding saint for the last fortnight, a sadist with a crooked sense of humour, had finally been left behind. Simultaneously, on disembarking, I had lost the feeling of watching an exotic film show from a murking auditorium. What had that saint been up to - and those boats? At the time when I had most need of a smooth passage, physically and morally unfit for adventures, the saints had so outwitted me that I was condemned to a chapterful of journeys lasting half a week. Grounds of ill-health, which had seemed a little euphemistic at the time of writing, had been proved correct before I left the institute, underlined while I was packing up my house, and reconfirmed through the last harrowing experience. Now I found my bed damp - Mr N's wife had made it for me assuming that I would come on the day I said I would in an over-confident telegram. I could not have been less concerned. That bed, the sheets, the blankets were all mine. I had arrived.

Six hours later I shot out into the day, in old jeans, an old shirt and an old sweater, all that I had pulled out of my suitcase in the night before leaving it at Ormos and walking up. I'm not sure about the walking, it felt more like coming on a funicular. Mr N had left with his second daughter for some obscure trees which I did not try to find. Any trees would do that day, I was going to the olives, that was all. My soles trod on tufts of grass which had sprouted in the autumn rain. I felt connected, I was living in the country - already that was happening - I was not a city person any more. I could feel the Langathans' day being like mid-morning. Where they could not be seen among the trees they could be heard. I was walking into their time, and from now on I would be out among the first.

It's real. It's live. There is no auditorium, I'm here.

Across the gorge Eleftheria had a grove. I had picked there with her five years before, she might be picking there today. Short Phanis who is wise hailed me from a tree-top. He told me that she was. He was surprised to see me walking down the gorge, but not amazed. I said, `I've come to pick the olives,' and that seemed logical.

`Eleftheria!'

`Carolina?'

`I've come to pick with you.'

That wasn't really true. The moment that I reached a standstill, my body started to complain. I dared not climb into the branches. Something was wrong with my co-ordination even on the ground. I lay down on the sack-cloth and when I closed my eyes I was staring into a kaleidoscope. It seemed best to keep on moving slowly, tugging at a sprig of olives here, a single olive there, collecting a handful off the ground. Eleftheria told me that I was tired from the journey, I should be resting, she respected my enthusiasm but it had been precipitous. She was glad of a companion, even a disabled one. Short Phanis reported in the evening that her voice did not stop from the time I joined her until I left her in the afternoon.

Eleftheria told me that Athens makes you dizzy, it works like poison through the system and eventually destroys the health. I was glad to hear that, I would have little trouble in explaining my reappearance to anyone, for whoever stays into the winter is a real islander and thinks the same. She told me that my director was a good man because he understood about my dizziness and had emphasised that he would gladly have me back. She told me that she would have liked to adopt a little girl, who would call her Aunty, be given all she wanted, and look after her and Vassilis in their old age, but that he could not agree to the idea. She told me that Anna was picking with Michalis like the best of island women, everyone admired her, he was a lucky man. Mr N had more trees to pick than anyone. It was right and proper that I should go with him my first week, but there was one distant grove where she - Eleftheria - would like to have me with her afterwards.

There was no awkwardness about her being unprepared for two mouths at midday, for she always brought herself a hefty helping of what she cooked the night before. Her complaint was only at seeing what a fragment I could eat, so we had some pleasant old-time argument, and more talk about the boats, while I lay on the sack-cloth feeling ghastly and content. She told me that Langatha across the gorge was beautiful, I saw that it was so and I was here to look at it. Bells would ring and boats would hoot, I could not hear them, they were not my business. Eleftheria had her company, and it was of no importance how my body felt.

In the early afternoon I walked through groves and fields down to Ormos to collect the only piece of luggage I had carried with me on the last boat. I had filled a small removal van when I gave up my house in Athens, and was trusting that the rest would follow after an unfair quota of mishaps on the way. Right now I could not feel concerned with objects. I was walking in the country, passing friends and breathing island air. The father of the Laki girls - the ideal island father, I always think, and so do they - sat down on his ladder, offered me a cigarette, and gave me a lecture of congratulations when I refused. A little further on, Anna jumped down from a tree.

`Please, please, come picking with us soon,' were words exploding with a dozen urgent questions when I appeared, confirming some mysterious reports about a telegram to Mr N. Olive days were joyful to her when Michalis could leave his village work and come, but more often she went out with Sophia, her mother-in-law to all intents and purposes, and Sophia always yowled at her when she swung from the branches upside-down. I gave my word to come and swing beside her. It would be good to have whole days together - essential, for there was so much thorough talking to be done. In olive season there's no time for that except among the olives, and I wanted every detail of her autumn news in exchange for what I had to tell, a story which no other islander could comprehend.

At some time after dark the feeling of arrival was completed when I sat down in the place which I had long been picturing and needing, in the little creaky shop where all that mattered was the here and now, the relief of it all, the balm of it all, over a familiar table and plates of home-raised pork. I could no more have taught an English lesson - or so it seemed if I made a conscious effort to picture doing so - than I could have taught Chinese. Why bother? That way of life has gone, so let it go. And do not force the issue of going out to meet the future. That will come. Perhaps among the olives it will resolve itself. So I said in Athens when the only thing that counted was extricating myself from a seedy situation without making a mess. Now I was here and that was done.

Here is my commander, laughing at my adventures, pleased to have me back to pick with him. Here is his wife, in Maria's old place, not expecting any other for herself, glad to have someone in need of kindliness and smiles. The second daughter is whiny about becoming a Maria, but now that Demosthenes is six his mother can bring him to the shop, and Mr N is still more of a daddy than a tyrant to this last child. He's a grandfather as well, he's only been one for a month and already he is talking of next year's olive picking when he plans to have the baby in his own house and Maria in the trees. His elder son is still at school, going twice through most of the six classes, so he'll be there for a while. In the shop Yorgos the policeman is still top customer, but he's part of the set-up that I'm having, so I'll go along with him as well.

When I had fallen out with the world five years before, I had found my ointment here - in another shop, but the difference was that I preferred this little one. And this time I knew, intimately, what I would find. This time I had my own house, to be lived in, not just exclaimed at but enjoyed. November was a new month for me, the month - they said - to move downstairs. Upstairs, with its high ceilings and four windows, would soon be uninhabitable. I might have added that the sweat of nightmares, for the moment, was my only sleeping problem, up or down. My sheets were screwed-up rags with far more sodden saltiness than comes from island air. But every reawakening was new reassurance, every night became more peaceful, more concerned with ordinary dreams. How could I not feel quickly healed when every morning I woke to bright reality? - Get up! It's olive time.

`Can you reach that branch?'

`Of course I can.' I could reach any branch that had an olive on it. I pulled my way up and was in communication with leaves, olives and the sky. I'll decide on the next thing in the olives, did I say? I'll decide which sprig I'll pick. Mr N, as always in the trees, was dour and taciturn. The girl was less of a prattler than her sister, she played the radio, but what comes out of that is mostly island songs and sometimes boat news, not incongruous. I tried reciting poetry to myself, I tried to be methodical, rubbing up old favourites by night and polishing by day. `Had we but world enough and time...' I began well, wandered, and always ended thinking about olives. 'Why not just enjoy it?' Anna said. She meant the picking, not the poetry.

Except for her style of swinging, she was so much the real islander that I hardly saw her for more than fifteen minutes here and there. She was always rushing off to feed the pigs or look for a lost goat, reminding me of our promised days for conversation in the trees. This is a basic difference, that at dusk on the return Anna gets straight on with the next job, whereas all I do before suppertime - I don't aspire to change this habit - is to work on getting clean and dry and warm. I don't mean that I doubt anybody else's cleanliness, though I might wonder, but the only way I know of achieving a comfortable warmth is a slow and thorough hot-water wash and change of clothes such as good village housewives do not have time to indulge in every day. Perhaps they have an ingrown thermostat. Anna seemed to have one. She was looking forward to her first island winter without any of my doubts.

Why not just enjoy the olives? I would do exactly that. Whom I would pick with was the only serious problem to be faced. I went with Eleftheria to her furthest trees as promised, for five days, and then *Kyria* Mouska pushed Anna down the waiting list, begging me to go with her daughter for a day. That day led to a hopeful suggestion for a second, but I sensed a rousing of displeasure in Mr N. He had his contract with me for alternate weeks at first and full-time later on, but now when I mentioned Eleftheria he looked at the ceiling, which is always a bad sign. I had had to go with her, I said.

'Why?'

'Why? She's someone I know.'

`No, she isn't. I am.'

I was in no state to cope with that sort of situation except by stepping out of it. Because my true friend in my own language was a person whom I could make excuses to, I never picked with Anna for one day. `Where are we going tomorrow?' I asked Mr N half an hour after that interchange. He answered with a grin, and I thought that the best thing to do about getting well in Langatha was simply to get well in Langatha, where my commander's little shop was equal in home feeling to my house. Rocks are rocks whatever their blemishes or roughnesses, and homes are homes rather than Utopian resorts. If Mr N - who automatically took time off to meet a boat I did not come on, and twice again to deal with my luggage when that came - was jealous of my picking fingers, then let them pick for him. Besides, whoever I went with gave me supper, and I liked this place best, even though having Yorgos with us was rather like having a television set.

Yorgos was one who saved himself from the desolation of being stationed in Langatha by developing little-Hitler characteristics, being an outsize fish in a tiny pond. He was long and lean with eyes and gestures charged with electricity. Even when he wasn't speaking - which was not often - he was aware of being in the screen. When he stayed to do his big witty fish act at his table he would spark off Mr N, who had grand feelings about four-stripe companionship, especially when Mr Four-Stripes let his singing voice carry around the village like his commands. What he said could be amusing, but he mistook harangue for conversation, and Mr N would enter into a verbal competition with him, stimulating to themselves and bemusing to the audience. I preferred to move to Mouska's shop to be bemused.

Sitting at Mouska's was having private time, almost as private as my last waking hour at home, and that was something which I was learning to enjoy again. It was a happy reason for choosing not to stay at Mr N's until the evening turned into a *tête-à-tête*, and it was the only reason, for seduction never entered his agenda now. That would have been a stopper to the tube of balm that I was squeezing, but he had given up. His properness had stretched into such eccentricity that he refused to view my winter quarters when I moved downstairs. Now that I was in occupation, he could not take one step into my house.

Downstairs was homely and autumnal, with curtains on the windows, rugs on the floor, and all sorts of embellishments from Athens provoking the admiration of any passer-by. Dimitris and anyone who had done a hand's turn claimed the right to curiosity, while others were just curious - why not? But while Mr N was using Henry's lower room as a barn, the bakehouse as a parking place for goats, the main room as an area for drying fish, he could not cross the path when he came through that gate to see the results of works which he had commanded on my side. A compromise is easy with our stable-style doors, but he would not even lean on the bottom leaf and stick his head in, with his feet outside.

He had not roofed or plastered Henry's *cabiné*, or concreted the path, but there are so many good reasons for not-doing in Langatha when the concern is building works that I accepted whichever good reason he produced.

Before next August he would find the wherewithal and time.

Mr N was not making only a daytime exhibition of his properness. On the evenings when we left the shop together, he did not try to touch me unless I needed a helpful arm half-way. I considered myself a good night-time combination of goat and cat, but there was one rocky patch where on a moonless night I was glad of guidance if I had not brought a torch. One September he had made a request for an English police torch, when it suddenly became necessary for him - I do not know on what occasions - to see two hundred metres in the night, but normally he did not carry one. I have never known anyone so infallible in the dark. As we rounded the worst corner he dropped my arm, accelerated his pace outside my house, and barked goodnight. That was lovely. I lit my gas stove and enjoyed unruffled private time.

The passers-by had two reactions to that stove. Each was simultaneously admiring, and saying that I ought instead to burn an open fire, to make charcoal in the proper fashion for a brazier. Athenians have stoves or central heating, and Amorgots use the *mangali*, so I was rather sternly being told. The attitude was not unreasonably conservative, when we have chronic shortages of calor gas. The art of good *mangali*-making depends on timing and the type of wood. It becomes obsessive, you can boil a kettle on the best one, you feel obliged to live on toast and baked potatoes, you can keep it going all day. I felt apologetic, but the whole business of getting a new process going, especially when I was out all day and half the evening, seemed overwhelming in spite of its appeal.

I firmly put my gas cooker in the fire-place to make an inside kitchen, preferring not to raise the question that Mr N, who did not mention open fires, had stored all our old wood.

I was not brooding over that, or being timid, it was only that my antidote to strain in Athens was to bypass an area that I did not feel like walking through. And after two or three weeks of that sort of convalescence it did not help one bit that one dark night, when the sloping paving stones from Mouska's end of the *platia* were a downhill skating-rink, I fell on my back and broke a rib.

I crept on home without much trouble. The damage, I thought, could be investigated in the morning. It was only when I woke up thirsty some hours later that I realised that there was real damage to be found. I put out my hand, was seized with pain and could not reach my glass.

Help could not come to me unless I got it, when the day came, for my door shut with a bolt inside. It took about half an hour to stand up, but being vertical was no worse than being horizontal - and that was lucky, for having got into that position, reached the door and opened the top half, I had to stand there in the cold for as long again.

The first person who came along the path was Michalis' aunt, my nearest neighbour and former owner of my lower field, a kindly grey old woman in a shawl. She had so many aches and pains herself that someone else's made a change. I think she liked to find me standing in the doorway with a broken rib.

Clearly that was it. I manoeuvred myself back onto my bed, she found a lump, compresses and every kind attention were quickly brought. So was Mr N's wife, who came with fish soup and concern. So was Anna, who suddenly managed with the greatest ease and willingness to have time in plenty to be a district nurse. She and Aunty divided sick-room duties in their different manners - it was Anna who had to be told that there was a ban on laughing for a while. Aunty tried to put the fish soup into my mouth herself and was continually in and out with titbits of her own, tidying my kitchen corner with competitive sighs about her aching back, and legs as well. In the evening Mr N broke his own regulations by dashing in, stayed to have half a dozen questions answered, and instructed his wife to help me in every way she could. If one must break a rib on a Greek island, one could not do so with more active sympathy.

Anna and I had been lamenting that we were deprived of olive-picking days together, when there was so much to be said. Now that I had had an accident she even brought Michalis for an evening visit, such as was never managed while I was well. I had them sitting like a married couple at my bedside being leisurely about their news and plans. When they had their own home, they were telling me, I would be a constant visitor. And they knew where that would be now. That had been a problem and was solved. A house, with a little courtyard, not far from the shop, had been offered to Michalis by some relatives in Athens, in return for looking after a middle-aged dependent - Dotty Cousin was Anna's name for her. She was not very dotty, but childish-minded, and miserably out of place in an Athenian flat. She had her own house in Langatha, but needed food and kindness, and as her idea of heaven was Aiyiali with casual outdoor work and animals, it looked as if she might be an asset in herself.

Anna was longing to have her own home to arrange and be a housewife in. She had, in effect, been a daughter-in-law at Sophia's for eight months, and would be for as many more to come. The house needed renovation, including plastering throughout, and that could take not longer than the unravelling of red tape. The mechanics of their wedding was giving rise to much confusion and many varying ideas, from the priest, the police, anyone who liked to be concerned. Did she, for instance, have to be baptised into the Greek Orthodox Church? She would have to go to Athens after Christmas to sort out such questions and deal with paperwork. When we talked of that, I began to think that I would go with her, and on to England, to accept the kindness and the comfort that would be offered in a choice of family homes.

When asked if I was staying for the winter, I had been answering, 'Probably.' It was easiest to be evasive. Why pack another suitcase? Why go anywhere? But the toughest part of winter begins after the New Year, requiring Anna's physical constitution and a great many enduring qualities on top of that. In delivering myself and my possessions to my own property I had completed the first part of the mission that I had set myself. Olive-picking was a happy Stage B, and there would be more of it. When that was finished, let Stage C be English, let it take me to my mother's home in Dorset, or to Henry and Catherine's in Essex where the family doctor was a specialist in the sort of problems I was having - which were not to do with broken ribs.

Anna, my new nanny, encouraged me to go. She was far more worried by the punishment I gave myself for breaking a rib than she was about the rib itself. Not having a nervous breakdown, I had assured her when I came, was what I was purposefully doing when I threw up my job. I might have a tendency to throw myself off precipices, but I was well-known for bouncing back. However, she was anxious that week. She understood that while I had been doing well with the rightness of Aiyiali I was armed with a peanut-shooter against vicissitude.

Kind as my neighbours were to me, I was not kind to myself, so it was fortunate that I had broken nothing more serious than a rib. It has left me with a small lump still sensitive to cold damp weather, but only two days passed before I was creeping up to Mouska's with a walking stick. When Mr N's wife saw me outside she first reproached me and then encouraged me to come and eat lunch with Yorgos in the shop. A great many people shook their heads over our paths and told one another about the necessity for nice flights of concrete steps. Oh yes, it was a gentle life, but I had not had it on the programme. Six days after my fall - or downfall, as I looked on it - I gathered myself together and went back to the olives.

Most villagers had finished picking. December was approaching, the ploughing season was beginning, the remaining olives were falling fast, and Mr N still had twenty seven well-laden trees to strip. It was clear why he had been disgruntled when I had gone with others partly to be sociable. Yet on the day that I came back he took a noticeable amount of cigarette breaks, and while I climbed gingerly and the girl stuck to the lower rungs of the ladder, he started picking like a child off the ground. Towards midday he broke his heavy silence, `Eat now, you two, I'm ill,' and went abruptly home.

`I put out my hand,' he told me in the evening, `and I couldn't get hold of the olives.' He demonstrated the wayward behaviour of his fingers. I have never see him look so glum.

Rheumatism at the beginning of a winter is a bleak outlook for a farmer who has to spend most of his time ignoring it. After that day he was hobbling in the evenings, muttering to himself, rueful in his jokes and ruthless to his wife. She always got the brunt of his worst humour. Once he threw a chair at her.

I hated that, of course I did, but it was no reason to dissociate myself. It would have been no help to her if I had refused my place in protest - that would have been abandonment. I knew that she did not mind my sitting down to supper with her husband while she did the work, for we had developed an understanding that had nothing to do with who was serving and who was being served. So I took up each of her remarks that he ignored, and hugged her for abuses, I kept my place and told myself that Mr N was sick.

I do not know if ploughing is kinder to rheumatism than olive-picking. With those heavy animals dragging an ancient plough-share through the stony earth of tiny terraced fields, I would have thought not. But that was where he moved now, leaving the remaining trees to his teenage daughter, who was afraid of climbing, and a foreign woman with an injured back. 'Don't pick off the ground,' he said, 'and don't pick high. Collect what you can and stop.' I was shocked. I had never heard anyone speak about the life's blood of Greece like that.

Those twenty seven trees were not his own. I had assumed that he was picking for half-share, but now I discovered that the work was in lieu of rent for a field he had used. This was not an annual arrangement. Whatever crop he had grown in it was harvested, and ploughing paid. The girl and I could - more or less - complete the debt. The elderly owner of the field and the trees was in the shop most evenings, looking patiently injured, and I made it my project that he should get his due in oil.

Most island women hate picking by themselves. Anna loves it, so do I. I might not have been so high-minded about Mr N's upsetting attitude if I had not found the olives such a healing pleasure, but one Sunday I made a small atonement for my absence by going out alone. There was no poetry that day, unless it can be said that lone picking is poetry itself. If so, there's rhyme and rhythm in it - set yourself the most widespread of the laden trees for one day's work and your mind will be beating every moment on the use of ground cloths, apron, rope and walking-stick. I grudged five minutes at midday spent gobbling a chicken leg. I failed in my day's goal by one branch, and but for that there was one less tree vulnerable to the next gale. There will always be another gale soon.

I don't know why the English are the ones who have the name for talking about weather. Or, if they really like the subject, put the race on an exposed Greek island and they'd never shut their mouths. Weather! There is so much of it. You're always having it, whatever it is doing, and that's always changing, the whole time. It's a gale, you might as well be on a ship. There's a cloudless lull, you're soused in it. It's warm and damp, your hair looks as if you've just been swimming, and clothes hang limply from the line. The north wind blows with dazzling sunshine, the clothes will dry, but it's murderous to the fingers to peg them up. The south wind blows - that's sneaky - it makes the fire smoke. You're too hot in a T-shirt, shivering in layers of sweaters, always being caught out. Ploughing turns the fields pink, sunsets are ridiculous, it rains once and mauve anemones shoot up. You are constantly looking, constantly aware of what it's up to, living with it, woken by it in the night. Paths are torrents, stones clatter. If a shutter or a gate is banging, you huddle in your bed wondering whether to be brave outside or whether - if you stay put - the damage will be greater to your property or nerves. Then, on emerging in the morning, sniff fresh greenness - each one of your senses is perpetually being worked. It's beautiful, it's enervating. It's exhilarating and exhausting, for whatever the weather is, you are.

That's winter, nearly half the year. There's inconstancy for twelve months.

We do not go olive-picking on rainy days, but there are few of those. We have days with rain in them as well as all the other climatic happenings. When the clouds burst, out-lying stables fill with pickers in various stages of wetness and good humour, you cannot stand in them, half a dozen is a crowd, every discomfort is a laugh. Mr N, talkative again, is the joke-cracker in every muddy party - except once when he wedged himself onto a stone ledge and went to sleep under a leaking roof. By ourselves now, the girl and I are being rained on far from any stable. We grab the radio, our bucket of cold fish and mess of garments, and burrow with the lot under a sheet of polythene. Is it for this that I have given up my responsible salaried position in the capital? It is.

We finished all but the last pair of trees, the tallest that I have had to pick, and all the olives that had not fallen were dangling in the sky. `So we've finished. Daddy said -' I know, this is growing too familiar, `Don't pick high or off the ground.' And what was to be expected from a girl who dared not reach the top? On the fourteenth of December I picked the last tree for Langatha by myself. It was a happy day - a small bottle of oil for the owner, which was something real, but I was sorry that Stage B was at an end. `Are you staying for the winter?' - `No, I'm not.'

It seemed suitable as well as cheerful that I should have a nanny to escort me on the first lap into the beyond. Departure day, she had decided, should be New Year's Eve, and she would be in Athens with her wedding business and her shopping until after I moved on, impatient to get back to Amorgos herself, though a few days in the city should be fun. At the moment she was in correspondence with the British Chaplain, who would have to sign an affidavit that she was unmarried, and had begged the privilege of adding some personal advice. He had known many marriages between Greeks and English women, but never one that lasted longer than two years. She answered him with such assurance, explaining how she loved not only Michalis but the life on Amorgos, that he was convinced before he met her that he had found the exception to his rule. She was as definite about her life as I was being vague.

I could think of that in England. Now my only aim was to enjoy my final fortnight in Langatha as quietly as possible. In the mornings I went to write at Mouska's in a rib of sunshine with her *mangali* warm beside me on the wooden floor. It was nearly five years since I had abnegated my typewriter and all its works, and when I started, on a Sunday or a rainy day, to put words onto paper - not for a letter, for a book - I realised that, in England or Langatha, this must be the occupation for Stage C. If I was a writer, I was supposed to write. Not doing so had made me sick. I had to do so if I wanted to be whole. If I had no other ideas - and I did - I could write a text book for foreign students of the English Language, I ought to be qualified for that. But all that was important in this fortnight was the fact of making sentences again, remembering that I had a publisher in London wondering what I was up to after these blank years. For the moment I would sit at Mouska's getting into practice. *Life is a Suitcase* was the title of my thoughts.

Chapter 10

`Are you writing, Carolina? Are you writing?' Yes, *Kyria* Mouska, yes I am. Look at these pages. Watch my busy hands.

`What a lot of words!' the coffee-drinkers and the card-players exclaimed. `You'll make yourself dizzy with such writing. Are you writing about us?' The comments were so repetitive, and what I was doing was so remote, that they did not count as interruption, it somehow helped my concentration to have this mild distraction to retreat from, I could wind myself into a working centre instead of feeling lost in space. Every morning *Kyria* Mouska made me coffee and whispered, `On me.' After all, as she explained a few times, I wasn't earning money so it was unpractical to spend. That fortnight she sat sewing me a shoulder bag, like a nose-bag, such as all islanders - male and female - use, a parting present in brown velvet which I would carry everywhere. The men played cards, I wrote, we were harmonious.

Kyria Mouska's treating was an honour. Mr N's made me feel like a poor relation now. Since the olives had been picked I wished that he would let me be a customer. I wanted to order what I felt like, and sit at any table like anybody else. But what I ate or drank or where I sat depended on his humour - liberal enough but not my own. Carolina pay? - Certainly not. That sounded all right, and it often felt all right, but not when I was sitting at the corner of a table picking at a twenty-five-year-old policeman's leftovers.

Charity from a village butcher! And I was nearly thirty-nine.

`Village butcher' was my proud-moment epithet for my commander, and yet, however touchy I was feeling, I was presently shoving onto him the responsibility of getting another social occasion right. The day after Christmas was my birthday and I decided, as there's no Saint Carolina, to acknowledge it and have it for my name-day because it is the one who is celebrating who has the treating rights. I was so regularly treated in two shops myself that I was glad of this opportunity before I left. `We'll cook something,' promised Mr N.

He was sitting by my gas stove when he said that. The evening that he crossed my threshold, hearing that I had had an accident, he abolished his rule of not entering my house. Now, if I left the shop with him, he often came inside to warm his hands. It was a complication to my favourite pottering time, but the compensation was that rheumatism and puritanism seemed to go together, he never did more than murmur, `Paradise,' between some lines of conversation, or doze off in his chair.

I said I'd give him three hundred drachmas for some birthday-treating, and he could offer what he liked. Usually I sent a Christmas thousand, but I decided not even to excuse myself for not doing so this year, for I had come to an end of my feeling of indebtedness. Admittedly his perquisites from our estate were mostly on my brother's side, but `it's all in the family' ought to be a Greek expression, and Mr N had not done one thing to the property since Henry left, except to use it, in a year when his own well had cracked. As for my suppers, I had earned whatever happened to be on the evening table with three weeks of hard work.

Before Christmas he slaughtered a pig in Henry's field, which is a much more gruesome business than slaughtering a goat. Goats are delicate about the neck. Pigs take time. There are a few villagers - Michalis is one of them - who won't slaughter any animals, and some who will slaughter others'

but not their own. This pig was Mr N's, and it sounded as if he was having satisfaction. Even his wife and daughter were being merry about holding down the legs. Well, I was going to share the meat - wasn't I? - and enjoy it too. Keep placid. I walked down into the gorge with *The Metaphysical Poets* in my pocket. `A wondrous life is this I lead...' I ought, more appropriately, to have been collecting firewood.

Christmas is a mild occasion, with no rockets, coloured lights or tinsel, it's a glorified Sunday when the groceries are open by inclination and in the other shops there are extra-good titbits for the drinks. At Mr N's I told the regulars to be sure of dropping in the following evening, and did not lament the pig which had made the brawn which is the speciality of the house. The celebration was more involved with the Phanises than a policeman. We got happily drunk, not plastered, and danced to the pick-up. Then Mr N leaned over and whispered to me, `I want you tonight.'

Bloody almighty hell, Mr N, I don't have this on the programme.

I did not speak or make a reaction. I left within ten minutes with short Phanis to drink coffee at Nikolakis'.

`One day you will regret what you are doing,' Phanis had told me four years before at Ormos. `One day you will remember this evening at this table, and you will say to me, "Phani, you were right."'

I spent my birthday telling myself that I could take this incident as one that had not happened. I had had so many conventional goodnights from Mr N this season, and so often clambered out of a similar predicament, I could not believe that this one would be different.

Never believe any such thing if you are a single foreign woman living in a man's world. That lesson was taught years ago on Mykonos. It ought to have been learnt.

But supposedly he would go on as he always had, simply going on. He would have to. We had a social date that could not be postponed.

In the evening everyone who came into the shop, according to arrangement, was treated to a drink. A corner table was laid with forks and glasses for a few. `Sit here,' Mr N pointed to the far side of the table and I climbed in against the wall. Everything was as ordered, but for a certain something, coming from him, about the atmosphere.

`Many happy returns!' Not too many, please. I find all this returning rather wearying. `She's forty,' Mr N said. All right, I'll be forty. I was forgetting that in Greece you count the year you are facing, not the one you close. There's a wallop for me. I'm too old for this situation - and it is the situation I suspected, after all. Despite the birthday table, my senses are aware of it.

I do not know what happened next. I remember some isolated moments, nothing about sequence of events. One day I nearly fell down in Mouska's because I had not had a drink. One night my door burst open, a police torch shone over my bed. I was alone in it. As soon as that was ascertained, the door banged shut again, and Mr N's pounding footsteps - always at night there was that pounding - flumped away. How could that have been? My door shut inside with a bolt. How it happened is as mysterious as what was happening. I had offended Mr N's manhood, war had broken out, the world was in collapse about me, and for five days before the boat was due I was not half so drunk as the village thought I was, but nearer to insane.

Chapter Eleven

I did not lose control between that Christmas and the New Year because I had quarrelled with a village butcher. I lost control because I had no weapons. And having done so, I was so incensed by the failure of my mission that I flung myself into a vicious circle of making matters worse. All my gentle time had been nothing but an anaesthetic. I had tried not to make a mess and failed. I have failed - let me disintegrate. Chasms opened - let them swallow - I'll go down. There goes another of those foreign females who get licked by false romance on their Greek islands - yes, I'm proud, I do care what the world says because otherwise I've got Aiyiali right. What otherwise? There is no otherwise. One major blunder devastates the lot.

Why now? Why was this worse than any other item in the five years that I had known the man? 'Never mind,' he always used to say in this same situation. 'Everything else remains the same.' Why now? Because instead of saying no thank you I went off to Nikolakis' with short Phanis? Don't you believe it. He had to kick me because I was already down.

One night - early, I suppose in those five days - he came into my house again to say now and forever let us have this matter out, as quietly as if he had been discussing whether we would have the ceiling in bamboo or boards. Fine, but the ceiling question does not need compassion. Haven't you got this into your head yet, Mr N, I'm here because I'm sick? I was released from my contract in Athens on grounds of ill-health. And you know what the cure is - it's quietude, it's having the way straight. Mary, Mother of God, leave me in peace.

Oh yes, Mr N knew all that, rather better than any other villager. However, that was not his business. All he wanted was for me to tell him yes or no to what he cared about. 'No,' I said. 'Good night,' he said. After that the pounding came. The weasle became a mammoth in the night.

He was mad and I was mad. He hated me. He could have knifed me on the home path one dark night as easily as he had knifed his pig. Job satisfaction. But I had not come to this harbour to look for hate.

Mr N's feet were enormous, or his boots were, out of all proportion to his frame. I walked into Nikolakis' and saw him in the middle of some rowdy table - here, not on his own premises - here, dogging me, having an evening out. I have no place in his shop, and am I to have no place in this one either because he is a customer? I sat at the side with tall Phanis, I think. Mr N immediately got up, and he stamped out of that shop as I have never known anyone stamp. He forced every other person to look and listen, he was going cap-first at an angle of almost forty-five degrees, and the toes of his boots were right under the peak.

Flump - flump - flump - flump - what do the observers think? I can't say, 'I won't go to bed with him.' He can't say, 'She won't go to bed with me.' I am not looking for erotic love, I'm looking for loving kindness and all I find is boots. Trample, village butcher, I shall write an ode concluding, 'Goat, where is thy bounce?'

He's crazy, he's been twisted since he missed Maria's wedding, and he has the rheumatism too. Is that my business? He talked about his rheumatism, he did not listen to my sick mind.

Why now? In a lucid moment I saw one good reason - I was not useful any more. I had bought my place in his shop with Senior Service, a Christmas tip and other presents - let alone the promise of a house, which was officially his own in any case. Now he did not have the goodies, he had me - a poor relation - in their place. He had had to make a meal for my birthday for which I paid cost price. My house had been completed and the olives had been picked, I was an incubus.

How dare he? If he's so impressed by a four-stripe policeman, let him consider who I am. Let him make a phone call to the proudest director of any school in Athens, one who has been known to say of his own premises, `This place is a church,' and ask him for a testimonial. Let him do that and he'll hear about respect. If I go into that school in Athens, I'll be offered my old position on the staff.

He hated me, I hated him. Five days were consumed with my hatred for Mr N. The relief was not to have to excuse whatever rankled any more, his carelessness of olive debts, his truculence to his wife. `My only mistake is that I married,' he once announced to the whole shop. That's not just being boorish, that's illogical. He adores his children, he's a doting grandfather. Privately I took it up with him and he answered, `Ah, but she had no dowry.'

I lamented my place in the little creaky shop. I did not lament the man. I lamented one part of him, but not so much as half. And which part? - the part that was concerned when he noticed that I had my pillow growing mouldly against the dampest wall? Very easy it was for him to point that out to me. Why instead did he not mention my timber which he stored in his yard? 'He's a villain,' I told Anna. So far as I remember, she wrung my hand. 'Oh I am glad you've come round to that.' She had only restrained herself from using strong words out of courtesy to me. Now she had an unburdening of ferocious adjectives, not from old resentment - that's not Anna - but chiefly provoked by the cold war of the moment, when neither she nor Michalis knew why they were having a cold war.

Christmas is the official time for paying debts or interest. Mr N owed Michalis seventeen thousand drachmas, most of it since Maria's wedding when he had sent his wife to appeal to the kindness of Michalis' heart. And now, the following Christmas, Mr N ignored the loan, and his creditor as well. His cutting was so pointed that when Demosthenes, on an errand, bought a packet of rice at Michalis' shop, Mr N sent him back to return the rice, reclaim the money, and buy the same thing next door from Eleftheria. Why? Out of pride because he was in debt?

Anna, the only person in my confidence, was happy in her adjectives but not in her charge of me. She cannot tell me what I was doing in the daytime, but she knows that she had anxious evenings feeling responsible for averting a gruesome end to a sad tale. If madness is preferable to drunkenness, 'mad' may be a euphemism, or perhaps the two had gone in partnership in the mixed cause of defiance and despair. However that may be, appearances were clear to Anna who made a pretext every evening for coming up to Nikolakis', calling me out and taking me home without mishaps worse than broken ribs.

During those five days I must have packed up my house and packed my suitcases.

I still had difficulty in carrying my big water-bucket. I should not have filled so many cases, I would need help all along the line. That would be a long one, too, for all this luggage was over-weight for the air. Anna and I would share Michalis' donkey for the first lap, there would be no more telegrams for Mr N's. There would be no more telegrams - full stop. I began packing summer clothes as well as winter ones. When in doubt - that's all I remember - hurl the garment in. Life is a suitcase. I don't know the destination. There may be no more unpacking in this house.

Mr N had told me before Christmas that Kostas, our second policeman, who had left the island to get married, was interested in renting my house for perhaps a year. If I were to come back only in the summer, I could use my lower rooms, which would not be too restricting when I spent time on Henry's side as well. What would I be doing after all? I would have to - wouldn't I? - go back to work? I couldn't - could I? - retire at thirty-nine? He seemed to be putting these questions to me in presentation of the case for Kostas' living in my house. I could not answer them, and had no inclination to. I had stuck to 'if', 'we'll see', 'we'll talk of that again'. And now I could not communicate with the man who would act policeman's landlord if he chose.

Chapter 11

Who likes messes? Here is one. I'm having war with my owner of my house, and of my brother's house, which is full of hens and hay and fish. I bought that second house for Henry, presented him with his commander, and refused to try to keep it safe. The man has his animal possessions over there - let him have his policeman here - let him have parties every night. I'll go to Africa. I'll take a long trip down the Amazon. I'll be an astronaut.

So I went on until we were in every way ready for the end of it. On New Year's Eve Anna and I left our luggage at the harbour, with our sleeping-bags in a room there to begin the night in before the boat came in the early hours, and all that remained for her to take down later was ourselves. She must have felt relieved to be nearing this last responsibility before her journey, which was not a problematic one for I only wanted to kick dust off my heels. But there was no mercy anywhere, for either of us. Rough winds had turned into a gale, the boat was stuck at Piraeus, and Anna - full of dread, she says - came round to tell me that there was no departure for anyone that night. She could not have known then, it would have been too much to know, that we were not leaving for five whole days again. No boat, no journey, no reprieve for nanny. It was Force Nine on the Beaufort Scale.

We waited. The boat was held in harbour for so long that when Force Nine dropped to Seven, it set out on its next round of islands excluding Amorgos. Anna returned to daily life, I camped in my house and turned into a daytime troglodyte.

Five days' aggression may be a skirmish, ten is not. When the storm was over and I had survived, we found among the wreckage one compensation for having to endure the double blast. Ten days made me comprehend the force of Mr N's hostility. There would be no ending to it - this had to be accepted - in a handshake and a shrug. All very salutary, but not to the physical frame. That paid. And then it said, `Enough.'

It was on the third of January that the gale began to die. At the same time, suddenly and lucidly, it came to me that I had given up my job in Athens to look after myself, so as not to make a mess. Unless I took some iron treatment I was not going to embark on any boat. Anna could help me but she could not carry me, and I did not want to be carried, by her or anyone. Let me scrounge from the morass - since my body went on living - whatever style could be found. I would not be done out of that by Mr N.

There were two days to go. I prescribed one for hospitalisation and one for walking. I would spend the first in bed with grapefruit juice and baby sleep and the other on the mountain. No shirking. The sun shone calmly on the first. It seemed an insult to fine weather not to be in it, but I was also glad not to be a part of any weather, glad to be confined. My mind, a little rested, was growing logical, but that was no alleviation, for it pointed out how many problems lay between this house and Henry's in an Essex village, days ahead. I would have to travel overland across Europe, which I was in no fit state to do. Right now it seemed too difficult, alone, to bring in a pair of socks that I had hanging on the washing line.

`Nanny!' Immediately, between my house and Ormos, I had to look for help. I was lying in bed and thinking, there is a pair of socks on the line and before the end of this day, in case it rains tomorrow, I have to take them down. The chore reached proportions which seemed far beyond me, and I lay there waiting for my nanny.

Anna burst into the house from sunshine. I broached the subject by mumbling about suitcases. She pointed out that I had been through the major leaving process, almost everything was down at Ormos, I was only here with oddments, the house was ready to be locked up. I had to admit that this was true, but I had a problem about a pair of socks. `Well,' she said in her district-nurse voice, `you'll have to go out to the loo sometime, won't you? You can take the socks down then.'

My disappointment gradually gave way to admiration of Anna's unbounded commonsense. When the time arrived, I found that there was no difficulty at all in going down into my field and unpegging one pair of socks. Some people are so sane that they make the dotty feel dottier than before, but Anna's sanity declares that the world is on the whole a balanced place. When I bleated, `Nanny!' she did not squash me, or remind me that I was seventeen years her senior, she simply retorted, `Yes, Aunty!'

After that, everything I had to do seemed more achievable. The weather held the next day, bright January-warm. I went down the mule track to give myself the maximum of uphill ways, I walked and walked. I climbed to the top of the ridge above Langatha up a back gorge where I had never been before, and sat on a rock looking down on the place that I was leaving, with such new calm in my sadness that it had some obstinate ingredient of happiness as well. I would go down to collect the oddments from my house, leave the key in the door for the official owner, and shake hands here and there. At dusk I would walk down to Ormos, to go ahead with the arrangement that Anna had made five days before, to use our sleeping-bags in the room where we had left them and catch a boat before dawn.

But on my way down through Langatha I met Mr N's wife, my ally whom I had not been able to hunt out. What explanation for absenteeism - to her of all people - could be made? Yet in some manner or other, if only with a message, I would have had to say goodbye to her, so I was not sorry to be forced into an impromptu greeting now. She was almost tearful when she asked me, 'Carolina, why don't you come to the shop?'

'There's no place for me any more.' What else was I to say? I'd be damned if I told her I didn't want to come.

'Nonsense! How can you say that?'

'I'm afraid that if I came in, Mr N might throw me out.'

'Bah! You know how he talks. Don't pay attention. Come this evening. Come for a glass of wine before you go.'

I promised that I would. For her sake I had to do so. Promising was easy, my voice was lightly undertaking that. Presently my deeper horror gave way to anticipation that was almost pleasurable.

Now I had to dawdle about the village until after dark, keeping my equanimity tight about me, I had to do this right. I would flabbergast Mr N with my composure. I would not allow him a kinkle of a smile.

As soon as it was time, I picked up my basket, locked my house and walked slowly to the shop. It was important that the right people, and not too many, should be there. Some stage-manager of a saint would have to attend to that.

It was all right. When I reached the doorway there were five characters inside, well-chosen and well-placed. Mr N's wife was frying whitebait at the stove. Demosthenes was playing on the floor. Yorgos was sipping a preprandial ouzo. Another of the regulars, a Yannis, was being an extra at the side. And Mr N, standing upstage with his back to everyone, was lighting a fire in the top-wall fire-place.

'Is there a *bon voyage* here?' I asked.

Mr N's wife, with determined independence, sat me at an empty table, placing in front of me a glass of wine and saucerful of fish. Straight from the frying-pan they were delicious, fortifying to an abstruse conversation about the dying of the gale. All of us had lines. I could sense that Mr N enjoyed it - I did myself.

The wind had been Force Nine, now it was Two or Three. It had raged from varying points of the compass for days and nights. 'And has it fallen?' Yorgos asked me, as if wanting to verify the point.

'Oh yes, it has fallen from the north, and from the south.'

`And from the east?' asked Mr N, not turning.

`From the east too, and from the west.'

His wife filled up my plate and glass. Tension and relaxedness were in a conflict which had no effect on sudden appetite. `So you're going north?' That came from Mr N. Yes, I was going north to see a doctor, since the south had failed to heal. Then I gave his wife my keys and said, `It's time to go. There are five right hands in this shop, and will they all shake mine? Demosthene -' The boy responded obediently. `Yanni - Yorgo.' Each gave me his hand, Mr N's wife a hug, each gave me *bon voyage*.

`N?'

He had still not turned his head. `I'm sorry, Carolina, my hands are too busy and too dirty with these sticks to shake yours.'

So I wished the shop a happy winter and walked away to Ormos.

Chapter Twelve

f ever you need children, these are yours.' The boys were two, three and four years old when Catherine made that statement. I needed them when they were turning seven eight nine. It was birthday season in an Essex village. The doctor's prescription was for nephews. If I made a cake the family was pleased, if I did not no one was critical. I was allowed to read eight-year-old literature and play eight-year-old games, or to sit goopily in an armchair staring into space.

`Do not look more than twenty four hours ahead.' - `Do not push yourself.' The doctor was well-known for firmness, but as I had - by a whisker - brought myself to him instead of being carried, he was not stinting about such sentences. I stayed among my nephews until late in March, as long as I was certified unfit for work. `Debility' was the word for my affliction, which I thought euphemistic, but it was not unpleasant once I could succumb to it in this kind home, where at that moment Catherine was the best full-time companion I could have. Afterwards my best companion was my mother, in her kind home in Dorset, when the doctor had dismissed me - there's an unkind word - because I had begun to write.

It might be improbable for anyone to be glad to be goopy for two months on top of a sister-in-law who is writing a thesis for her Ph D, but Catherine and I did not look on it like that, and she was quite as illuminating about my symptoms as she would have been on the History and Philosophy of Architecture, if she had not spared me from anything so pushing to the intellect. A parcel of upset hormones since the birth of Zachary had taught her too much about withdrawal, and rougher things besides, all undeserved, of a variety that I had inflicted on myself, but our situation was very far from the blind leading the blind. She was in good form while I was in her house, and helped.

It was just as well that I had left Aiyiali, for it was having a flu epidemic, ferocious weather, and the gas boat hadn't come. Everyone who could stand up was cooking on wood fires. Anna could, and she is a prolific correspondent so we were kept informed. Mr N's mother was one of the two who died. His family from Athens who came in for the funeral were lodging in my house. In February the Norwegian couple who had stayed in Henry's for the same month a year before, came bravely back. Mr N had made his symphonic agreement in the summer to co-operate with Anna about putting tenants in, and he did hand over the keys, but there the symphony stopped. Very soon she was writing - as distraught as I had ever heard her - that she would not be able to bring herself to ask for them again.

The main room had been cleared, except of mould and dirt - and a few fish scales, perhaps - but the Norwegians felt that they were living in a public park. Every other part was used, right up to the front doorstep, and that was the noisiest place of all. Regularly at daybreak Mr N's wife and daughter, obedient chattels, came clanking buckets to do their washing there. The tenants pleaded that there should be some warning, some agreement, about laundry days and hours. Anna bore the message, at which Mr N came storming round. He would not have it dictated to him when his womenfolk could do the family washing at his own house.

Henry did not reproach me. I never heard the words `I told you so.' When I made my full confession, admitting that he had always been right about our Mr N, his first reaction was brotherly concern. He also felt relieved that he no longer had to make a tactful effort to support a man he did not like or trust, and that at last the three of us could think concertedly about what had to be done. A fractiousness of feeling, which had hovered uncharacteristically between me and Henry ever since I bought his house with Mr N tied in, evaporated now. Mr N himself had freed me from my promise, and from my faith to him. We had a great clearing of the air.

And what was to be done? Henry said, `As soon she's married, we must get the property transferred to Anna's name,' in the tone that no one would use on resolving to repaint the window frames. That only meant persuading Mr N to take a trip to Naxos with her, and put his name to a new contract handing over his favourite facilities on his home path. Yes, Henry. Very nice. And how do we go about doing that? `We'll find a way.' We would do that in August when he came. For the moment, being set on non-aggressive pressure, he had us sit down to compose a couple of friendly letters to Mr N, which I translated and Catherine copied out. They included no mention of reports from me or Anna, but hope to hear of progress - which we knew there had not been - with the *cabiné* and path. If we had expected any answer to these conscience-prickers, they would have been a waste of stamps.

Anna's next report was that Kostas the policeman
and his wife had been installed on my side on the first of
March. I would have to spend part of the summer in my
lower quarters - like a Mykoniot, letting the best part of
my house. Well and good for one year. I would have no
complaining rights when I had jeopardised my brother's
whole estate. But I had better have access to Henry's
house when I arrived. I had better be given my own rent.

When I arrived? Of course. There might not be
another telegram announcing my arrival, but there would
certainly be more unpacking in that house. For here was
the tough lesson learnt at the doctor's desk, there is no
such thing as metamorphosis. Life would go on, in all
departments. When facts cannot be changed there is
nothing left but style. And therefore, on the day that I was
sent out into the able world, I wrote to the director of my
old school in Athens asking if I might consider myself on
the staff again, as from October the first. Since I had to
earn my living, and could not be another person, I thought
it would be satisfying to walk back through those portals
with more style than I had fallen out of them. But I would
not load my life with private lessons, and I would leave
at the right time.

So after all I had only taken a year's holiday, and the
best part lay ahead. The doctor had made no ban on
pleasant daydreams, I started making them before I could
confidently resolve to make a birthday cake. They
developed, they became preposterous, I had to speak of
them. Over a supper table I made them sound as
hypothetical as possible, and then they grew so tantalising
that some days later I had to angle to have them put into a

factual statement that I dared not make myself. 'I wish I could visualise what I shall be doing in May and June,' I said. And Henry answered, 'I was under the impression that you'll be on Crete with Julian.'

I was. There was my daydream, and it was not a dream at all, it had grown into a fact. On May the seventeenth I had the eight-year-old cub scout beside me in the air. His almond eyes that day were very large. And I for one was flabbergasted with incredulity and joy.

Julian's teacher had only raised one problem when I abducted him from school, that she herself was green with envy, and one stipulation, that he should take his reading books with him. Jason said he'd had his turn the year before, and did not seem to be weighing whose was the best deal. Zachary thought himself too young for this one, which sounded a bit adventurous, but would like his own turn next year, please. Catherine's reaction, apart from generous enthusiasm and the feeling that she would miss her middle son, was to buy tickets for those other two to fly out with her ahead of Henry and join us in the middle of July. That depended on my meeting them at Athens Airport, since her own sick years had left her wary of such matters as connections with boats to Amorgos. It was strange and wonderful to me that Henry's only complaint about the whole arrangement was that his holiday from his Polytechnic was too short. He saw it as an advantage of the expedition that I would end up in Langatha with a sturdy nephew for a bodyguard.

At eleven o'clock on our first night, in a Heraklion hotel, Julian started polishing his shoes. After that every sign of cub-scoutism completely disappeared.

His parents had been left with three poste-restante addresses of dubious date on Crete, and none in the Dodecannese, which would be our way of approaching Amorgos. It was not the sort of expedition to have a fixed itinerary, and I had not given it much more forethought than delight. Another subject had taken over in Dorset for the best part of two months. I had been working on a text-book about word-formation, seriously enough to interest Macmillan, while my mother was writing, for the Lutterworth Press, about the origin of words. *Words Words Words* was the title of her book, and also of a very happy time we had together, with open dictionaries on every table and gardening for our intervals. Then not even the glories of Crete could move my mind from suffixes and prefixes. On the road to Essex those gave way to tales of King Minos. In the air I was in a happy state of shock. It was only on the fifth day after landing that manic panic struck.

It came as physically as the migraine, with whirring wings and not two minutes' notice, beside the swimming pool of the Maleme Beach Hotel, where the manager's daughter, through some unlikelihood, was a second cousin of Julian's. He would not otherwise have been brought to this setting, which was not my idea of Crete, though it equated with his idea of Paradise. It was also a mild background for an attack of manic panic, but that seemed to be irrelevant. So was the fact that during our first five days I had spent eighty of my three hundred pounds. Those were breaking-in expenses, with hotels along the north coast from Heraklion to Chania. We would soon get our tent erected, we would find our own level in the south. If necessary I would fall upon my autumn fund in Athens, all that I had left when I threw up my job, to start me off again. This was a once-in-a-lifetime trip, not to be spoilt with niggling about cash.

Then what's your trouble? This is Crete. It's rugged, it's beautiful, it's real. Julian is having his dream of bliss, you should be having yours as well. Think what an injury you would be doing him if you turned him round and sent him home again.

I could, however. Our tickets were seven-day returns. I had not thrown them away.

I'm crazy. I don't know where my mind is, but wherever it is it's been raving since the day it elected me the vagrant mother of an eight-year-old. Very nice that seemed when I sat on my sofa with no responsibility, beyond the day, that I did not choose to take upon myself. Four months ago I was hardly able to make a train journey straight through Europe. Now -? Take the boy to Heraklion, put him on the plane, and then... Then what?

I prowled round the swimming pool talking myself out of that. Do not look beyond the morrow. We could always make our way round Crete on that advice. It fitted well with Julian's style of life. Put your mind on what he'll have for supper. Tell him bedside stories. Tell him about Daedalus. You know all the answers - the doctor says you do - remember that. Hang the autumn. Hang next month. So I talked until Julian ran into a lamp-post.

He came dashing towards me with blood streaming down his leg. I pulled the band-aid from my bag and heard my auntly voice. Two days later, when the return plane left, a weight of doubt took off with it. I threw away the tickets and concentrated on enjoying Crete.

That bag was the brown velvet one which *Kyria* Mouska had made for me. On the sixth evening, when we first got the tent erected, and Julian realised that I meant to sleep outside, I tied it to my wrist with a long piece of string, placed it by his pillow, and told him that he could tug it, if need be, in the night. Our beach was at the mouth of the Gorge of Samaria, lonely - awesome, one might say, as well as stony - I saw his point. That system lasted for two nights. Afterwards I was allowed to stroll in any direction within calling range. I could sit at a taverna table after supper while he slept twenty feet away. But the Mouska bag had to be near us, always. It carried passports, cash and travellers' cheques. It carried life's three other essentials, band-aid, felt pens and a snack, and always had room for the moment when any small object was shoved into my hand - `Keep that.' Hanging on a chair it meant, `I'll be back in a few minutes.' Sometimes Julian would be left holding it himself. It would have been as unnerving as a series of earth tremors if I had lost my Mouska bag.

We cheated on the Gorge of Samaria. We walked half-way up, turned round and came back. Here and there we met a group of hikers, all properly weighed down with knapsacks, when only we walked light. The bottom part is the most splendiferous. For a month we tore round Crete, here-and-now people cheating a good deal.

When there were no roads we went by boat, and once on a bumpy army truck that was to build a road, and once, when the bus came to its inland terminal, we were carried on down a dirt track to an unofficial place, Frangokastro on a beach of oleanders, because the driver wanted a swim. We kept a travelling scrapbook, did our daily reading, and those two duties - for all the pleasure of Julian's pictures with their hallmark of a sun smiling in the top left corner - would raise the daily panic pressure because there was the threat that we might fall behind. I learnt to live with that panic below surface, I kept pushing it down. When Henry came in August it could be released, and that was August's problem, if it turned into a balloon. Do not look ahead. Julian never did.

His interest was intense in the bus that we were travelling on, and in our destination when that came into sight. 'When are Catherine and the boys coming?' was his first reference to his family, on the sixth day. 'Where are we going next?' meant that he needed the next line in the conversation with a new friend. He was always making friends, and according to their movements - or whether or not he found pedal boats, canoes or table football - he wanted to stay for ever or move on at once. He had no inhibitions about asking for anything he wanted, but was also grateful when he got it, and he never ran off without permission by himself. We each knew exactly how we stood, and that often surprised me. Crete offered diversions which I could never have discovered by myself.

In the mornings I would wake beneath an increasingly hot sky, with plans for explorations to be made, but not a step to be taken outside the permitted circle yet. I pottered a little, filling the billy-can with water to make tea and boil eggs, until a wriggling from inside the tent announced the morning's first conversation, a daily ritual.

`Carolina!'

`Hallo!'

`All right.' And that was all.

The sun, which was making me look Swedish, was bringing out the true American Indian in Julian. He was a striking eight-year-old in size-ten clothes, with jaunty good looks, and a gentleness when he befriended younger children and animals. Life's greatest danger for him was of becoming spoilt, and for me of calling him `my boy', which was true for the moment but would not be for long. He came through so well that the consensus of opinion was that a season of being an only child had been beneficial, that two months' gallivanting round Greek islands with a fairly dotty aunt had somehow made him calmer than before. I came through deciding that awareness of my danger would have to be protection in itself. After all, apart from returning to the bosom of his family, the boy would grow. His size-ten clothes did not contain spare flesh, they promised gianthood, he grew out of his boots before reaching Amorgos. His body tired him suddenly. Once I had to carry him, and he went to sleep immediately on my back. I staggered, but my encouragement was thinking that he would be carrying me before too long.

`Carolina, shall we climb that mountain?' Neither of us was any good at lounging. I would always say yes, we would always find our mountain higher than we thought, puffing as we shouted echoes all the way up, and always told each other that it was worth it afterwards. `Carolina, how far shall we swim? Shall we swim out to that rock?' Let's swim out to that rock. It was always further than it looked, but I knew that Julian would not tire before I did. I wanted him to dive. I was as proud as he was when he finally plunged in head-first. `It's a matter of confidence,' one of the day's friends explained to him, and Julian struck me with an awe that made me tremble by throwing himself down on top of me proclaiming, `This is my confidence.'

I was sure then that he had no inkling of my jitters every time we struck or packed up camp. And I was not hoodwinking him. You cannot easily hoodwink a child, and this was an uncannily perceptive one. He made me be the rock he needed. I needed him to make that rock of me. The jitters left me when I was facing him. A minor injury, a prickle in the foot, a stomach ache, all these were instant therapy such as had saved me at the Maleme Beach Hotel. One prickle from a date-palm had to be taken to a doctor's surgery where a frightening array of instruments was brought forth and each one rejected in favour of a razor blade. Julian loudly preferred to limp through life. `Hold my hand,' I said, 'as hard as it hurts.' He did. It hurt. But not like a village butcher's boots.

'Carolina, where are we going?' We were always going going going, from north to south, from west to east. Where are we going? Wherever the table football is. Wherever there are Minoan palaces. We made a tour of Malia and Gortys, spending connoisseurs' hours playing hide-and-seek. That's not being disrespectful. That's understanding about labyrinths. Where are we going? Wherever there are beaches. We mapped beaches with strong currents, special pebbles, nudists, stepping-stone rocks, rocks for the best dives. We made a fire for a feast of shish kebab, and that was the evening when Julian wasn't hungry - but he's the carnivore. We went to tavernas because that was simplest and friendliest, we also needed access to water and tables for our scrapbook. What we did not have was bedtime stories. We were going going going and bedtime meant falling into sleep. We were always panting and in need of refreshment. 'Carolina, where are we going?' - To the bank.

Four weeks after our arrival at Heraklion, on a mixture of calculation, mood of the moment and what was dictated by the bus timetables, we came to Sitia, the eastern port. I had carried my happiness between my teeth, but there it was intact, and so were we. I had given up being shocked by our financial progress in favour of calling it a triumph that we had enough of the summer fund in hand for two splurging days with hotel nights on Rhodes. There were tantalising spaces on the map, but I preferred those to a claim to having 'done Crete', which is in any case ridiculous. I thought that one day - given the opportunity and the means - Jason or Zachary, or both together, could have their turn on Crete. Something else told me that the opportunity and means would never come together, but at least I would be able to locate my new daydreams.

`Carolina, why don't you tuck in your shirt?' So we're appearance-conscious, are we, now that we're on Rhodes? We shower twice a day and spend time at the mirror - Julian does and I take glances - I had not realised what a black-and-white couple we have become. Julian, waists don't suit me, I don't really have one. Why don't you wear your blue cap? It's been my disappointment that he hardly ever wears it. When he lost the first one, a sinister version of Mr N's in khaki camouflage, I was glad to fork out for another, but he's so proud of this blue one that he's afraid it will be blown away. It's the excess item on the list of articles to be kept permanently available and safe. My Mouska bag is confused with those already, the top of the picnic basket is reserved for the teddy bear who was the last-moment necessity as we walked out of the Essex home. It will be a relief at journey's end to stop having these problems, though there will be others in exchange. The cap is one too many, and I am not going to impress on Julian, who is so interested in the mirror, why it is more important than my shirt. God have pity on the world's teenagers in ten years.

We don't have a ball now. Rhodes with all its seventh-heaven pleasures - the kind that are supposed to make good philhellenes bewail how it is spoilt - is too diverting for us to need another here. When the first two had been punctured, and I said that balls could not be called necessary expenses any longer, Julian gave up five days' ice cream to buy a third. Then every other anxiety gave precedence to my dread of a third puncture before we arrived at the fifth day. We had it. And that meant two days with no ball and no ice cream, and no excuse that I could find for slackening my rigidity. I must remember, when I go on alone, that it is not devastating to walk down a waterfront without stopping for a drink. I could do that easily when Julian had foregone his ice cream for a punctured ball. Really it would be a salutary arrangement - for the adults - if single people regularly borrowed a child for two months.

'Carolina, where are we going?' - 'Carolina, can we have bicycles?' We're going to Kos, we're going to Tilos, we're escaping from the rich man's seventh heaven, where Julian would stay for ever, there are reasons for a frantic zigzag, yet it is frantic, we are here-and-now people going going going, and the way that we and the money are careering we are going to Aiyiali sooner than I thought. On Rhodes there are too many joys for hire, on Kos there are bicycles for ten dracs an hour. September is paying for them, I've broken into the autumn fund and somehow we don't seem to be camping any more. On the way down from the temple of Aesclipios my brakes gave out, at the beginning of a two-mile downhill road with bumps. Where are we going? Please not to a hospital. Don't let me be killed today. If I'm killed today I don't know what my boy will do. If I'm killed before Henry solves our problems - can he solve them? - Mr N will claim my house. 'Carolina, can we have a tandem?' Let's try a tandem. We're hopeless on a tandem, let's trade it back for bicycles, let's set off again, let's catch another boat. On Tilos, which has a feeling of Aiyiali, there is nothing to be hired, not even a ball.

`When we get to Aiyiali, will Mr N be at the harbour?'

`No, Julian, not this year.' I was practising answers for the questions which would probably come on the boat. `You see, Julian, Mr N has been behaving very badly. He isn't a real friend any more.' You see! How silly! No child of this faithful nature could be expected to see any such thing at all. `We have Anna there instead now. And Michalis. They're our friends.'

We gave Tilos twice as long as Rhodes, with a room which did not feel like a room to let to tourists, but rather a little old seaside house that no one happened to be living in. It was all so far from Julian's latest idea of Paradise that he hardly noticed that. He began putting words of Greek together and made so many friends that he had his moment, here too, of not wanting to leave. Where nothing was for hire, anyone who had a rowing boat would lend it, and anyone who had a motor boat give rides.

Tilos might have a feeling of Aiyiali, but I wasn't sure what Aiyiali was going to feel like this time, except that it would be much better for having Julian. Two years before, when personal freedom had seemed to be of first importance, I had handed Jason over to his nanny as soon as we arrived. There would be none of that this year. Thank you, Catherine.

`Carolina!'

`Hallo!'

`All right.'

credit |
34,500 | PAID

Nikolaras, coigne	600	(commented on elsewhere)
House, last instalment	8000	
Nikitas commission	1000	--- some of which he insisted on using
Laki	2871	immediately for the priest's blessing feast
Carolina	5 5500	--- eventually to be reduced
Michali	4500	--- unfortunately reduced at the
	600	last moment from 5000
Dimitri, builders	800	--- 4½ days work.
workman's wages	2700	total of 28½ days
Nikitas	2500	completion of above work - in advance
	100	SEE OVER.
Priest	100	
* 20 dracs buried		
loukoumi	20	
	24	
Permit	83	
Cement, 21 bags	735	To complete all pre-winter works
" carriage	140	
2 cans	10	
well-cleaning brush	80	
	29 463	
coffee + ouzo approx	37	they've drunk a lot but I've
		enjoyed it
	29,500	+ sometimes in the evenings I say 'Enrikos
unaccounted for	5,000	--- to be accounted for
	34,500	by Xmas with regular report

	454	
HOUSE	15000	
garden	1700	
Nikitas	1500	plain cash. (plus Xmas
contract	2800	
blessings etc	450	
mattras 56	11200	
workmen 78	12660	& 1st winter
carp. work	590	
carriage	2210	
materials	17185	
scaffolding/inst	1000	
household	10200	about
winter	1350	
Xmas - Easter	5450	
Easter - Summer	4642	
	90527	To Sept '73
	92730	sand 3100
Xmas-Easter	*420 (-tiles)	beams 4190
		ouoopola 2160
	5000	cement 2100
ouof	4500	gravel 975
	102650	(325)
		bamboo 400
		lime 3150

Chapter Thirteen

J ulian and I came back to Langatha with Markos the muleteer. In spite of a strange feeling, I thought there was a great deal to be said for paying a sum of money for a service and having the way clear. Markos, the uncle of the Laki girls, which he sees as a connection - 'You, Carolina, opened the mind of my first niece' - is small and gentle, a speech-maker when he is drunk, though I have never known that make him independable. He's straight with a few swerves. His two favourite subjects are his dependability and his respect for us. He once told Henry, enumerating the family virtues, 'I have never been kissed by a foreign woman, except your sister and your wife,' which was inaccurate for Catherine had kissing rights that I do not. She used to claim them regularly for arrival and departure in preference to my handshake with Mr N - 'used to' -, I would have to work on that expression. From now on Markos could have his licit kisses - two a summer - with his fee, and Mr N, who used to get them with his Senior Service and his whisky, could do without.

Now, inadvertently, half-way into the village, Markos staged a confrontation which was as well to have behind us right away. At the turning to Mr N's shop, a few paces down, he had a sudden errand which left me holding the donkey while Julian dashed off to look for Anna, and at that moment Mr N walked out. If he'd had a telepathic message he would have stayed inside - it couldn't have been that.

We looked at each other. I considered saying good afternoon. According to etiquette it's the one who passes who should make the greeting, but since he had refused a handshake and a *bon voyage* when the etiquette of a farewell demanded them, I was hanged if I was going to say good afternoon on the return. I hoped he would. He might even say, 'Welcome.' He did not. We stood looking at each other for what seemed far longer than a few unnerving seconds, then I pulled the donkey on up to the *platia* where everyone in sight waved and welcomed with great vigour and no stickling for the proprieties of who was where. The rule collapses if you've been away for half a year.

Mr N's wife gave me a hug and the keys to Henry's house, and thereafter we exchanged the smiles of restrained saints as if we thought the situation inexpressibly sad. It was. And yet it was impossible not to feel a happiness at being back again, whole-minded, with a nephew, which everyone thought as proper as could be.

Julian came back from his first run hand in hand with Anna, who was discovered in a state of radiant elegance, thinking that we ought to see a halo round her head. That morning she had been baptised into the Greek Orthodox Church. Our new priest, just ordained, a zealous young man who would do no good in the World Council of Churches, had insisted that baptism was a technical necessity. The British Chaplain in Athens denied that, the Bishop of Santorini recommended it, Anna and Michalis made the decision on the side of thoroughness. It was the right choice for Langatha. 'We love you all the more,

Anna,' declared Mr N's wife with an embrace. `You're a real Christian now.'

There was as much doubt as to how as to whether she should be baptised, and finally the priest, who had never been through the performance with a baby - let alone a foreign female adult - gave her the works. He had her arrayed in a white holey robe - meaning holey with holes in, though I suppose the homonym would do as well - which got soaked, but in his agitation he forgot to bless her clothes until she had put them on again, so she had several changes in a corner of the church. She got back in the wet garment while he blessed her pink skirt and other items, and those were to be worn regardless of activity and hot weather for three days. She was not allowed to wash for nine. It was her external elegance that radiated, pink and white, while the inner self was being valiant. Following donkeys up and down the mule track, or charging up the mountain after goats, she only had some little conflicts about whether or not God would really frown on a dab in the armpits.

It was good to have a friend with donkeys, especially one with constant business at the harbour. Being a student muleteer at her side made the uphill mule track as easy as the down to Julian. He was vigorous all day, an independent beach-boy, befriender of foreigners and locals, Anna's helpmate, and in the evenings he flopped. At the time when Mr N and I had regularly broken bread together not even a coca cola would have lured the boy another step. Then I was tied, and I was glad of that. Having a nephew had become the reason why I did not break bread with anyone outside the house.

But I was not in need of fortifying motives. I liked Julian and having Julian in any case.

Living on Henry's side of the path did not seem unnatural with the son of the family in the house. Mine was alien ground, with Kostas the policeman upstairs and everything that had been in those two rooms heaped or strewn below - even the bed, which is not strictly speaking portable. The boards can be lifted off, but it had been a structural job to gouge the beams out of the walls, and it would be another to put them back. I did not mind my chest-of-drawers and a wall-length bench, made to measure by Michalis, being lent to Henry's house - they became indispensable to us at once. But I was irked by the treatment of the bed beams and the way the books had obviously been hurtled downstairs, and most of all when I discovered two island maps tightly folded beneath the heaviest. Those had a rarity value. They had been presents from two thoughtful friends.

Kostas, in a splendour of plastic flowers, was being a grass widower while his wife was having a baby in Athens. There was whisky in the cupboard now, and I was politely asked in for a glass, not feeling like a guest in my own house because that was unrecognisable. I was impressed by how total anyone can make a transformation, but did not tell him that his city sofa was more comfortable than my island bench. It amused me to drink whisky sitting on it, being congratulatory about the birth of his first son and discussing all the problems that his wife would find when she came back, but there was not one object that I coveted and not much else to say. Clearly I was regarded as a neighbour rather than a landlady.

I was interested in rent. I was relying on it, three or four thousand right away. He was paying either eight hundred or a thousand a month, on the first day or on the last, both of which details I spent some time trying to resolve, but could only say for certain that reasonable terms for a long rental meant winter terms all year round. From him I got the information that it was all in order and I should apply to Mr N. I applied to Mr N's wife, who delivered one thousand for a sop, and whom I sent back with a demand for clarification, or for more. Poor woman, she could never have illumination on what had happened. We could both have done with illumination on what was happening now.

I reckoned that the rent was a thousand, of which Mr N - who would never take one drachma - got two hundred for his cut. But as he had it all in any case, what turned out to be the summer's question was whether I would get my cut of eight.

A little immediate cash came from a German Walter and his girl-friend who rented Henry's lower room. I was living from hand to mouth, but when nothing more - neither money nor clarification - was sent from Mr N, I still played a quiet game. It would have been so easy to go berserk, and Mr N so probably expected me to go berserk, that I decided to defy us both and concentrate on being an aunt.

Making the decision was simple. But I had to keep remembering it, every moment of the day.

During our first week tall Phanis happened to tell me that he and his mate were coming the next morning to whitewash the two houses, an annual job which means upheaval for two days. Kostas refused the turmoil inside, but I had no more say in that matter than in the matter of the date. The commander-in-chief had spoken, and it was fortunate that I found out beforehand, because Phanis with his long nose and his cheeriness and his cries for coffee, beer and ouzo and sweeping out of cobwebs always arrives as soon as it is light. We carried everything outside - furniture, bedding, crockery, the lot - making a street market of the courtyard, and were chatting among the jumble when Mr N threw open the gate.

He stood in front of us. Perhaps he had been goaded by my silence and non-appearance, but while the three of us above were being dumbfounded, he did nothing - just by appearing - to put the silence right. He nosed about. I decided to speak. Rejecting the other things I might have said, I offered him a cup of coffee. He walked across the terrace straight towards me, looking down - he must have got past us, up the steps and round to give himself the height - `I don't want coffee and I don't want ouzo, and I'll take you to court for renting a room.'

I was glad that the whitewashers were with me. They were immediate cheer, they were witnesses, they were a piece of village sympathy, and in the absence of real weapons that was something we would need. Whatever a whitewasher heard the village would hear, and whatever he heard in Mr N's shop I would hear too. Right now Phanis was being a first-hand reporter, and confirmer of my most serious suspicions. Mr N had openly announced that in the autumn he was going to sell my house.

Or was it both our houses? He'd miss Henry's. If he sold mine he could afford not to give the other up. I only half-believed the boast, it would be too audacious in Langatha to put into effect, nevertheless it was one to snatch my breath. I gasped and got it back. Julian was soused in whitewash. I mopped him up. I poured out workmen's ouzo, we nattered and went back to work. I am always impressed by how much Phanis achieves in spite of his consumption, and how fast. He did a good job on my side, where Kostas would allow him, and when that was finished I rented out my lower room as well.

The week's tenants were an elderly, rather frail couple, friends of my one surviving uncle, whom I wanted to treat well. They had plenty of books down there, and spotless walls. Comforts were more dubious. I had just explained that they would be sharing their well and bathroom with a policeman when Kostas called me inside to say that they would not. The water level was low that summer, his wife would soon be coming with the baby, babies use nappies, nappies have to be washed. I said that I was under the impression that he had rented the top part of the house, and that top and bottom share the well and *cabiné*. He informed me that he had rented the whole house, and it was only by courtesy that he allowed me the use of the downstairs rooms.

Courtesy - at eight hundred or a thousand a month?

Carolina, do not lose your temper. The month's decision is for dignity. Don't you forget.

I would never be able to quarrel with my tenant because he always referred me back to Mr N. And you cannot threaten half the police force, 'I'll go to the police.' My elderly couple joined the run on Henry's doorless, roofless, unplastered *cabiné*, and made a delicate request for a chamber-pot.

I am sure that Mr N intended to complete the *cabiné* at the time he took the money for it, and he might yet concoct some reason for not giving it a roof, but a reason for not replacing Michalis' bricks that had built the walls would have to be ingenious. Michalis was in no hurry for them, but he did observe that two caique loads had come in without provoking one movement or one statement from the man whom we had left responsible. About the only sentence that Michalis had had addressed to him by Mr N in the last few months was, 'When is that mad-house coming?' in the middle of a shave.

Up and down the mule track behind donkeys, which means at conversational pace, Anna and I tried to work out Mr N's psychology and purposes. He was either extremely cunning or extremely confused, and we voted for confusion but others disagreed. The Laki family, having a grand time with 'I told you so,' believed that he had reached the hatching of a long-laid plot to do us out of the whole property. Father was being self-reproachful for not speaking to me forcefully in the beginning - he had five daughters for practice, after all - or not offering himself for the paper ownership. 'Never mind, I wouldn't have listened,' was my standard answer, for this kind of conversation became one of life's common features as Aiyiali's interest grew. But I did not believe his theory because five-year plots are too carefully thought out to be confused with twelve hundred bricks or the pocketing of a little meagre rent. If that family were correct, Mr N had turned from a first-class confidence trickster into a bungling one.

Anna thought it was the winter tenants who had been provocation, just by being there. Mr N had realised that he would not have a free estate for his own use unless he did his best to turn them out and make it clear that he wanted no other occupants. I could more easily agree with that. Revenge for wounded manhood? That was being carried rather far if it was the sole motive for iniquities on two sides of the path, but it would be encouragement. Throw in pride. Throw in debts. Throw in everything that goes with twistedness. I don't know why I had stumbled on the only villager who needed a psychiatrist.

He might demean himself to get his stubbly chin shaved by Michalis, but what in this world was going to make him sign over his property to the barber's wife, a woman who had once committed my own unforgivable offence? The crucial wedding was to take place on the first Sunday after the Panayia, the twentieth of August. And should Henry go to Mr N on the twenty-first, `Our dear friend is married, she's a Greek, give us your signature'?

What convenient timing, Anna! Somehow on the mule track, with Julian diverting us with donkey-talk, we were always less worried than intrigued, and laughing too. We were not one-track-minded. There were the wedding plans for us as well. Would half a dozen people be invited or five hundred? There's no compromise. And do you remember, do you remember...? How much better this month feels, whatever catastrophe we may be facing, than January's Force-Nine gale.

Let the Beaufort Scale do what it liked, I was not rising above Force Four. That's a promise - Nanny! But I did mean to lay my hands on more of Kostas' rent at the beginning of July, and that might be a testing moment.

Kostas was playing a careful game of mollifying me by calling Mr N either villainous or crazy, while remaining pals with him. It did not suit him to take my side in more than private speeches, and when I persuaded him to take a message he looked smug at the answer he brought back. Mr N was offended by my use of a third party. If I wanted rent, I must go and ask for it.

I? Go to his shop? Walk into that place with all the used-to of old years about it, and all the hostility of Christmas winds? I would. I was not evading Mr N, I was only avoiding chasing him. I even wanted to know how it would feel, but Julian would have to go with me.

Julian had almost outgrown the childish appeal that he had once made him one of Mr N's biggest weaknesses, but there had always been a liking, which should be a pacifying influence, and I was not lying when I told him that he would help to make me brave. What was I afraid of? Mr N might knife me in the night on our home path, but he could hardly knife me publicly in his shop. So we walked in boldly, striking silence round the walls. Mr N looked up.

I said, `Kostas told me I should come to you about the rent.'

`Yes of course, and you've done right.'

`Then what about it?'

`There've been expenses.'

`What expenses? Nothing equal to the rent.'

`Carolina, this needs pen and paper.'

`Then get them out.'

`Not just like that. I'll prepare an account and send it round.'

`Be quick about it. I need cash.'

`Go home, don't agitate. It will come.'

Ten minutes later Demosthenes was at our door. Mr N had got his pen and paper the moment that I left the shop. `It' turned out to be a bill.

Debit

Whitewashing	2,100
Manure for the flowers	80
Watering of flowers	300
Digging round trees	150
Carriage of things	200
Meal for the workmen	200
25/6/77 (sent with his wife)	1,000
Total	4,030

Credit

Four months rent	3,200

So I owed him money? I owed Mr N seven hundred and seventy drachmas? Calm there, Carolina. Tell him to go to the police.

The expenses for the whitewashing were detailed and in order, except that Michalis thought one item stiff. I allowed the manure, though two sackfuls could hardly have been unloaded onto eight carnations, this year's total sum of flowers. Trees? What trees? Some had been planted and they had all dried up. And as Mr N had freely used Henry's property for his umpteen purposes and mine as a lodging house for his relations, he might freely in return have watered eight carnations.

Carriage of things? What things? This item turned out to be the removal of my own furniture and other possessions from my own upper rooms, to the injury of some of them - never mind my feelings - which Kostas had done by himself. I got another whisky in my ideal-home upstairs with that piece of information, and Kostas wrote in red ink in the bill, 'Get that from me.' As Mr N had it already, this could be called a Kosta-style flourish.

These small items did not add up to financial ruination - I was having that without them - but they were enough to make me mutter about it being the principle that matters, and I found it diverting to work out what they all meant. Meal for the workmen? I asked Phanis about that. Mr N, he said, had waylaid the two of them on their way home for the meal that their wives had been preparing, and insisted on giving them a plate each of what was in the pot. That was bean soup - good stuff. They also shared half a kilo of retsina and a few dried sardines. This was a masterly piece of bungling on Mr N's part, if his ultimate aim was to rob us of two houses. Phanis was stunned. The villagers loved it. A hundred drachmas for a plate of bean soup and minimal etceteras? I got the money's worth. Mr N paid for it.

I had agreed on leaving action to Henry, but I could not accept this account without retaliation. On the one which I drew up and sent back, Mr N owed me over three thousand drachmas. Kostas had told me that he paid the rent - one thousand - on the first day of the month, so I put down five months at eight hundred. Let the commander have his twenty percent, but let me have my eighty. I also included a refund for the concreting of the path that had not been concreted, as I had contributed to that, but left Henry's *cabiné* to Henry.

Mr N's response to this account was that the whole matter had to be discussed. See how well my policy had worked - we were arriving at the obvious. He would not have agreed to a discussion if I had suggested it ten days before, and here he was, not running when I yowled behind, but asking for an invitation. I have a flash picture of him telling me by word of mouth that he would come to Henry's house if he was bidden there in writing.

So I wrote the bidding, and went to the beach with Julian. We had my little room in Laki until the middle of the month - it went on being mine except in season when all the rooms were let - and in a haphazard way we continued the midday and afternoon that I had been leading for ten years. When the fifth daughter was free and in the mood we had an English lesson, and sometimes Julian attended, co-ordinating rather well, if briefly, with a Greek ten-year-old. Sometimes I paid for what we ate and sometimes I did not, there was no discussion about what was on the bill and what was on the house. Julian became siesta-trained, and when July's demand for beds reduced our two to one, we stretched out sardinewise with his reading books and the incentive of finishing them before we went to Athens for Catherine and the boys. It was a narrow bed, and the Aiyiali beach is long. We had a fine time shooting apart and together again.

`Has Efdokia had her lesson yet?' - `When will it be lunchtime?' - `Can I go out with the fishermen tonight?' Julian was always good about asking for permission. His behaviour was, in fact, an all-round credit - except when Mr N came to our house. Throughout that hour he bounced on the platform beds and yelled, in a good exhibition of bad boy's wilfulness.

`Stop that, Julian!' But if this was a bad moment for abnormal disobedience, it was the moment itself that was responsible. Poor boy, the whole performance was a laudable reaction against grown-ups being horrible.

Mr N had been his hero. He had been My Friend, holding him on his knee, giving him donkey rides. And here was the friend and hero with his aunt, talking interminably, talking and talking, and it did not need more than eight years, or a knowledge of the language, to understand the nature of that talk. Julian could not have said that this was an ironic laugh or that a rueful one, but of the three of us he was being true. He knew.

The subject was our grievances. I thought that mine beat Mr N's, but we were having to compete for whose were worse, with particular zest for minor ones. My arrival the first day was very bad. There I had stood with Markos' donkey, I was the one who was passing and I didn't even say good afternoon. An attack of flu was a perfectly good reason for his ignoring every communication through the winter, but - whether or not he had refused to say goodbye to me - there was no pardonable reason for my refusing to say good afternoon.

'You were the one who passed.' At least that was a fact. The next complaint, that I had been discouraging foreigners from coming to his shop, was not. There were few foreigners in Aiyiali to discourage, I hadn't mentioned his shop to anyone. It's not one of Langatha's attractions, though it might be if he welcomed foreign customers, and he does not. I'd go myself, I said, if I was sure I wouldn't be insulted or turned out.

'Who'd insult you?' he demands. 'Come.'

'All right, I will.' Let Henry find a non-aggressive front. Let my loyal and carnivorous nephew have his Sunday feast of goat. It only seemed to me that we were moving from the trivial to the fictitious to the irrelevant. Let's try bean soup. Julian yelled and bounced. Our workmen - 'Quiet, Julian!' - got ouzo, they got coffee, they were always satisfied. There was no reason for bean soup. And at that price!

'What price?' Mr N, tossing away half my argument, had to leap to his feet, so as to lean on the table with more force, and bang it, while haranguing me about the rising cost of living. I thought he had come to talk about the concept of commandership and here we were quarrelling about the price of beans. Don't forget the oil. Calculate how much a liberal-handed islander allows per bowl. 'And you, Carolina, go round the village talking about it.

You talk at Mouska's.' Now that was more like the heart of the matter at last. `Stop that, Julian!'

Phanis had done as much of the talking as I had, and it seemed to me that if Mr N was so touchy about the subject, he must be ashamed of it, and also that either of us talking publicly about bean soup was not half so offensive as Mr N talking publicly about selling my house.

Now I was hearing it, what I'd been waiting for. `I'm going to sell your house on the first of September. And I'll give you back every drachma you've spent on it, from the first day. It's all written down, to the last cup of coffee. You'll have it all.'

Why does the statement you have heard indirectly jab so much deeper when you hear it straight? I wondered what was so special about the first of September. It was probably just a circumstantial detail, but I didn't like the sound of it. I wanted my house. I couldn't live on the money as a tourist for a year. The value of the property was ten times what I had spent. Shouldn't Mr N's notebook take that into account? And anyway - hell, damn and blast - what I wanted was my house.

That was not his business. `Things,' he said, eying the ceiling, `are not as they should be.'

`I'll say they're not.'

`For one thing, there's the matter of tenants.'

`There is.' I said a great long say about the matter of tenants. He had his say about caretakers being paid for their services. Services? What services? We might instead talk about property owners being paid for the use of their indoor and outdoor premises.

Mr N lent across the table. 'See here, I'm responsible.'

'So you are, and that's the point. You agreed to co-operate with Anna about bringing in some rent.'

'But there are limits, Carolina. I have a teenage daughter to protect. Now these Norwegians, they were sun-bathing in the nude.'

'In February?' There might, of course, be interesting glimpses to be caught if the daughter had to do the washing on the doorstep, but brief ones in that temperature, and certainly indoors. So, having got back to the well, I had my second say about the laundry.

'When are you two going to stop talking?'

How right you are, Julian, how right. All this was a small part of what we had been saying, and there had been no real communication except about Sunday-evening goat. But suddenly, as if to produce an active example of non-sequitur, Mr N pulled out a loaded handkerchief, extracted from it two one-thousand-drachma notes, unfolded them and laid them neatly out. It was not all that I was out for, but I was taken by surprise. Then we got back to the bean soup and another hundred followed, that one with a thumb. We wasted a little time shoving it to and fro before we finished. Whichever of us kept it had to be the less injured, and as he left it there he won.

How was it that the whole palaver had been like old times in his shop? From beginning to end it had been an hour of talking with Mr N, an hour when the strangeness of my being on the village scene, while not a part of his, had been exchanged for a sort of companionability. In some perverse way we had dug our satisfaction out of this new interchange.

`How can you laugh?' demanded Julian.

I laugh because otherwise I would cry. If I could not laugh I would not be able to call this fight a game and look at my opponent across the board. Or if I could not laugh I would not be able to call the man a villain, kidding myself that there is enjoyment in the war. If I could not laugh... I would not be here if I could not laugh. I would have expired when I left my job in Athens, or long before.

While I was feeling this necessity for laughter, Henry wrote to me that Catherine had been very low and would need all the support that I could give, and Catherine added an apologetic note to say the same. The doctor would only allow her to make this journey with the boys if I met them at the airport, which we had agreed on anyway, but the addition of doctor's orders to my mission gave it a bonus of solemnity needing a big joke to go with it. And here was one with no concoction - this was the doctor who, in the immediate past, had certified me as suffering from debility, unfit for work.

How can this brother of mine, who saw all my weeks of goopiness, elect me as the column for his entire family - so much precious life? I did cry out, but not in protest, just a cry, with a large element of thanks. If Henry and the doctor had such confidence in me, I would have to have confidence in myself, and I still looked forward, with love, to meeting Catherine and the boys, but I looked further forward, with need, to the father of the family arriving too.

And what are we to do now? Carry on as usual. We join a family of Julian's beach friends for Sunday supper in Langatha, and that means roast goat at Mr N's. Being a customer there turns the little creaky shop into another place, while what it used to be is locked away into the past. On other evenings, despite all my worries, I have an obdurate feeling of content at being with the boy at home.

I doubt if any meal in the village was ever more politely ordered or more politely served. Everyone enjoyed it, the goat was succulent and the bill astonishing. It was so low that I dutifully reported that at Mouska's, which was doubtless Mr N's intention, and my disappointment if I wanted injuries. At that moment I did not, but more were coming. He may have got me there one Sunday for the pleasure of falling in and falling out again. I know that I gave up aiming for the non-aggressive front and went back to the non-appearance and the silence, while Mr N's last words to me in this phase were, 'Neither to you nor to your brother do I have a word to say.'

Michalis, my shadow commander, saw humour in each development reported across the counter, and passed it back for a smile. 'Big problem.' It always makes the problem sound more supportable when he says that in his way, and Michalis' way is one of the reasons why he did not settle down with an Aiyiali girl. He has a private flair for mimicry, convulsing Anna and me but never quivering himself, and his judgement, which is part of the same quality, is more pointed and less sweeping than in most islanders.

Mimics, like cartoonists, may be among the world's natural judges, but Michalis could not tell me whether or not Mr N would sell my house.

Sudden whim would be enough for that. Selling a house depends on a good offer, it does not need a five-year plot.

If I could not laugh...

Julian and I had three weeks from our arrival to get ready for our next journey, leaving the house welcoming for Catherine and the boys, and what should have taken a couple of days on the domestic front took me all that time. It was fortunate that Henry, who once said that his only complaint about me is the fuss I make over where to put one tomato, could not see me getting the scene organised. I was also so much aware of natural hazards threatening our boats, counting engine trouble and collisions as being as natural as the weather, that I took Julian off with me on our expedition allowing for a hurricane.

Being on the mainland was still no certain safety. We had three days to preserve ourselves from greater or smaller Acts of God. Acts of taxi drivers in Athens turned even Julian into a back-seat passenger on the first afternoon. An insect bite on my neck blew up so fast that I stopped caring about looking like a football and wondered whether it was possible for pressure on the throat to cause asphyxiation, leaving one eight-year-old forlorn in the city streets. The Mouska bag became as important to us as on Crete. And Julian, who was growing daily more conscious that the first aim of this trip was not to spend all our time and money on bumper cars, ice cream and hamburgers, began looking on the morrow with unprecedented awe.

`Are you going to sleep outside?' he asked suspiciously, when I had brought us to the safe distance of Chalkis to spend two nights in a cottage belonging to an old friend, in a lonely olive grove.

I was only going to stretch across the doorstep. It was too hot for me inside. Julian likes to be tucked up even on nights when the heat is a whole eiderdown.

`What about the snakes?'

`There aren't any snakes. Anyway, I'm on the doorstep. I'll be protecting you.'

`But what if you're bitten by a snake? What would I do? Catherine and the boys are coming, and I don't know how to get at the airport.'

Thinking this point of view extremely practical, I wrote a note to whom it might concern giving the essential details of their arrival, flight number and all. It ended, to Julian's dictation, `And Carolina says that if she dies in the night it's not my fault.' After that we both slept well.

Chapter Fourteen

'Go back!' I brought my brother's family to Aiyiali in an island-hopping way, and it was on the beginning of the last lap, from Katapola to Ormos, that I let out my shameful yell. 'Go back' is the most idiotic plea when a caique is heading into the first wave. There is no way but onwards once you have left the harbour, so do not beg the captain - who knows what he is doing - to capsize his boat. Squeezed with the boys among a cargo of beer and lemonade crates, which weighed us almost down to water-level, Catherine and I stared at each other, 'There's three of them and only two of us.' That too was silly. There could have been no life-saving with any number of adults in that sea.

One occupation was trying to decide on the winner for worst moments, careering up a wave towards the sky, or trembling across the crest looking down into the narrow chasm before the next, or the slam of landing at the bottom, walled in on both sides. I disliked being in the stern watching what the boys were doing. I composed a telepathic cable of apology to Henry for leading his entire family to death by drowning, and dismissed the temptation of promising St Nicholas a new church, though he did get candles afterwards. As there was an afterwards, there was nothing to be regretted, except - possibly - the discovery that nerves do not toughen as they age.

Nobody was sick. It was not that sort of roughness. The boys, with their average age of eight, were grinning when we disembarked. Catherine, who had successfully made an effort to seem better than I had expected, thought that if she did have nightmares they would not be a high price for the reunion and return. We rollicked up to Langatha where my first discovery was that Mr N had been using our calor gas drum in his shop.

I had left the kitchen open for our tenants, Walter and his girl-friend, who were cooking in the lower room on camping gas, but had asked them to be extremely economical about their use of ours. 'When the gas comes' is a mini-version of conjecture on the construction of the road, and none had come this year. It's illegal to bring your own drum on a passenger boat, and I was one of the few who was not cooking entirely on wood. Walter promised that they would stick to one dinner party's worth of gas. On that evening they prepared the ingredients, brought them up and found an empty space beside the stove.

This was not conclusive evidence against the obvious suspect, but Walter was an efficient spy. He spent an evening at Mr N's shop, noticed the number on the drum in use there, and that was the number which reappeared in our kitchen just before we all came back.

Not one insult, not one threat had roused me to plain livid fury such as this. That drum had not been bought in any old Langatha shop, I had had it brought from Katapola at great expense, and the next thing would be the supply at Katapola running out. Fuck you, Mr N. You may be the owner of the house that the gas drum is standing in, but the drum and the gas that comes out of it are bloody well mine.

What do you do then? Go to the police? Kostas' chortling on the side when he saw where Walter's eyes were moving had only been a piece of corroborative evidence. Fuck you too, Mr Policeman, who sits by and thinks it funny. I'll - no, I won't do anything. Chalk it up and wait until Henry comes. At least it makes me feel better about making a villain of an old friend.

When Henry comes... Whatever he might do about the warfare, I would not be the stoutest column anymore. Then I would relax, though while I said that I was whole-hearted about everything I did. We were a happy family of five of our varying stages of childhood and lack of confidence. This was Catherine's last sick season. After that the misbalanced hormones were diagnosed and put in place. Coming to Langatha, anyway, was always good for them. I felt that she only needed a hand put out to her, to pull her back into the world. I put out a hand and she became daily less withdrawn. She had been the right person for me in Essex, and I was not the wrong person for her in Langatha. I would not ask her - as she had not asked me - to buy a kilo of potatoes without understanding what a tough achievement that might be.

During those two or three weeks we all slept in the main room. Catherine and I had three over-excited boys to settle down, with Julian in a turbulence of mixed feelings of being one of three again and hardly knowing who his mother was, but when the swimming and the mule track had knocked out two of them the third would go off fast. I slept on the outside edge of Henry and Catherine's wide platform bed, to give Catherine a wall to turn to in the morning and to cope with night-duty myself. That was not being sacrificial, but rather claiming rights, for I was used to a cry, `Carolina!' in the night, and there would be an end of that when Henry came and I moved across the path. I daresay that was a soppy way of thinking, but I was about as confused as Julian after two and a half months.

When Henry did come, the column crumbled. I had to take a stroll behind a real one to let the tired professor have a family reunion which was bumptious but not emotional.

Henry was with us, I moved into my lower room where now the cries came from a month-old baby, not my business at all. Kostas' wife had come back to a load of problems, there were nappies hanging on my terrace - spectacular in the north wind - and I had no personal resentment towards her for needing all the water in the well. I lay in bed and listened to the baby crying overhead, to the policeman's footsteps, his choice of bedtime music, and lullabies from her native Epirus.

Eight thousand would not have been an unrealistic rent in August. It seemed hard to have given up the main part of my house for eight hundred, which I might not get. Kostas had promised, after the beginning of July, that from then on he would pay me direct, but when he produced nothing on the first of August he looked surprised when I came reminding him. Oh sorry, he had been mistaken, he had not been quite clear before that he had rented the house not from me, but from Mr N. Plain, vivid fury again. After that Mr N's wife did bring me the eight hundred, which disappointed Henry who thought that every injury would be strengthening to our case. However, it was a summer for every little helping, and in this case I preferred the notes. The dubious point about them was whether they belonged to August or July.

`When Henry comes...' We had often said that in reference to the warfare, but what was the missing half of the sentence now that he was here? He needed and deserved a few days' holiday, but our problems pressed about us, they could not be forgotten longer than each visit to the loo. `When are you going to finish it?' the neighbours called. How should we finish it? If Henry felt disposed to fork out the cash a second time, the completed *cabiné* might end up as another present for Mr N. Besides, it would take a daring builder to come and work for us. Mr N had threatened Dimitris that if we called him in to do the work, he would send the police to throw him out.

Henry's imperturbable answer was still, `When Anna owns the house...' which made me self-conscious about choosing between `when' and `if'. Determined to begin with a man-to-man encounter, he covered pages with relevant vocabulary, conciliatory phrases and - far more difficult - some possible responses to whatever Mr N might say, in Mr N's own style. He had picked up a good deal of builder's Greek apart from every-day politeness, but the problem was to find the opportunity of using it.

Catherine had exchanged one goodday with Mr N, the boys had been too nervous of his aura to do more, Henry found an expansion hardly possible. The first time that they met, on a narrow stretch of the mule track where there's no turning aside or crossing paths without one word, Mr N jumped off his mule, shook hands, jumped back, and whacked the beast on in the nearest he could get to mule-track gallop. After that he spent some days of masterly evasion.

You might ambush a man in his own house if you are fluent in the language, but not with a few studied phrases and doubt about replies. It ought not to be necessary in a small village, when his shop and house are at two ends of one path and you live half-way along. But that week Mr N was having back-street exercise, and Henry sacrificed sunsets on the terrace to hours of coffee-drinking in the shop, served by his wife. When once Mr N did make a date, and kept it, he admitted that he owed some money but was in a hurry now, he would go through the details the next day. The next day he joined a policeman's outing to Tholaria. Or perhaps that was when our friend Adonis, then ex-president of the Aiyiali Society in Athens, was waiting in the shop to have it out with him on our behalf. In any case, Henry never got a chance to use his man-to-man vocabulary, and Adonis ended that evening of his holiday as a solitary customer for fish and chips.

He did not complain. And rather than boggle at appearing as our open champion he killed some time making speeches at whomever he found in the *platia*, hammering on a table and proclaiming that it was outrageous for a foreign family to be so served. It was a blotch on the name of Langatha, the priest should call the populace together and tell them so in church. Hot stuff, I thought. No doubt everyone enthusiastically agreed. Everyone was with us, we were even doing a favour by producing such a gossip subject, down to the details of bean soup. But they did not actually rise up and tear the villain's eyes out as one Ormos widow thought they should. And it would have been tough on the Phanises to have to boycott their familiar shop.

Where clannish spirit is a virtue, and public spirit given little thought or commendation, how could we, who had no blood relations in the village, expect more support than back-slapping and smiles? This is a place where a man who wants to watch his television does not care two hoots for his suffering neighbours when he turns his generator on. If the sailor above us lived here regularly, I would be insane, and I hear a mere humming compared to what is inflicted on the old couple right next-door to him. They might as well be trying to sleep in a hammock hung from a ship's engine as in their own bed when he decides to entertain himself. Don't think that worries him. He's so little worried by such considerations that once, when the machine was running at five-past-two siesta time, and I charged up to yell about the laws of peace and quiet, he angrily retorted, 'Half-past-two is the official time. Go to Athens for your peace and quiet.' He's worse than anyone, but he's not exceptional. All these charming people are concerned with their own four walls and fields. If there was public spirit someone would repair the patch of mule track that's cracked up. Every able-bodied man has to put in two days' work a year for public causes, and no one makes for that one, they all manage to find a public cause at their front door.

But Adonis, who saw further than the local people, and who was made irate by them, persisted in his mission until he caught Mr N alone. Afterwards he came back laughing at the load of baloney he had heard. Henry, who had just managed, in his own one-minute encounter, to get in a word about Michalis' bricks, and had been answered, 'My wife was sick in the winter,' could easily imagine that 'baloney' was the term for it. Grievance, again, had been the retort for grievance. Why did we have to send an emissary instead of talking to him ourselves? Why? - Poor Henry, who had be missing sunsets! - And the rest was as laughable as that.

Mr N had denied saying that he was going to sell either of our houses, but he refused to part with them. We decided that it was time to put some heat into this war. What about Christos the scribe? Was he a boggling type? Or might we receive more from him than the smiles that he awarded far more sparingly than other villagers? Adonis agreed that we should try him for our resident champion.

Christos, the one dapper figure of the village, if dapper figures can go through life without a tie, was not a customer of Mr N's and I had long been disillusioned about my first impression of xenophobia. Apartness is what I had mistaken for aloofness - how could one immediately know? Even on Panayia night he is inclined to sit alone, sometimes on his little balcony outside his office overlooking the *platia*, less Christ than God. At family parties he often ends up by himself. But each time that I came back to Langatha he would rise to make a formal greeting, stand the first drink from his distance with little more to say, yet not intimidating after all.

Henry and I went up to his office, which is small and dusty, Langatha's deposit of reference books and files of documents. Christos did not look surprised. His look said, `I was wondering when you would come.' There was nothing that he did not know about our woes. He had been blaming himself for not preventing them. And what were we to do now? 'You'll have to go to Syros, find a good lawyer and take Mr N to court.'

'But we're foreigners, we have nothing on paper, it will cost a fortune, we don't have a chance.' A court case on Syros? That's a horrendous thought.

'It's the only thing to do,' Christos insisted. 'There are no promises on paper, but how many thousand of drachmas have you sent through the post office into his hands?' The post office was Christos' house. He knew. 'That's all recorded, and I'm your witness. You go to Syros - quick.'

We had found the villager who would do more than pat our backs.

Panayia week was approaching, the middle of August. Henry and family were leaving in the first days of September, which allowed absurdly little time for conducting an assault through an island eleven hours away on the next boat schedule and meaning an absence of five days. The last chance of a reprieve was for Christos to make his own attempt to terrorise or soften Mr N. Did he mind being publicly of our faction? His answer was a gleeful laugh.

When he came back, his face looked very like Adonis' after the same interview. He had asked one direct question, 'Will you sign over the property to Anna?' with a threatening 'or else', and got an equally direct reply. 'I'm not buying and I'm not selling,' snapped Mr N. 'Let these people get out of my way.'

'When Henry comes...' After all, the ending of the sentence was, 'I'll be lieutenant in an open war.' Most sympathetically he and Catherine wished that there was a choice about which of us should go off on this campaign in peak season and peak heat, but there was not. I pulled out a small suitcase and told myself that I was leaving on a jaunt.

Even now Henry was adamant that we should first, by some means, have one personal talk with Mr N, whose behaviour seemed more sick than truly villainous. It was as if he had found himself cast for the villain's part and was doing his best with the performance, but making an awful hash of it. I remembered that he had once come to the house by written invitation, so we tried that again. After all his evasive tactics, it was as easy as could be. One of the boys was persuaded or bribed into delivering the note, and within a few minutes Mr N came hurrying through the gate.

Catherine and Henry, who could only catch at phrases, at first wanted every line translated, but gradually I gave up and they did not badger me for more. It was obvious that he was talking - in Greek idiom - Chinese. `Why this change of heart?' said Henry. `Ask him that.' The answer was all about the night I broke my rib. Finally, when we tried to push him into a corner, he flashed back, `But what do you expect? I'm mad.'

Then I would go to Syros. We had nothing else to say, but having once got hold of him it was difficult to silence his Chinese monologue. The boys did not yell or bounce, but there was unhappy fidgeting. At last, `Take me to court, then,' and he was stamping out. Henry, who had been against him, or never in favour of him, through his five years of commandership, now took to saying sadly, `I think I'm rather sorry for Mr N.'

`Leaving for the Panayia, Carolina?' I was asked ten times down the mule track and at the harbour. `I'm going hunting,' I said.

Chapter Fifteen

S yros is a ridiculous place on August the fifteenth. Rooms are full, so are the scraggy beaches, public offices are closed. I spent far too much time sitting about at tavernas and cafés, not lamenting Langatha's Panayia, for Anna's wedding the next Sunday would be our festival, but - because of that - feeling frustrated by ineffectuality on the Syros waterfront. It was suddenly so imminent - only five days ahead. For the first and only time Anna was showing signs of feeling remote and severed from her Northumberland family. We had to do our best to be that family for her, my business was to be a sister or an aunt, and now I had abandoned her. At the least I ought to have been helping with this week's chore of painting one new house throughout - not just doors and windows, but right down to the floor. She would be a blue-fingered bride if she wasn't careful, or unless she left both coats of white ceiling to the end, but that is lonely work for the eve of wondering, if you haven't been or seen one, what Greek brides do in church.

However, here I was on Syros being a lieutenant on a public holiday. I moved through the cafés down the waterfront and drank Campari at the bar of the hotel where eventually I found a room for most nights, with more comfort than I might have chosen if there had been a choice. Henry had decided, or discovered, that from now on we were sharing in a commonwealth. I liked this, there was no thine or mine about our resources any more than there was about beach towels or boys. Both houses spent what they had on what was needed. None of us could be finickety, and one necessary item - so he insisted - was a style on Syros that would be good for the morale. My hotel was good B-Class value, especially as the barman accidentally charged me twenty five for a sixty-drachma glass of Campari, as he found out one day when I came back. Fortunately I drank a good many glasses, and those were valid expenses, for the barman was opinionated about lawyers.

Suing one's neighbour may be backgammon to the Syriots. Every other door is a lawyer's office, and every man who hears the subject mentioned can support his own ideas with first-hand experience. This island is the capital of the Cyclades, and Grand Central Station for Aegean boats, but its waterfront is just a blown-up version of other waterfronts, you run into an old acquaintance, you drink an ouzo, enquire for a room, and everybody knows your business. In the present situation this was what I wanted. It was all very well saying, `Go to Syros and find a good laywer.' I could find fifty lawyers without looking, but how should I know which one was good?

The trouble was that since Opinion A was as emphatic as Opinion B, and each damning to the other, I was not having much illumination, nor from the differing views of C and D. However, I was influenced enough to decide against what I had heard on Amorgos. Our native lawyer, after all, was just the man not to employ. Probably his nephew's mother-in-law was Mr N's wife's second cousin, and he was labelled as non-energetic anyway. Energy as the first essential was all that was agreed about.

There are bright young lawyers who are interested in fees and innovations, without experience. There are sleepy old lawyers who nod wisely and put their cases on the shelf. I heard of every kind of strength and weakness, and opted for the barman's choice, which meant that my hotel gave me not only comfort but support. The next morning I was knocking on the door of a middle-aged lawyer whom I was promised to find serious, solid and experienced, with energy and determination still pumping hard.

I was received by his clerk, a cheerful young man properly surrounded by more books than space. He listened to my outline of my story and made an appointment for me to meet the big man in the evening at nine o'clock. So much for the morning's work.

How is one to kill twelve hours of this windless swelter, feeling as dotty as I feel and bewildered by despair? I cannot think of any consolation except that Catherine and Henry are the people that they are. They will not say or think unkindness when I have lost them their Greek property. That's just thousands of pounds and a piece of satisfaction tossed away by poor Carolina's misplaced confidence - something like that is all that they will say. And I shall be a teacher looking at holiday brochures, for nine months of every year making little economies for the sake of something I don't really want to do for three. I shall be speaking to myself for twelve months about Mr N and my misjudgment, if I must live to eighty I shall be saddled with that village butcher for all my years again.

If I could not laugh...

The trouble is that there, on Syros, I hardly can. My sense of humour is being a deserter. If I don't grip onto that, then all is lost.

In the evening I put on my best dress and went back to meet the lawyer. Solidarity of figure he did have, with a round, bland face which I felt misleading in some way. I had an inkling that we would get somewhere more purposeful than the first pat on the head.

His own office had more space than books, he liked to stride about. He did not find it difficult to believe Mr N's part in the story, but he found it extremely difficult to believe mine.

`And you never made an agreement of any kind on paper?'

`Not the smallest.'

`Nor wrote any receipts?'

`Not one. I sent part of the money through the post office, that's all.'

When he had gulped that down we had to go once through the sort of speech that one expects on such occasions, that is to say, he was extremely busy and usually dealt with nothing but the big stuff, but he would take on this case because I was a misused foreigner, and he would take it on to win. But having said that, he had said it. More often it's a speech that circles round.

He kept talking about finding proof of whose money had been spent, but the best record of expenses was in Mr N's own notebook, with no denial from him about the source of funds. If that was the issue, what did winning mean? A court order for the refund of the sum that we had spent, which might just buy a stable in 1977, would be our disaster, and a triumph for Mr N. We had to have both houses transferred to Anna's name.

`They will be,' the lawyer promised, `and by Christmas. Now I need copies of the contracts. Where are they?'

`I have no idea.' Hope for massive achievement on this mission was about to disappear.

They must exist, probably at Katapola. I would have to go and get them, then we could begin. Go and get them? That's not running upstairs. That means -. Yes, I would have to go back to Amorgos and bring them to him, copies of the copies, however that was organised. Without them he could do nothing, not even enlighten me on one detail of how we were going to win this case that we were going to win, at what sort of court, or what the costs would be.

`Bring me some receipts, too,' he added as I rose.

`I told you, there are none.'

`Well, dig up something. Come with whatever you can find.'

So much for my five-day outing. I got onto the next boat with nothing much more to take back to my family but green peppers and courgettes.

Christos thought differently. He knew the lawyer by name as `a good man', I had put wheels into motion - what more could I have done? The copies of the contracts would be on Naxos. Yes, Naxos, not Katapola, he knew where. And we could get all the main recipients of our money to sign affidavits declaring that they had known that it was ours. He'd write his own as well.

Something on paper, something to please the lawyer, that was all that this would be. Well, Greeks love paperwork. Anna's name by Christmas? That's the lawyer's promise, let it be believed. Now this business was being extended into the next era when I would be - would I really? - a teacher in an Athens institute. I was feeling far less certain about that engagement than I had been in March, and it did not seem a promising beginning to be asking leave to attend a Syros court. 'You have no choice,' repeated Christos, which made us feel better - a dire situation does not seem quite so dire when there is no alternative. And right now we had a consolation, a wedding, vital to our campaign with joy for six Matthewses thrown in. On the eve of that day the subject of Mr N and lawyers was suppressed.

The eve is the beginning of a wedding, with ritual such as goes with every possible occasion, at this point concentrating on the bridal bed. Under the guidance of her new relations, Anna was spreading hers in proper white and lacy splendor with a borrowed baby lying on it, where gifts of money would be scattered round. She and Michalis were both exhausted with major works by the time they came to deal with frills, but frills were necessary, for it was in this new house that the wedding guests would be received. He had done the plastering himself, and installed the lavatory seat that morning, as well as being their own carpenter. She had been painting, hanging curtains, beautifying fundamentally and through to flowers until, in the middle of the afternoon, the dressmaker arrived. A proper island wedding requires three wedding outfits for the bride. When those had been delivered, our Cubby became concerned with rites that were mysterious to us.

Michalis had lost his voice. He had sung through four nights in succession, not as a bachelor making the most of Panayia week for a final fling, but as a lute-player earning sugared almonds - he was spending sixteen thousand drachmas only on liqueurs and sweets. Throwing his own wedding was unprecedented behaviour on the island, and I reckon it would be almost true to say in Greece, but after seeing Anna for two years, no one queried it. And there was to be no stinting from Michalis. He would not take her off to Naxos to economise on treating wedding guests. 'After all, you only marry once.' He's an Amorgot.

Only the sugared almonds caused eleventh-hour panic. Five hundred little white muslin bags of them were ordered from a Naxos shop which failed to put them on the first boat, and the second was held up in a storm. 'You can't have a wedding without sugared almonds,' Michalis was agonising Anna. They came on the eve.

On the morning of the same day Stephanakis' boy was sent round Aiyiali inviting almost every inhabitant to the ceremony and the evening feast. The idea of having only the attendants and family, with us representing Anna's, was also flawed by Michalis' saying, 'But I must ask So-and-So.' As soon as one extraneous So-and-So was included, the five hundred were, and the bridegroom only had to give the word for the people to come, his goats to be slaughtered and tall Phanis the whitewasher to turn into a chef. I was tremendously impressed by the calm way in which he was able to provide a feast for the masses at one day's notice.

After the bed-decking ceremony, Anna was sent to spend the night with us. She slept on a camp-bed in my room, and I thought it greatly to her credit that when we found ourselves whispering like schoolgirls after lights-out, she said, 'We'd better go to sleep,' and promptly did just that. She was prepared a special breakfast on Henry's terrace in the morning, and it was also to her credit that she ate a boiled egg. But despite her calm appearance she had a panicky idea that she would faint in church. Her normal position in a service is beside the door.

It did not help her that the wedding day was the hottest of the summer, with not an attempt of a breeze to fan those who were coming from the other villages in their best clothes. The ceremony was to be at three, but no one could get married at such an hour on a day like that. Langatha is not Athens where on Sunday afternoons taxis in swift succession carry up their brides, and off again, while the priests - like dentists - work through their appointments, and in a surge of two-way traffic the church steps are the waiting room. Our priests would not go away. There is hardly a village wedding in two years.

At three o'clock the first of the advance guests were arriving at Anna and Michalis' house, where the bride in her jean skirt was handing round liqueurs, and goodies wrapped in silver paper to be consumed or pocketed. When the interior was crammed the courtyard took the overflow, and then the street. Somewhere in the midst Stephanakis and the day's lute-player found elbow room to strike up a merry tune. Finally Anna and I retreated to the bathroom with her wedding dress and several other females who were having a competition with me to get her into it. The bathroom window outside was half-way up a flight of steps leading to the roof, so those immediately became a desired position for little boys, our own displaying their devotion at the front, and thus the bride - swiftly - was arrayed. Michalis, still husky, wandered into the main room from his mother's house, tie in hand, wearing his only suit, which was a heavy winter one. He had his tie put on and was ready for the bride to be put into his hand. By whom? A cry went up - `Enriko!' - and Henry, who was being the day's photographer on the roof, was hauled down, pushed through into the bathroom to be the father and lead her to the groom. He looked paternal, he felt paternal, he was touched.

This was what we had done in Langatha, we had brought it Anna. And we had planted for ourselves an ambassadress, not just a nanny and an agent, our one enduring attachment. Goodness knows, our comings and goings would always be peripheral activities, but Anna, having plunged into the centre, was there, Langatha's and ours. Henry, whom I had baptised Enrikos, was having his village confirmation, and Catherine - Katerini - was relieved of going through the Greek part of her life as `Carolina's sister-in-law'. They were liked, they were real people, and the boys - who spent the day proclaiming, `It's all our fault,' - were having fewer mistakes to complain of as to which was which.

Everything that seemed haphazard about this day was the island's sensible way of dealing with circumstances as they arise. When the musicians led the gay procession churchwards it was five o'clock, but no one had complained or gone away. And there Anna became a woman of Langatha, and the priests did not - like priests in Athens - attempt to forbid the flinging of rice as the couple were led dancing round. Mr N was one of the few villagers not present, or we might have shouted out, 'Now will you sign on the dotted line?'

After the ceremony is sugar-almond time. Immediately the bridal house received all who had come before and all who had not, with more cakes and more liqueurs, and the newly-painted floor was now so trodden that Anna had stopped worrying about its stickiness. Afterwards came a little time to gasp.

In the *platia* tall Phanis, the annual master-in-command of the Panayia feast, was being master-in-command again at Nikolakis', which must have involved a great scrounging of plates and chairs. The high tables were set inside, but the outside temperature was kinder, so the fringe guests had no complaint. As feasting turned to dancing, more and more moved out, and we saw a rare sight, Michalis the musician in the dance. Being the tosser of bank-notes was an unusual role for him. With gusto, in spite of blistered feet, he tossed away a generous amount of what he had lost his voice for at the receiving end. Anna, in elegant grey-blue, was dancing in the authentic island style with which she loads donkeys and milks goats. She only wilted when the musicians had led her and Michalis home, where they had to have a blessing from the priest. After a dizzy day that seemed like one item in excess.

The rest were left to dance into the small hours, but that was not the end of it. On the third day of the wedding we were to reassemble at Nikolakis' before noon to eat gut soup. There was a sluggish air around the *platia* in the morning while Phanis was rounding up hands to chop the bits, and Evangelia opposite - whose shop had shared the evening's work - was wandering round muttering, 'Who's going to do the washing up?'

Who would? It was just a matter of two or three hundred plates congealed in heavy grease. I put away my knife, went home for Enrikos, and for the next hour or so Michalis' mother and the two of us bathed our hands in water which turned to gruel and then to porridge before we got through to the final rinse.

Business-like in aprons, we carried plates through the *platia*, while Christos, who had given his own daughter this same thoroughness of a wedding, drank coffee and looked on. And that is how he is, one of life's onlookers. But he is also an absorber, and I could not help feeling pleased that he was there.

Henry and I felt deserving of the light, tangy soup that a smaller gathering sat down to. Anna took one spoonful. It's almost the only island taste she has not acquired. But she led a children's dance, which was far more important, looking more like Anna in simple red-and-white check, and danced the *bállo*, which is a twosome with Michalis, the dance we had been waiting for. He tossed notes until the early evening, when Langatha - having had its wedding - crumpled, and the lights of the *platia* were out by nine o'clock. Anna and Michalis took one day off, and I conferred with Christos about affidavits.

We were lucky. The two former owners of our houses, instead of having gone off to Salonika or Australia, were both in the village at this moment, Katina visiting and the other resident. They and Dimitris, Michalis and Nikolaras, still President of Aiyiali and our first supplier from his shop in Ormos, would all - if they could be persuaded - state that they had received such and such a sum from Mr N, knowing that the money came from Enrikos or Carolina. Michalis signed his form with enthusiasm and no questions. The others, sympathetic though they were, showed natural wariness about committing themselves to forms.

The least literate were just plain wary, the others scented the danger of being summonsed to a Syros court. I could not see why they should be, if it was only to repeat one officially stamped statement, especially when each was so repetitive and the penalty for untruth was two years' imprisonment. We wanted Christos there. We needed him and could be sure of him, he received our offer of first-class boat tickets and the best hotel accomodation with impatient scorn. That was no issue, he was going and that was that, though he was the one who had had no dealings with either house. Michalis and Anna would have no reluctance. Michalis could always find other business to throw into the expedition, and all being well they could rush Mr N to a notary as soon as they came out of court. We wondered whether Christos and Michalis would have to drag Mr N onto the caique, and who would be keeping company with whom. Every time our imaginations started working the result was increasingly bizarre - quite bizarre enough without more characters.

Yes, I was dramatising the scene on Syros, but unless I tried to see it as hilarious I could see it only as a heap of bills and anguish, physical and mental wear and tear. So, Julian, we laugh. We do our best.

Christos appointed nine o'clock in the evening as the hour for Dimitris and the two whom we had bought our houses from to do their stuff. We began at his office where he, Dimitris and I converged by separate routes, and if secrecy was the object, the fact that his office was dimly lit at such an hour and that the three of us were lurking on unaccustomed paths raised doubts about the scribe's stage-management. Dimitris put on glasses and looked worried. I had never seen him in glasses in five years. `Ah, Carolina!' was his rueful refrain that summer. He likes us in his way and would not - aloud at Mouska's - have lamented the moment when I came into his life if he had felt real regret. He was loyal and he signed obediently, but not with zest.

Christos and I now padded down the moonless street, taking separate ways where it divided, and meeting at the bottom of the village where in a surprising style of an ideal-home kitchen, waiting with points and plugs for electricity, an illiterate Kaliope - the former owner of my house - lived with her daughter's family. Illiteracy involved a great many explanations and much encouragement from the younger generation, whisky for us and conspiratorial handshaking. Christos, whom I had never seen so lively, was obviously enjoying himself. 'My only complaint,' Kaliope said, 'is that Mr N did me out of two thousand drachmas. We settled for twenty and he only gave me eighteen. Well, it's too late now.'

Eighteen? But he told me nineteen. I sent him nineteen.

Christos gave me a knowing look. There you are, Carolina. Everyone told you Mr N was eating your money. Here's proof that he swallowed one good note at the first course.

Old Kaliope was having a small grumble. Her two thousand would make little difference to the splendour of her kitchen tiles. But I, with my loss of one, was having a revelation.

Kaliope's daughter signed for her, and there was no talk here of Syros. But Katina, the final object of our back-street business, was already brooding over that. Yes, of course she would like to help us, she was outraged by Mr N's behaviour, she would be only too glad to sign if she were not afraid of a summons to Syros in the autumn. So, regretfully, she was deciding to refuse.

'You won't have to go,' I promised wildly. 'Christos will be coming, Michalis and Anna will be coming, we don't need everyone. And if the lawyer says you must, I'll tear up this form in front of him.'

`It's the children, Carolina. I don't care about the expense. I'd gladly go to Syros to help you and Enrikos, but what am I to do with the children? Really, I cannot.'

`Shut up, Katina, and put your name down, there.' Christos jumped up, and that meant speech-making. `I'm going to Syros, and I've neither sold a house nor bought one nor built one - not one of these. But I know what this woman has been through, I know how she's worked and how she's been wronged, and you're going to help, as the others are, to save her. It's a disgrace to us all. One evening I saw her crying, and my heart bled, I swore that when I was needed I would do what I could. Now sign your name.'

This was hot stuff from our scribe, and took me by surprise. My hysterical behaviour one year before, when my moral system had begun to crack, was not only shaming to me but irrelevant. Never mind, we got our signature.

We left, as we had done everything that evening, stealthily. But all that appeared wrong about so much stealth was calculated to be right. Christos, twinkling smugly, told me later that he had made quite sure that our mysterious progress was observed by at least one policeman, and anyone else happening to be around. Two and two plus stealth makes a far more interesting number than the two and two of any daylight stunt, and anything known to a policeman would quickly be known to Mr N.

This was also our policy about my journeys. There was nothing to hide from anybody when I appeared with a suitcase on the mule track, but we allowed only a sufficient leakage of information to encourage conjecture in the right quarters, of a rattling kind.

I do not want to go to Syros, I do not want a day on Naxos breaking the journey on the way. I feel like a commuter. I'm not a tourist, hustling with crowds on rubbish-bin boat decks for the sake of viewing the beautiful Aegean. Family time is precious, journeys drain the Commonwealth. Please, I don't want to -. I don't feel well.

The Commonwealth was scraping the bottom of its purse. I had had my splurge with Julian on Crete. Henry had come provided for a family holiday. However, he put in an order with Nikolaras for twelve hundred bricks to replace Michalis' hoping that Mr N would not suddenly produce them or the cash himself. He also encouraged me to keep on with the Campari treatment and eat well. As we all said, it was far more cheerful for me this second time when I knew what lawyer I was going to, with documents, and what good hotel. Once again we would be leaving Amorgos with debts behind us, but neither he nor Catherine would ever murmur that while the funds were the Commonwealth's the fault was mine.

'Dig up something,' the lawyer had told me. I dug and found one letter from Mr N, the one reprieved from the rubbish tip when in a regrettable act of tidiness I had thrown away the rest. Here in one long sentence Mr N had received some thousands of drachmas from me, paid for gravel, was making building progress, wondered how I was, and was sending me some eggs and hard-baked bread. Christos was delighted with this when I went up for my last instructions. He gave that letter the same glint of satisfaction as he gave the ending of his own affidavit, a description of his interview with Mr N, quoting with a final flourish, `Let these people get out of my way.' He stamped it purposefully, and I apologised for burdening him with all this work. As a civil servant he could not charge a fee.

That brought him to his feet again. He had to shut the balcony door to give himself scope for what was coming next. `See here, Carolina, you've been coming to the village for years, and I've seen you for years. You have written a book about us, taught our children, brought a good family and good people. You are -' translation breaks down here, but I was overwhelmed at what I was. `I don't talk, you know that, but I watch and I see and I know. And right now we're having warfare. I don't want your thanks, I want to win. And don't you go putting spokes in the wheels by letting these people out of going to Syros. Did you tell Katina she wouldn't have to go? Let her go, and let them all go, Dimitris, Nikolaras, the lot. Don't pity any of them. Who has shown pity for you? I'm going, and at my own expense, - don't talk to me about tickets and hotels - and it will be as much of a nuisance for me as it'll be for them. They'll all come, and you will win, and I shall be your first witness, I, Christos the scribe.'

Chapter Sixteen

'T he ship no leave the port...' Captain's English revives an itch for my red pen. 'The ship no leave the port until better the weather.' My second journey coincided with the season's gale.

When a boat is stuck in port, the passengers are stuck close to. There is no statement making it safe to take an hour's walk. The announcement either means 'until better the weather' as it says, or 'until we persuade the port authorities to give us sailing permission, as we think fit.' The company loses substantially on each delay, and I suspect that the green light depends partly on money passed under the table. Finally the boat hoots - it may be after an hour or two days - and fifteen minutes later leaves. Sometimes the wind seems as high as before, sometimes even higher. But after so much sitting one does not care how rough it is, one only wants that boat to move.

'The ship no leave the port until better the weather.' My first boat had arrived I cannot remember how many hours late at Amorgos, a night on Naxos felt like a night in a ship's cabin, the second boat managed to put in at mid-morning, and in the early hours of the next reached Syros, three hours along the line. I felt as if I had travelled from Piraeus to Rhodes.

If anyone had told me that the keeper of the Naxos archives was away on holiday and that the photo-copier was out of order, I would not have been one bit surprised. That the man was immediately to be found, that our contracts existed in the shelves behind him, and that the machine had just been cured of whatever ailment it had

had, took me aback. The swift efficiency of the whole business left me with a tourist's day on Naxos, an island which develops a familiar face for anyone who lives on Amorgos. At a lotus-eaters' beach taverna I composed a list of Mr N's iniquities and peccadillos for our lawyer, and in the town I took a broken sandal to a chatty cobbler, which turned out to be detective work.

So I came from Amorgos? Aiyiali or Katapola? And which village in Aiyiali? Langatha? Very nice. Then he got to `which part of Langatha?' - here was more than usual topographical familiarity - and finally `which house?' Once more, very nice. He had stayed in it. He bought goat skins from Mr N, and when he came on business my house was his free hotel.

I had always encouraged Mr N to make use of my house when it was empty. He did so much for us, such as watering eight carnations.

Our lawyer on Syros was pleased with the affidavits, more so with Mr N's letter, and brushed off my attempts to add to them or go through Henry's list of questions, informing me that all the details would be clarified in due time. But even when he was didactic and refused to listen to me, I still had the feeling that he knew his business and wanted to get on with it. That meant being ready to take me to the courthouse the next morning to smash the champagne bottle or whatever one does on launching a case in a Greek court. And he knew better than I did what was relevant.

`Now, when this Mr N took matters into his hands, he said that he would make a contract in your name?'

`No, he couldn't, foreigners aren't allowed -'

`But that's what he said?'

`No, I've told you -'

`But you believed it, didn't you?'

`No.'

`But as a foreigner -?'

`I didn't.'

`Come now, you believed it.'

`Yes.'

`That is what you will say in court.'

He was standing in front of me snapping his fingers like the conductor of a truculent orchestra. I felt bewildered. I thoroughly disapproved. And now his ferocity turned into a beaming promise of a good-conduct prize. This particular line, he instructed me, was the only one to ensure that our property would be transferred to Anna's name - speedily and with low costs. But I would have to be obedient.

And what about those costs? I craved a statement.

He refused to make one. Perhaps he didn't want to shake me. Anyway, Mr N would pay.

But Mr N didn't have money. Ah, didn't he? The lawyer grinned. Now he was in a hurry, and there was work to do. He called in his clerk and with much striding declaimed a statement in the sort of Greek that's classical to me, pages of dictation to be typed out by the evening, with my signature at seven-thirty, please. In the morning we would take it to the courthouse, then I could catch the midday boat. The hearing would take place some time in the autumn, and now did I have two thousand drachmas for stamp duty? That, apparently, was the bottle of champagne.

The tone of the question assumed that I would not have it. I cheered myself by calling that astute. He was unperturbed by my being impecunious, he would put down the sum now, and in the end - as he had said - it would be for Mr N to pay.

One of my Syros occupations was phoning Henry, which was possible by the system that sends notice in advance, having him sitting by at eight in the morning when calls go through comparatively fast. I decided to disrupt the next day's breakfast and had the notice sent, but only in case I should regret not having done so otherwise. The safety of our houses and our gambling funds depended on this day's decision, and I was sagging, I had such need to talk to Henry that I made the telephone appointment for the morrow, even though it would be too late. What gambling funds? We hadn't raised them yet.

What do I do if I break down again?

You're not breaking down again. That's out of the question today. You're just growing soggy with all this sitting round at cafés. Nevertheless, sit down again and think this business out.

If I sign to a plain lie, we are no longer the injured innocents, and surely that's all the claim we have to the protection of the law. On the other hand, if I refuse to sign we will not - except by a longer and more expensive process - be given the protection of the law. That sounds dotty - can it be correct? So the lawyer says. I am weary and sometimes doubtful of my senses, and this evening I have to go to the dominating man and sign or not sign his document. I think he gives me confidence. I can't decide, I can only wonder what - by eight o'clock - I shall have done.

To hell with etiquette, I'll get a second opinion before signing anything.

'What's new?' The waterfront was not quite the waterfront of Mykonos in the days when I was to be seen following police summonses up and down, and yet there was something evocative about it, with the growing number of greetings and demand for bulletins. And again I did not mind my problems being other people's pastime. Opinions were what I wanted, motives were immaterial.

All lawyers use twisty methods, there was no disagreement about that. My latest drinking companion added, on the point which everyone did disagree about, that there was one who stood apart from all the others, whom I must, if I was in my right senses - (but was I?) - go to consult at once. He was homosexual. That piece of information was handed out as if of great significance, and since the whole speech was in his favour, that must have been as well. I could not say it was against him, I had resolved on one more consultation, so I went.

He was forty, which put him between the fuddy duddies and the flashy new boys, he seemed efficient, and he was immediately going off on holiday. But he listened to my story, he took the time to tell me that all lawyers use twisty methods, and exclaimed, 'Oh, that man!' when

I mentioned Mr N. 'Go the way you're going,' he advised me, meaning 'sign'.

My way was dithering, but since not signing put us nowhere minus all the money I had spent, I went back to my lawyer supposing that I would sign his document. He himself was engaged with other clients at seven-thirty, so I was looked after by the clerk, whose business was to read me three pages of the sort of Greek I could not understand and turn it into the sort of Greek I did. I did not think that I had come to listen to a story, but this was narrative and fictional. I heard how when I came to Amorgos this summer I took it into my head to sell my house. Firmly believing that my name was somehow written into the contract, I went to Mr N to ask him to make the negotiations, and to my horror and astonishment he answered that it belonged to him.

Horror and astonishment? There was plenty of that - right now. So I was to put my name to being so much more of a bloody fool than the bloody fool I was? That irked me as much as the question of perjury upsetting the case of the injured innocents, or perjury itself. And now the clerk was handing me a pen, 'Sign here.'

I insisted on seeing the lawyer first. The clerk was alarmed. His master was busy and did not want to be disturbed. His master would have to be disturbed. He was. And he was displeased. It cannot be an offence to be in need of time, but when I made my plea for time he was displeased. I told him that my brother had phoned forbidding me to sign anything he had not seen. I would have to take the document to Amorgos and come back the following week. I did not believe that, but it might be

true. Everything I was saying was so nearly true that I had
no reason to feel guilty, unless I was under attack from
schoolday ghosts. I was handed the document reluctantly,
told not to be tardy, and escaped. When I phoned Henry
the next morning I had nothing to report except that I
was eating Commonwealth funds for the preparation of a
paper which I had refused to sign. Not even he could be
expected to be encouraging about that.

The rest of the morning was a void before the
midday boat. My whole inclination was to retreat into its
emptiness. I wanted to curl up as I had curled up on an
Essex sofa, but the time did not belong to me, it was the
Commonwealth's. I asked myself why I had only made
use of the barman on this classy premises. He had not yet
discovered the correct price of Campari, so there had been
more glasses with more of his advice, but now I went to
the manager. In his office I was back with the opinion
that the young lawyers are best because they are more go-
ahead and with-it than the older men. All right, I'll hang
etiquette again and try a younger one. Second opinions,
apparently, are free.

At noon, with two hours of Syros time to go, another
lawyer's clerk came to the hotel door. It was Saturday, a
court day, it had taken a great many phone calls from the
manager to get hold of him, and having him was clearly
hazardous. Escorting me to his master meant escorting
me to the courthouse, where I knew my own lawyer and
his clerk would be. But I was not going to leave the island
without having this document read by someone else.

The courthouse of Syros is what one calls an imposing
building. You are as exposed as a ginger cat on an iceberg

going up its marble steps. I had reached the top, and there were columns to hide behind while I waited for Clerk B to bring the new, young lawyer out, but at the moment when he appeared, walking purposefully towards me, Clerk A came trotting up the steps. The lawyer swerved behind a column. Clerk A made straight for me.

What was I doing here? Just passing the time of day, taking a look at the scene of impending battle, waiting for the boat. An imposing building, this courthouse... 'Tourism,' I grinned.

'But you'll be back soon?'

'In ten days.'

I would have felt better if I had not been clutching a certain scroll from his own office, but we smiled our way out of the situation and I put it - situation and scroll together - into the young lawyer's hands.

'That is the only course.' It took five minutes for him to read that version and hear mine.

'Is there no other way out?'

'None. None at all.'

I did not care about the proportion of expediency in his statement. I had filled the morning with Commonwealth business and had a boat to catch.

Walking along our home path in Langatha, I found myself caught by the summer's local hazard - walking straight towards Mr N. There are certain patches where nothing in the way of evasion can be done, narrow enough that you must brush shoulders or bend aside. `*Yiasou,*' he flung at me, a provocative `hi there'.

`*Yiasou.*' Yes, Mr N, that's called careless defiance. Are you wondering just how defiant you need to be? You'll have your information soon, direct from Syros. In not so long you'll be travelling there yourself.

Henry and Catherine reassured me that I could not have done more or differently. Consultation with three lawyers, and no bill yet from any, seemed more of an achievement now that I had them to tell me so. As to this document, it was not a question of ethics but of whether it would work. If ignorance of the law could be used as an extenuating circumstance, then let us use it. However much we might dislike playing fooled and foolish, we had been fooled and foolish - at least I had. The wording did not make much difference.

I could picture Mr N's outraged interruption at the hearing. `I never told her that - she didn't say that.' No, I didn't, it's all fabrication. Bang bang bang. Silence in court. And I should not be able to look at him. Then don't. Look at Christos instead.

We decided that since we had put ourselves into the scribe's hands, we would stay there, doing what he said. He read the document and asked, `What's wrong with that?'

So there we were, there was nothing wrong with it. My horror and astonishment had only had some shifting, and what had been inserted was mild stuff to what had been left out. So after all I had told the lawyer truly that I was going back to Amorgos to consult my brother before returning to sign the document. It would cost two thousand drachmas, borrowed from Michalis, only for the stamp duty. Heaven knows what else - not only in money - it would eventually cost, but we were back to seeing it as the one and only way to go, a way very like our own home path.

Now in these last days I wanted nothing but to sit in the sun talking with Catherine, or as an alternative to talk with Catherine in the shade. It was September, my family was leaving in a few days, and we decided that the best thing would be for me to go with them, turning my next trip to Syros into an extended holiday. Let us have a two-day change of air together before the wrench when they got onto their plane. We could find excuses of chores for me to do in Athens, away from Mr N.

I could make a prospective hunt for my new lodging, to move into in October, I could borrow money from my school director - a characteristic beginning, that would be. I might see ex-President Adonis and ask for what Henry called the ascetic affidavit, since he approved of our way of renovating island houses, with stable-style doors. And so back to Syros to make my signature, and back to Amorgos for the remnants of September before the next sortie into working life. Now that we began to picture it, it seemed essential that I would travel with Henry, Catherine and the boys. We could go to Aegina and sit in the sun together, or sit in the shade. Now while they packed and cleaned their house I had nothing to do on my side but not to put away my suitcase, and my aversion to that case was leaving me, for it seemed that this was life's occupation, carrying it down the mule track and bringing it up again.

We ordered Markos for the noon of our departure, to give ourselves a last fish lunch at Ormos and a last swim before the boat, which was due at about three o'clock. At eleven-thirty I took a detour into Evangelia's for one quick ouzo, where vice - if outcome has anything to do with it - was rewarded. That was all part of the plot.

Evangelia, whom I may chat with half a dozen times a season, was alone, and sat down for a gossip that had an air of something more than idleness. `I have heard,' she said, `that it's Anna herself that Mr N objects to. You never know, he might sign some other sort of paper, a long lease if that can be, or for another name. Why don't you ask him - now, before you go?'

`It's useless.' What could I say? The wheels were turning, our papers were prepared, Markos was due in half an hour, we were weary of Mr N's jabbering, our plans were set. It's too late, Evangelia, too late.

`Come on, Carolina, call him round again. Do you know what you're in for if you go to Syros? Trouble, worries, expense, and you may lose your houses in the end. Try him just once more. You never know.'

`Well, I'll tell Enrikos what you say.'

The house was in a state to be expected twenty minutes before the arrival of a muleteer at the end of a summer holiday with three small boys helping to pack up. They were interested in preserving objects such as stones and plastic men from crisp packets, Catherine was interested in not preserving them, and Henry - a great man for last-moment activity - was putting up new kitchen shelves. The idea of getting the Chinese jabberer into the middle of this scene did not appeal. And yet? Oh well, why not? I got out pen and paper while Zachary was cajoled into being the deliverer of the final note. After an extremely short interval, he and Mr N came running - this time really running - through the gate.

For five minutes we heard such a garbling of his own language that we nearly said, `Get out of this house.' Suddenly he switched to a clear channel and at this moment Markos came. Catherine had to go out and officiate over the demanding business of loading boys and luggage just as we reached the climatic statement, `I don't care who the houses go to, Anna or anyone. I'll sell them to Anna tomorrow for fifteen thousand each. I only want to see thirty thousand on the table. Tomorrow. All of it.'

That was clear enough for Henry, he only wanted to verify that he had got it right. Thirty thousand, tomorrow, Anna's name, say four hundred pounds. Catherine! Thirty thousand for Anna's name tomorrow? Catherine among the animals and luggage called back, `Yes.'

I remember our reaction coming in one big shrug. Somehow or other I thought of saying that my own suitcase should not be loaded with the rest.

`Come on,' said Mr N to me, `we'll go and talk to Yorgos.' We left the others, charged up to the *platia*, marched straight through, and on to the police station.

Everything was happening so fast, I hadn't even brought my cigarettes.

Yorgos was busy. 'Come back in fifteen minutes.' Mr N and I looked at each other with only the most fleeting awkwardness. 'Let's go and drink an ouzo.' What else was there to do?

We might have looked for Christos, but I preferred to do that by myself. 'All your friend cares about,' said Mr N, 'is worming out a couple of drachmas here and there.'

Evangelia's was fairly crowded now. Our entry was as silencing as any two exhibitionists could wish. We pushed our way through to the back. Evangelia! Ouzo! We clinked glasses. 'Good work!' was his toast.

'Good winter! Give me a cigarette.'

'What! I'm treating the drinks and you want a cigarette as well?' He gave me one.

I ordered a refill, with a wink for Evangelia who was grinning on the side. Later Christos told me that Mr N had put her up to the job, relying on my dropping in some time. He must have been desperate, for Mouska's is my shop. It was a last chance very nearly lost.

Mr N put all his attention on a card game while conversation started up again, quietly enough for anything of interest to be overheard. But there was nothing offered, unless from my clattering mind, until Mr N looked up, 'Shall we go?' - 'Let's go.'

Yorgos was ready to be helpful, but pointed out that all he could do in his official capacity was to act as witness to an agreement, he could not draw one up. Mr N, therefore, had to concede to my bringing in Christos, who was leading a mule up the street that very moment, coming back from Ormos after a perfectly timed trip. I ran

to him. He gave a quick reaction of triumphant surprise.
`He's got the wind up,' we told each other. We - not Mr
N - had won.

What had been the mutterings and confabulations and
the ponderings in the little shop, that had made him sneak
off to Evangelia? We were told that someone's lawyer
relation on a visit had added prison to his other prospects,
while all Christos' back-street business and my journeys
to Syros had done effective work. When we had time
to pause and ask ourselves why we had not offered, at
the beginning, to buy his signature, we also saw that the
answer would either have been no, or yes for a hundred
thousand.

Christos joined us at the police station where he and
Yorgos entered into deep discussion about whether or
not Anna was yet Greek enough for the transaction to
be made. Identity cards are not handed out at a wedding
ceremony, and hers was having all due hold-up with red
tape. Each consulted his own tomes and leaflets, and
finally decided that she should sign an interim contract
the next day at noon. Later on she and Mr N could go to
Naxos to a notary.

In my hurry on my way home I did remember to tell
her that she was going to buy two houses the next day,
and that buying meant putting down a thirty-thousand-
drachma loan. There was no hope of any immediate
contribution from the Commonwealth.

Henry was waiting for me, sitting by the well in
the silence of his evacuated house and courtyard - now,
suddenly and far more truly like his own. We spent a little
while being bewildered side by side, realised that we had

lost our fish lunch, hoped that Catherine would give us up and have a good one with the boys, made ourselves a salad and wondered why we hadn't attempted bargaining with Mr N. When he said thirty thousand we might have answered twenty, and ended up with twenty five. It would not have been worth the effort, we were unburdened, and when all the other luggage was removed my suitcase had been left behind.

I was not travelling that day. I was not going to Syros, to Athens, Aegina or anywhere. Instead I was to be bereaved - immediately. I had been with all or one or some of this family, my family, except for some weeks of the spring, since January, and we were not even having one last fish lunch to say goodbye. Objectively we were triumphant, subjectively I could only think that I would be left waving at the port.

We looked around and saw two houses, four fields, a courtyard, terraces. We would never have owned this place, we would never have achieved so much if it had not been for Mr N. We would never have had one complete and one half-finished *cabiné*. Really, he deserved his thirty thousand. Call it the agent's fee. He might have asked for fifty thousand - why hadn't he? But he should have named his price six years ago on offering his services. As it was he had bungled things in every way. Once I had promised him my house for one of his own family. Now, without wronging him, I had righted my nephews.

Mr N - he himself - had saved me from the rashness of my promise. My gift of honour could be directed as I pleased.

Thirty thousand drachmas... There would also be the contract, and later on the purchase tax. I would have to write to our lawyer, whose bill would not be wasted money, but it was another bill. At least I had refused to write a two-thousand-drachma signature.

`We'll send you money for Michalis quickly,' Henry promised.

`And I'll borrow a lump sum from the school.'

`Poor Mr N, he's lost his storehouse.'

`And his laundry.'

`And his garlic-field.'

`And his hen-house.'

`And his slaughter-house.'

`And his cobbler's hotel.'

`He could pay for the bricks now.'

`He could pay for plastering the loo.'

`Call that money his ticket to Naxos.'

`He's got all the timber, too.'

`That's a tragedy,' said Henry. And now that we could feel something, we sat in dazed euphoria lamenting the loss of two old houses' worth of beams.

Chapter Seventeen

At twelve noon I knocked at the door of the police station. Christos was in his office, Mr N in his shop, Michalis and Anna were in theirs. `Bring them along,' Yorgos said. Christos came. Anna and Michalis came. Mr N, whose single occupation had been inspection of his ceiling, made sure that he kept us all waiting for ten minutes before we heard his steps.

Christos read out the terms of the receipt he had prepared. Mr N would have his thirty thousand drachmas, but he was bound, as the author put it, hand and foot. Michalis handed Anna a wad of notes. He had not boggled, so soon after his wedding, at having to produce so much. Anna counted them. Mr N counted them. Yorgos held out a pen. Was everyone content?

`There's just one thing,' said Mr N. `I don't want any monkey business after this, no more sneaking off to lawyers or -'

`Shut up, N.' Christos and Yorgos crushed him in unison.

Anna signed. Mr N signed. Christos signed. Yorgos signed. My business was to produce a few drachmas for the stamps. *Kalo riziko*! That's the proper salutation to the new owner, so it was said - to Anna - by one and all. *Kalo riziko* - good destiny! And, hey presto, my commander had turned into a Norland nanny.

`Anything else?' asked Yorgos, looking from face to face.

'There's just one thing,' I piped up, and turned to Mr N. 'What about Michalis' bricks? Are you going to get them, or would you rather give me two thousand, and I will?'

'They're on order. That's my responsibility.'

I knew perfectly well that they were not. Nikolaras had told me so when we ordered them ourselves. 'I just thought you might prefer to have that off your back.'

Mr N was doing a quick calculation, and decided that it would be as well to hand over the notes. We would never have got hold of them if we had not put them into his hands to give back.

'And you have your ticket to Naxos,' I added with as much significance as I could get across. He knew that I was referring to the money that should have built the new *cabiné* a roof. The journey to the notary public was generously financed, he'd have a first-class ticket - don't let's haggle over that.

Mr N nodded. And I thought that we had said the last thing to be said to each other about our house. I really did think so.

Later on in the day Michalis got his interest, someone else was repaid another debt, and the next morning there were new shoes on the family feet. The village was divided between calling it outrageous that Mr N should have this sum of money and thinking that, if so much had to be paid out, it was far better for it to circulate around Langatha than to disappear into a lawyer's pocket on Syros. At some point Mr N's wife and I gave each other a mute hug. 'Mute' was the word for my own feelings, which were in a state of shock.

The boat had come too early, hooting at two-thirty, when Henry's family was carried off. It's a natural law on Amorgos that boats come late, but occasionally they catch you out. I did not have the time to share with Catherine any of the day's euphoria, which was being spoilt by this sudden severance. I watched Julian as he dashed in all directions for his back-pack and the bits and pieces that had been pulled out of it since lunch. My here-and-now boy, do you realise -? No, don't say it. Keep that to yourself. But when the passengers had crowded onto the caique, and rather than standing back to be a waver I jumped on too, Julian pushed round the side towards me as we were moving out. Instead of any of the things he had not said, such as, 'I had a very nice time, thank you very much,' he muttered in a manner jellifying to any sort of aunt, 'I want to be near you.' I was glad that I was wearing my bikini. Half-way out into the harbour I dived off.

How good it is to have an Anna at such moments, to fly to in her kitchen or in her little courtyard, which is - more than any other courtyard that I know of - like an outdoor room without a roof. How good it is to have a friend of my own kind, without the need to fly. It's all been rather like looking for a bluebird, I've found the way back home.

Anna is not a good advertisement for woman's liberation, but to do the washing and the cooking for her husband does not make a chattel of her, she knows her own mind far too well for chattelhood. She's not a carpenter, a barber or a lute-player, she refuses to be a full-time shop-keeper, she does not sing in church, and since Michalis has all those occupations it would be extremely mean if she did not have a meal in the pot for him when he came home.

When he opens the door, or looks in through the gate, he is the one whose eyes are full of wonder, while each time - and most rightly - he congratulates himself. If he is sitting tired at the table, he may say, 'Get more bread,' or, 'Where's the cheese?' but that is the Greek idiom, it does not make him wonder less. If the cheese is on the top shelf, Anna will jump onto a chair and take it down. This has nothing to do with the who's who of sexes, she explains. He's forty and she's twenty-three. Respect is due to age. Besides, his tone of voice is not one bit like Mr N's, or like Maria's fisherman. Maria's was a love-match, she has a second baby on the way, everything is as it should be, and yet - somehow or other - she is a pathetic little fish-wife at the bottom of the hill. In Michalis' house respect is not one-sided, problems and plans are discussed over this table, whoever has put the cheese on it.

Sometimes a dish is placed before him such as he has never previously sniffed. Initial suspicion gives way to a gradual, cautious acquirement of new tastes, and the new about his habits is not only on his plate. His main room and kitchen do not look like any other Greek interior, and yet there is nothing about them to shock the villagers. They are a compromise between Anna and Langatha, with a sparsity of plastic ornaments. And there is no doubt whatsoever that a baby in this house will be encouraged to kick its legs and even stand on them when other island babies would suffer fearful malformation of the bones. Anna's will be carried into the outside air long before they're six months old. That might shock the neighbours, but it won't shock Michalis. What has Anna done to him? He himself says, 'We don't want a butter-child.'

Strictly speaking, my commander had turned into Anna-and-Michalis hyphenated, and we could not be better off. I went off to have a word with Kostas about that - poor Kostas, who no longer had a chum for a landlord. He could stay until next March for a thousand a month, paid on the first, but I would want the house back in the summer, and when his year was finished there might be a rise in rent. So he was informed, and could not answer back.

I felt smug about that speech, and no longer resentful of nappies on my terrace or Kostas' choice of bedtime music, for I might be living downstairs but I was not the underdog. The baby cried, the mother crooned. None of my problems had been the baby's fault, the lullabies had never been cacophonous. Now it was not by courtesy of my own tenant that I was lying under my own ceiling. I might have drawn a bucket of water from the well, but - why raise issues? - I refrained. My compensation for remaining in my downstairs exile would be having the house lived in through the winter, which is good for it, with a steady thousand drachmas accumulating into a small Easter present when I came back. Look at it like that, it's not so bad. And what is bad? We're free.

So I saw it, and almost the next day I heard through other channels that Kostas had been reposted to Santorini.

The house would be mine again a few days before I left for Athens, mine only to shut up, and Kostas' winter rent had after all been rent for spring and summer. So much for my Easter egg.

Never mind about the loss of little compensations. The great achievement is what counts.

I know, and I'm not niggling, or being particularly sorry for myself. I see no reason for self-sorry feelings, but all this is irrelevant. I have a problem that is less emotional than one big glaring fact. I'm hardly in a fit state to go out and be a teacher. I'm as numb as a frost-bitten finger - in September, with the whole working winter ahead. If I had emotions they should be triumphant. I seem to have none, except for fear.

If you have just had pneumonia, will you take a cross-Channel swim? If your broken leg is just out of plaster, will you attempt the Marathon? The doctor says that `a nervous breakdown' is only a term that people use, there's really no such thing, but recovering from the affliction - whatever you may call it - is not like recovering from chicken-pox. It was less than four months ago that I set out with Julian, and I have been having the most improbable treatment ever since. I'm a perished guitar string - I'm talking about capacity, not inclinations - and I do not know if I can play again.

Oh yes, you will. You will take yourself to Athens, walk the streets to find accomodation, go up the stairs into the school that you fell out of, teach in it for nine months, thirty hours a week, to live and pay your debts. People work for their living, don't they? There's nothing so extraordinary - why are you kicking? - about that.

Work for two years, and then you may come and live in your own house.

'You know all the answers,' said the doctor, but that had been in March. If I do still know one, I know that I am back in need of January's advice, 'You're exhausted - do not push yourself.' And what am I to do about that now, when I must push? Let me lie here, listening to the lullabies. I am frozen. Thawing hurts.

The arrival of the bricks was rousing. It was the third shipment since Henry had borrowed twelve hundred from Michalis, and it was fortunate that we had put our order in, for there was an immediate run on them. Nikolaras wanted them counted and removed at once, and now I learnt why Michalis wanted to be repaid in kind, not in cash. They were craned in heaps out of the boat, and the dozen or so purchasers were trundling wheelbarrows about and building castles along the waterfront. I appropriated Ormos' rubbish barrow, a mini-dungcart, and a piece of space. It was amusing at first, trundling and stacking in blocks of twenty one, ten bricks high with one aslant on top. I could have done with boys. This was real Commonwealth labour, and sweaty though it was, it was also good to have a Commonwealth to labour for. The day was hot, the stacks rose weightily at noon, but I would be unusually deserving of a long siesta afterwards. Demolishing and removal of the castle was Markos' business. At last I laid the final brick and reported to Nikolaras, who came along to count. 'Carolina, that's not twelve hundred. That's six.'

Nikolaras does not find much humour in life, but he found this humorous. I was supposed to be educated - so he thought. `Knowing letters' is how he put it, but letters are not figures, I gave up mathematics at fourteen. `Get on with it,' he said. The weight of bricks was making a hole in Ormos dungcart, and I did laugh for Nikolaras, but I did not find the situation so laughable through the sticky afternoon.

If I could not laugh... Do not let me now, at this last moment, lose my sense of humour. Humour walking out makes room for manic panic. I learnt on Crete what that was like.

Where is Julian to run into a lamp-post? If Julian ran bleeding to me, I would hear the auntly calm.

Julian is going off to school now with his Cretan scrapbook and his memories, which are deep and superficial and have no middle layer. His teacher is admiring, I would like to turn the pages with her, to hear the fragments of what he will divulge, about pedal boats and table football and King Minos - so much can be expressed, but there is more inside. `Next year it's my turn' were Zachary's parting words. Next year it's his turn. Keep well for Zachary.

Writing is the only way of keeping well for me. If I know any of the answers, I know that. Not writing was the only wrong thing about my house before, but in the new era I shall not be running round in quite so many circles, constantly in need of a little creaky shop, or its proprietor. Even now I might take out the typescript of the textbook I began in Dorset, and try to put my mind on that. *Talking about English* was the title - I could keep doing that, on paper, for the remainder of my life.

I could guess the publisher's verdict, which I would hear in Athens, too surely to feel much more concern than I could about the subject of prefixes and suffixes, so absorbing in the spring. They liked what I had written, but it did not fit into a scheme or syllabus, they did not know what to do with it. Attend to the market. Find your category. But whatever happens, keep on writing, if only for yourself. The people of Langatha go about their daily business, and so shall I, the typewriter is mine. *Life is a Suitcase* - why not go back to that?

But life really is a suitcase. That's too near the point.

After a great palaver with myself I did take out a sheet of paper, but only to form half a dozen sentences on a happy subject to our lawyer on Syros. He had to hear the outcome of the battle. I had to thank him for his effort, which had been of help toward that outcome, and to ask him for his bill. It was not really difficult to write a letter once I had gone through the process of getting down to it.

What would the bill be? Two thousand 'for you' was my guess, two thousand at the least, but I was wrong. I never received any answer, there was no bill at all. My barman had sent me in the right direction, to one of the Cyclades' good men. Now I know my lawyer if I fall into new trouble. 'You wait!' Michalis grins.

'You wait!' Henry and I had twice bought two houses that could not be ours, and there was a long-term joke at Mouska's and Evangelia's about 'when Anna turns us out'. Christos laughs, more than I have ever known him laugh, whenever the subject is revived. His reward is the pleasure of post mortems and a top-quality English shirt. But the Greeks are better givers than receivers, he boggled at the present and is satisfied with memories. `It's a stormy day,' says someone, and he laughs, `But not for Carolina.' If short Phanis who is wise is sitting by, I get a knowing smile.

I went out for my laughter, not being good at that at home. *Kyria* Mouska greeted me with alternate sighs and cackles at the ending of our tale, stuffing little extras into the brown velvet bag that she had been sewing for me before the outbreak of our war. She is gratified to see how it is always hanging at my side, but she does not know that it is called a Mouska-bag. This is a gladness in my life, that she did not make me a purple one with orange spots.

Kyria Mouska has turned into a travelled lady in the last two years. She has not only been twice to Tholaria, she has a pilgrimage to make there every year. In accordance with a promise to the doctor saints Anargyri, when an eye infection turned one side of her face into a red balloon, she goes riding round the mountain on the day of their summer festival to light a candle in their church. I don't think she pauses for any other purpose, she is gone before the feast, but I wonder - when she turns round - if she looks across the plain and sees the beauty of Langatha streaming down its mountainside.

As soon as Kostas left I would be able to stand on my own terrace looking out at that grand church. Now in my restricted quarters I listened to him pounding round with packing-cases for his ideal-home furniture, and wondered why he did not ask a question, or make a statement, about September's rent. It was on the fourth that the treaty was made with Mr N, and I had not received a drachma's payment since about the fourth of August, when Mr N had sent eight hundred unprovoked. Finally I had to go to Kostas and query that myself. Deciding - I hardly know why - on a piece of island courtesy, I said that five hundred would do. Call it half a month, and never mind that he was leaving at short notice on the seventeenth. He answered that he had given Mr N the whole thousand on the first.

I had thought this tale was over. I was not in the mood for the smallest aftermath, but I went to the old commander in his shop. It felt like being stuck at a railway station with last week's who-dunnit, intimate with all the dialogue. He was agitated. Verbally he was forthcoming, but I did not want a Chinese arithmetic lesson, I wanted cash. My resources were so low that five hundred had taken on the value of five hundred when I first came to Amorgos.

Mr N told me to fetch Kostas. I fetched Kostas and we sat in a triangle while they took it in turn to do their sums. Each agreed with each other through every item and each came to the same conclusion three times over, Mr N that he had received nothing for September, since he was paid on the last day of the month, Kostas that he had paid the full rent on the first. None of us lost a temper, we just made a class of dunce pupils until we could not go through it once again, and the only clarity emerging was that, whether or not Kostas had paid September's rent, I was not going to get one drachma out of either of them.

`You can't leave it like that,' Michalis said when I had walked away. Oh can't I? Shall I go to Syros? Shall I go to Yorgos and see which Chinese dialect he speaks?

I shall lie beneath my bamboo ceiling listening to the lullabies of Epirus. So far as I am concerned, the woman singing them is living as a guest in my house.

This is where I lay eight months ago, looking at this ceiling, waiting for Anna because I could not take my socks down from the washing-line.

Yes, you could. You did, she made you do it. In the afternoon you went out and took them down.

But then she came to Athens with me. Now I have to be responsible for getting there without a swerve. Can I do it? I don't know.

That was the uncanniest boat journey I have ever had. Long hours, roughness can always be expected, hazards may be elemental or mechanical, but uncanniness - really, that is going rather far. And the gale had blown out. We were on the deck in calm January sun.

Anna was being the picture of glowing health that day, while I was being grey. Her hair was thick and springy, mine was dead - enough people have commented on a change in its condition to emphasise that I was not just being lugubrious about what the mirror said. She could not sit beside me, because she had to dance. Michalis had entrusted her with an assortment of jobs to do in Athens, and over thirty thousand drachmas in a bag which never left her side. His love and confidence were adding joy to the novelty of a few city days ahead, and all this pleasure flowed into her feet so that the dance was going on from the island to Piraeus.

It happened that the captain was a native from Aiyiali, and Michalis had written a note of introduction which she sent up to him. At some moment, while I was being grey and she was dancing, one of the ship's officers, all white and ribboned, ran down from the bridge demanding, 'Where is Carolina?'

'Here,' I said.

But I was not.

He was looking for a fair-haired English girl, and it seemed that I had been travelling on these boats for long enough that a hair-faired English girl had that title, like one of a species.

I was dead and Anna was the phoenix. Here was corroborative evidence. Anna was Carolina, and I was the ghost of a former incarnation given life with that name by the Mykoniots. I liked her far too much to feel personal resentment - that was fortunate. But it was strange, and it made me feel haggard, to be watching my lost youth dancing on the deck.

Presently she came towards me with her dancing footsteps, and stood in front of me. 'Carolina,' she said, 'you can't expect me to restrain my youthful spirits,' - those exact words. I felt ashamed and crushed. I slept for a while in our cabin and woke heavy with the need to apologise for having looked the look that provoked that remark. But she never made it. She denied the words with astonishment. She pointed out that it was not the way she talked. What I heard is what she had every right to say, what I deserved, no more, and the words are as clear in my memory as the springiness of her footwork and her hair.

Well, that's all very nice, but the phoenix story doesn't work. We have to be two people. I am here. I am. I shall prepare to go to Athens and be vigorous. Tomorrow night I may be sleeping under my upstairs ceiling with its pretty beaded boards, and I think I might feel rejuvenated there - if I could only have the time.

Mr N's mule and donkey were regularly at the door, carrying Kostas' cases and packages away. I had to ask Kostas about his departure hour. I could not expect it to occur to him that his movements might be of interest to me. But when he had drunk his last cup of coffee, he made the announcement widely with the worst sin on the record - he took his two drums of gas onto the path, turned on the taps, and blew the stinking remnants into the public air. There was enough for a little localised pollution - and how many cups of coffee, how many meals' worth of cooking too? There was not one neighbour who would not gladly have carried or sent back the empty drums to wherever they belonged. Some had been cooking over wood since January. I was eating fried eggs in preference to boiled ones because they save three cooking minutes. He could have told me where to send them and left them in the house. But I had a consolation, if I wanted him to be seen as villainous. He could not have damned himself so thoroughly or so fast as by publicising wanton wastage with precious and obnoxious gusts about the neighbourhood.

Then in one swift exercise he, wife and baby were removed. I walked up onto my terrace and into my upper rooms bemused. I was free of Mr N and free of Kostas, my house was mine, as nearly as it could be, and now

- now, at this silly moment in the middle of an autumn sunset - I had a surge of feeling sorry for myself. I wanted a holiday - here - before I left. I needed one, just for a fortnight, say for the length of time that I had had Kostas as a guest, seventeen days to be precise. Not having it might be my downfall. The week I did have would be for mopping up his mess.

I looked out from my terrace, and there was the view intact. The pike-backed island, Nikouria, had not shifted its position off-centre in the bay, and out beyond - between the tail of Nikouria and the tail of Amorgos - I could see the shape of Ios twenty miles off. Tholaria was still a tadpole, with the church of Mouska's pilgrimage a little too large among the village houses, cream among their white. The artist made a slip with his proportions, and I rather think with colour, but I may be over-critical, some like it just like that. I swivelled round, as always, and up there in the mountain, almost the last building eastwards in the Cyclades, the church of the Panayia was spruce with whitewash from its August festival. But lower down, where the gorge rises, there was no whitewash on the walls of the deserted village, no spruceness there. Stroumbos had been a message to the world for over twenty years. At the moment when my view was being such a short-term dispensation, I did not like its message very much.

As to that sunset, advancing in its autumn route from Tholaria into the bay, the less said of that the better. In any case, I could not linger, there was damage to be viewed inside.

The rooms were empty but for litter, and nails in the walls. Where the nails had hit stone, Kostas had left holes. There were two burnt patches on my pinewood floor, one from charcoal dropped from his brazier in March, the other in the neat shape of an iron. If I worked at it, perhaps I could make the charcoal blackness look like natural knots. I would bring up my furniture, make my arrangements as I liked them, and if there was a sadness there ought to be a balance of satisfaction too. The house was vacant. I walked through the emptiness and silence in such ineffectual circles that I only realised when it was almost dark that Kostas had not just deprived me of some gas, there was no kitchen stove.

I did think this tale was over. I really thought this tale was over. This is crazy. He's been supplied with seventeen thousand drachmas for the expense of moving, so I'm told, and he has to take my stove to Santorini too?

I had a second one in my inside kitchen corner, but that was beside the point.

Kostas had previously exchanged the missing one for Henry's, which has an oven, and I had found it with an eye gone from one of its three rings. He said, of course, that Mr N had taken that, and Mr N, of course, said that he had not. I always lost in these three-cornered arguments. But I did point out to Kostas, when he moved it back again, that if he borrowed equipment from other people's houses he was responsible, and for the sake of verbal agreement he agreed. He would have it fixed, he said. Don't worry. Lovely, but there are no replacements in Aiyiali, if anywhere. And now there was no stove in my kitchen.

It was late evening, by Langatha standards, but I took off in a swoop of fury down the hill. The boat had not yet hooted. I reached Ormos just in time. Kostas looked unhappy when he saw me, and unhappier when I got going with what I had to say. That was brief, but fierce. I did not care, as Kostas did, who heard. It would have been a terrible deprivation if I had not beaten the boat.

I was so angry that I threw the upstairs litter into my tirade. Kostas apologised and answered back. He had left money with Michalis to put back the platform for my bed and for Anna to sweep up. He had also left the gas stove with Michalis, for him to do something about the missing eye.

Anna is top landlady. She's not a charwoman. But Kostas' boat was due at any moment, and he knew I could not check his stories here and now. He did not care about leaving me with lies and rubbish, only about having a foreign woman shouting at him on the waterfront. And remembering my policy about my private Beaufort Scale this summer, I ended with a handshake and a *bon voyage*.

Now that Mr N was removed from one corner of the triangle, the tenant's statements could be verified. Kostas told two lies at the harbour. Michalis had received money to replace the platform, and nothing else. There had been no thought - why should there be? - of Anna sweeping up, and he knew nothing at all about my stove.

Out of curiosity, I wonder if Kostas did pay September's rent. It was the seventeen lost days, and not five hundred drachmas, that made the difference to my well-being, but I do wonder. There is no reason to suppose that those two lies were his first. Mr N told me that his payments were always in arrears.

And out of curiosity again, I wonder if Mr N was quite so unscrupulous as the people of Aiyiali like to tell me about our building funds. I know he made a thousand out of the purchase of my house, but he did not out of Henry's, and I don't see how he could have embezzled large sums after that. Large sums? There were none. We were dealing in remarkably small figures all the way along. I did check the accounts, and had a pretty good idea of what was what. He may have compensated himself for doing, say, a master builder's work with workman's wages now and then, but all that's wrong with that is that he should have paid himself correctly on paper from the start. As for his thirty thousand, he earned it as a commander, but he got it in the wrong way, he ought to go to Christos to take lessons in style.

It does not matter any more. He walks along my home path and barely grunts goodday - he seldom called out greetings as he passed. His wife walks along my home path and we exchange all sorts. She admires any new improvements and brings me eggs and cheese. She's easy, and whatever she may wonder, she never asks for mysteries to be explained.

The mystery of the missing stove became a village joke. No one could quite believe my theory that Kostas had carried it to Santorini, but no one could produce a plausible alternative. Conjecture was an enrichment to chitchat around Mouska's where he did not have defenders since he had so blackened his character with gas. Yorgos promised to make inquiries, and write to Kostas. Why not phone him? That would be difficult. Kostas was a driver, he'd be on the road, all over Santorini, every day. And so I was to leave without illumination, for how could it have occurred to me that all this while my stove was sitting in a store-room beneath the police-station of Langatha?

Chapter Eighteen

I lay on my mattress on the floor of my upstairs bedroom, which resembled a cell - but I liked that - in some ancient monastery. Michalis would have to hack stones from the walls to put the platform back in place. There would be no tenants making structural alternations in this house again. One of the boards had pencilled on it at one end, in English, 'This place only for cutting onions,' and on the other, 'And this place for cutting bread.' I have no more explanation for this mini-mystery than for any of the others, but it suggests a dispersing of my property such as makes me feel lucky that when Michalis did the job he found all the boards intact.

Through the window opposite my pillow I see Mount Krykelos, rising to the highest peak on Amorgos. I do not draw my curtains, I like to see it there by moonlight, and in the morning when I wake. The Greeks are great closers and lockers of everything that can be closed and locked. I must admit, I think I am enamoured of my open house.

Except in gales I never shut this door at night. There are windows on the three other sides. Upstairs looks out in all directions. These ceilings are high. The problem is how to shut your eyes, the inside shadows are so pretty and there is such connection with the great expanse of the outside. If you wake on a full-moon night you think it must be daytime, you have to step out onto the terrace to be a surveying eagle, it's transfixing - in colour - red roses are bright red. When there is no moon you have to step out onto the terrace to be an astronomer, or an owl, for if you call `pioo - pioo' you may be answered, so here's a question for a moonless night - do owls look at the stars?

I called in tall Phanis to deal with the nail holes. I could have done that by myself, but it was as wearisome a chore as I was weary, and he would do it cheerfully and fast. He came down with his brushes and his buckets, declaring that since Kostas had refused to have the upstairs whitewashed in July, those rooms had better be done now. With him about the house I was able to deal with such enormous problems as whether I could spare two teaspoons or a saucepan from this kitchen to start me off again wherever in Athens I would be unpacking next. We were light-hearted over our ouzo and our coffee - Phanis would make a wonderful commander for any foreigner who wanted to rebuild a house. He worked for the best part of six hours before lunchtime, and said, `That's a lot!' when I gave him two-thirds of a day's wage. Take it, my friend, but don't eat bean soup on the way home.

`Now you have your pigeon,' he exclaimed. Yes, my house is my white pigeon, inside and out, and I have to go away from it. Give me my seventeen days.

I know, the war is over, we have triumphed, and we will come back to the new era that Henry always gave a `when' to, while I was doubtful with my `if'. But there will be no such era for me if I cannot earn it first. And the last one is still lurking. I have Kostas in the drains.

Washing-up water took fifteen minutes to run out of my sink, and then instead of running through its pipe into the lower field it mostly seeped out through the wall. I ignored that as long as I could manage to, that is, until the water wouldn't budge at all.

Michalis and I spent a precious, final morning being plumber and plumber's mate. For two hours he wallowed elbow-deep in such stinking muck that he had to wash in boiling water three times in quick succession and souse himself in perfume afterwards. Kostas' wife had done without the drain-top and swilled down everything, even a baby's dummy, incriminating evidence along with beans and melon pips. Incriminating evidence won't help us. I don't go to Syros now. I wiped myself with Michalis' perfume and went to work with suitcases.

I can't laugh today, but it would be an insult to my terrace not to proclaim that I shall come back and laugh on it. Babies' dummies, missing gas stoves, Syros lawyers will all be funny when the new era is in swing. So long as you know that you will have it, laughter in the future ought to be as good as laughter now.

Anyway, whatever may become of me, this terrace will be safe for my nephews to be eagles, astronomers or owls.

They will come, the houses will be here, the view will be here, I think that Stroumbos' message has to do with permanence. I do not see that anything in this landscape will change except that sooner or later there will be no generator above Henry's house. And come off it, Carolina, you really know that you will be here yourself.

So I kept talking, prowling round the house and round the village, in and out of Anna's, in and out of Mouska's, up and down the mule track, mumbling to myself. Once in the late evening I walked past Mr N's shop - I had got used to doing that in the way that he walks past our estate.

As I crossed the beam of light thrown through the open door, I was halted by a cry of `Carolina!' from inside.

That was Mr N. That was the ex-commander, sitting at his table all alone. It did not seem extraordinary to walk in and sit down. I had no inclination for disdain. He filled a half-kilo measure of retsina and brought a second glass. So, `Your health!' - `Your health!'

We could not talk about the weather, we could not talk of Syros lawyers, but there was a great deal about Kostas to be said. It was four-stripe Yorgos who could do no wrong. Kostas, in any case, had left. And I was thinking while we chatted that if I had to be wrecked on a desert island with one of them, I would probably choose Mr N. For one thing, he would be the most ingenious desert-island man.

There would be Sunday-evening goat in the new era, and if I wanted I could come in and order a glass of wine on any evening, like any customer. I did not think that I would make a habit of it, I was not one of the lads, I would be self-contained at home, but I liked to know that there were no longer any bars on any doors. That would be a feather in Mr N's cap, when I was seen inside his shop. Why be stingy about handing feathers? They are free.

I do like this crazy village. I've been feeling dour, but I don't think I could be dour in it for long. Sometimes I cannot make up my mind whether it is truly crazy or inordinately logical, but that I like it I do know.

So there were Mr N and I, leisurely with our half kilo - there would not be a refill - gloating over Kostas' wickedness with gas. The gas led to the stove and on to other peccadillos until we grew so chatty that we moved on to horticulture, leaving Kostas out. Mr N had to stop himself in the middle of an absent-minded sentence about a plan for Henry's flowers. He was not drunk, he is no drunkard, but he must have had a certain quantity. `Well!' he exclaimed. `I'm out of that!'

You are indeed, old friend, thanks be to Christos and the saints, you're out.

`Don't have anything to do with that man,' I was urged by one who knew our story. All right, that's sensible advice. I'm not having anything to do with him. That's why I'm here. He's not my friend and not my enemy, but only the proprietor of a little creaky shop. I am sharing a jug of wine with him in preference to not sharing a jug of wine. I do not care whether or not I shall do so again.

I'm free. That's freedom. I do not have to wait - I certainly shall not - until Mr N decides that it's time to shut up shop. I don't need his arm along our rocky, murky path. I do very well myself as a night-time goat or cat.

Besides, I had to go immediately, I could not wait. I had an urgent need to be at home, and by myself. I started running as soon as I was through his beam of light, glad that he had called me, glad that I had gone in, for it made me laugh, not ruefully or bravely, but with real laughing laughter from the moment that I reached the path. I scuttled home, and if I lurched or if I staggered, the lurching and the staggering were not due to wine or rocks. I bounded up my steps, across my terrace - which would not have been my terrace but for Mr N - to fling myself onto my mattress unrestrained. Laughter in the future will do very well, but give me the choice and I shall go for laughter now.

-*-

Addendum - The Magic Muletrack

In this book of Carolina's there is much mention of the arrival and influence of Anna, or "Cubby" as the family called her for many years. The following is Anna's telling of the trip she made with Carolina's brother and his family, when she first came to Amorgos as a Norland Nanny in 1974.

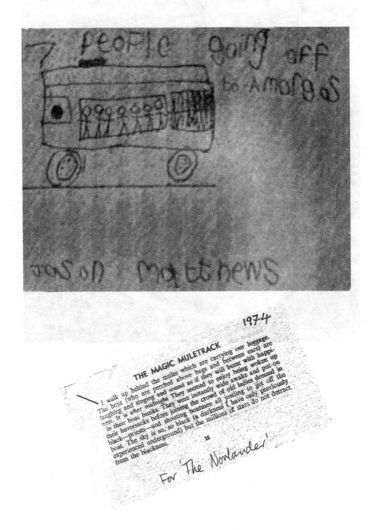

1974

THE MAGIC MULETRACK

I walk up behind the moles which are carrying our luggage. The boys (who are perched above bags and between cars) are laughing and singing and sound as if they will burst with happiness. It is after midnight. They seemed to enjoy being woken up in their boat bunks. They were instantly wide awake and put on their haversacks before joining the crowd of old ladies dressed in black—priests—and shouting boatmen all jostling to get off the boat. The sky is so, so black (a darkness I have only previously experienced underground) but the millions of stars do not detract from the blackness.

For The Norlander!

THE MAGIC MULETRACK
From The Norlander Newsletter
1974

I walk up behind the mules carrying our luggage. The boys who are perched above bags and between ears are laughing and singing, and sound as if they will burst with happiness. It is after midnight. They seemed to enjoy being woken up in their boat bunks. They were instantly wide awake and put on their rucksacks before joining the crowd of old ladies and priests dressed in black, and shouting boatmen, all jostling to get off the boat. The sky is so, so black, a darkness I have only previously experienced underground, and the millions of stars only highlight the darkness.

I can hear cicadas, mules braying, hooves ahead, and the happy sounds from Julian, Jason and Zachary. I can feel smooth, polished stones and prickles beneath my feet, I can see nothing, but tomorrow my eyes will have a feast! We have arrived on Amorgos (a small island in the Cyclades – a 10 hour boat journey from Athens) after travelling across Europe for 10 days. Four adults and three boys in a VW camper (nicknamed the Bed-Bug!), a journey that had been described to us as hell with small children, but of which we enjoyed every minute. The van became the children's home, and the fact that it was moving made it more interesting for them. They responded to being in a cramped space by being creative with paper, pens, scissors, by reading, telling and listening to stories, and singing. When we stopped they were immediately absorbed in whatever the surroundings had to offer. They chased each other round beautiful pillars in Vicenze, sailed anything that would float in the canals of Venice, played with a dead snake on a beach in Yugoslavia, pursued lizards and bright green beetles, scraped up bird seed from the pavements of Dubrovnik to feed the pigeons, ate swordfish cooked on a beach fire under Mount Olympus, "drove" lorries with bouzouki music blaring from them. . . . . . so many experiences and now here we are on this small island, with no roads or electricity, where we are not only going to have a holiday but really "live" in the true sense of the word.

The weeks that follow our arrival on Amorgos are full of walking, swimming, exploring the white villages and just wallowing in this simple living that so clears the mind of muddle and mess. Indeed, the children are greatly inspired and spend many long hours sitting on the terrace drawing – inventing weird machines, telling stories and examining the vast number of creatures that come along. Every night they flop into bed exhausted, full of good food, consisting mainly of aubergines, goat, potatoes, tomatoes, grapes, and goat cheese. Food here depends entirely on the season. Happy after a day on the beach playing with island children, and physically tired from their forty five minute climb up the mule-track to our village, they sleep immediately - no fears or worries as in England. Oh, for a mule-track in Essex! Indeed the mule-track is a story in itself - a whole book could be written about our travels on it with the children.

The track winds quite steeply down to the sea, lined with olive and fig trees, with lizards and snakes darting over its well-smoothed stones. Going down is often a race with stops to climb fig trees (tummies suffer from our travels down to the sea!) and lizard chases. The lizards are the species that drop their tails when caught, and though the boys do not want to hurt them, they are desperate to have a tail as a trophy! A mule stop (the Bus Shelter as we call it) provides a rest in the shade, and we talk to passers-by and practice our dancing. We travel barefoot up and down, and the stones feel smooth and warm.

Coming **up** the mule-track is slightly different - the boys walk very well if they are distracted the whole way . . . and the stories we tell! - from magic donkeys to Concords with noses that drop off, from chameleons to fire engines! The boys also tell us stories, the one that stands out in my mind was from Julian, about an old man with a waterfall flowing from his back. Often the boys are offered lifts on mules laden with figs, old ladies, wooden planks, aubergines, tomatoes and grapes. There was the day we were lent a donkey which threw the children off onto the track and bounded home with a bag of grapes and a precious camera hung on its saddle.....

I could go on for ever about the mule track!

Every Sunday evening we frequent Nikitas's shop for roast goat followed by violin, lute, and dancing. The boys reactions to this are predictable. Julian falls asleep on somebody's knee, Zachary livens up as soon as the music begins and dances around like a little insect, Jason drinks a little retsina and spends his time trying to persuade the island girls to dance with him!

We have our own feast one evening of stuffed goat cooked in our bakehouse oven. Brushwood is burned in the oven during the morning, the ashes are then raked out and the goat meat put in. The boys help to make bread and put their own loaves in to cook. The goat is ready after sunset. The round stone in front of the oven is rolled back and, looking into the dark bakehouse, one can see three small heads silhouetted against the glowing oven whilst Henry fishes the bread out with an enormous wooden paddle. What a feast on our terrace! The moon rises as we are eating and there is intense involvement and excitement in its movement. As it appears over the hills Jason (6) shouts "Look at the hinge of light!"

Many evenings we spend lying in our sleeping bags on the terrace watching shooting stars and satellites. For five weeks we are so aware of the effect nature has upon us, and the lives of the islanders.

August 15th is an annual religious festival in Greece (the Feast of the Dormition), and Amorgos has its feast outside a church half a mile from the village. As we walk towards it we can hear excited voices and people can be seen bustling around outside the church. Zachary (4) cries "Look - it's a jumble sale!"

There is a lot of work to be done around the house and the boys help by drawing water from the well, whitewashing walls, collecting stones for building, and trekking to the drinking water spring with numerous containers. On one water expedition Jason and I go on to explore the ruined village in the gorge. We wander round the old houses finding bits of pottery and looking down wells. Jason hopes desperately to find some treasure, but what we do find excites him even more. Beside the church is a small hut (an ossuary), and as we peep in and our eyes became accustomed to the dark we realise it is full of human bones. Jason cannot believe his eyes. This is the sort of thing he hopes to find every day of his life! I don't feel I can stop him going in, as he is so excited and curious. He creeps in and gently touches a few bones and then asks if he can piece them all together to make a skeleton! I do manage to deter him. On opening a large wooden chest he is confronted with numerous skulls, and then comes out of the hut willingly. He doesn't say much afterwards, but the wonder he expresses far outweighs the distaste that would have been the reaction of many people.

Perhaps the highlight of our time on the island for Julian (5) was the time he caught a fish. He was lent a rod and told exactly what to do if he felt a pull. He reacted immediately to the tug on his line and with a bit of help landed a good-sized fish. He did not leap up and down with excitement - his eyes just shone and he looked at it for a long time. As we walked along the beach he said,"do people ever cry when they are happy?" I said that they often do, and he said "because I nearly cried when I caught this fish." We walked up the mule track and, instead of stories, we had a long discussion about what the fish had felt and if it minded being caught to be eaten. He carried the fish carefully and, being Julian, dropped it several times in the mule dung and prickles. At home we prepared it together and cooked it. He sat alone at the table and squeezed lemon on it. It was gone in a second! As well as his excitement and joy over its deliciousness

I detected a little sadness in his face as he ate it. It will be interesting to learn later how he remembers his "first fish".

I could go on forever remembering scenes and incidents, but time to tell of our departure from Amorgos. We left on the ferry in the middle of the night, lifting the boys in their sleeping bags from the jetty where they were sleeping. I watched the moon set and fortunately fell asleep before our sad departure from the bay.

There are only two adults on our journey back to England and the extra space gives the boys more room to roll around like puppies in the back of the bus. On our last day in Greece we cook lunch on our little stove on the pavement whilst the van is having a window repaired. People are amazed to see us spread out like gypsies with fish sizzling away. In Yugoslavia I discover Jason about to sail down a deep, fast moving river on a piece of hardboard! We wash our hair in mountain springs reminiscent of watering-can washes in Amorgos. In Austria a wooded mountainside provides us with a feast of wild strawberries, raspberries and wood sorrel. In Rothenburg we returned to the van, all grubby with feet hanging out of our worn shoes and are stopped by a very smart couple in a Mercedes who want a photograph of us for an article on tourists in Rothenberg. I wonder what heading we will come under! The boys spend a very happy hour sliding round the Bishop's Palace in Wartburg on their bottoms and tummies. From their strange angle they scrutinise the splendid paintings on every ceiling. I wish I could do the same! We sleep in the dripping Black

Forest dreaming of bears and boars. Our last night is spent in Calais Hoverport car park.

We leave for England early in the morning. The channel is very rough, and the journey exhilarating, with screams of delight every time we whizz over a wave and down into a deep trough. A rainbow is over Ramsgate to welcome us home, and those beautiful merging colours seem to express what a wonderful time we have all had.

NURSE CAROL-ANNE HUGILL (Set 56)

Nanny to Jason, Julian and Zachary

Additional Addendum - Cubby's Wedding

Chapter 15 tells the tale of Anna's wedding in Carolina's voice. Anna's parents were not able to come to Amorgos for the wedding so Carolina's sister-in-law, Catherine, wrote a description of the wedding in a letter to Anna's parents so they could enjoy a vivid description of the events of the days surrounding the nuptials.

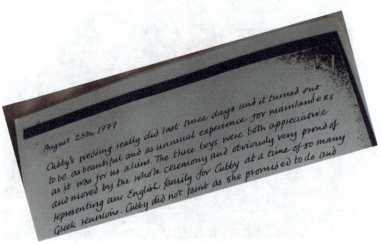

August 25th 1977

Cubby's wedding really did last three days and it turned out to be as beautiful and as unusual experience for mainlanders as it was for us aliens. The three boys were both appreciative and moved by the whole ceremony and obviously very proud of representing our English family for Cubby at a time of so many Greek reunions. Cubby did not faint as she promised to do and

August 25th, 1977

Cubby's wedding really did last three days, and it turned out to be as beautiful and as unusual an experience for mainlanders as it was for us aliens. The thee boys were both appreciative and moved by the whole ceremony and obviously very proud of representing an English family for Cubby at a time of so many Greek reunions. Cubby did not faint as she promised to do and, although a little nervous, carried herself through a very exacting 3 days with great aplomb. Right up to the last moment, Michali was fixing doors, windows, and, on the last morning, a lavatory seat. Cubby was frantically painting and longing to put her books on the new shelves. By some mistake of premarital adrenaline, curtains were made, wall hangings, beautiful shells, fresh flowers, the floor paint was only just down. As you can imagine, by the right moment it looked sparkling, happy, and very attractive. Cubby was worried about some Greek visual compromises, but it looked so fresh and so unmistakably Cubby it was lovely.

The first day was a bed ceremony of which Cubby will have to tell you more—but it started with a group sitting round (not us) such as The Priest the 'Combara' (a sort of lady in waiting come Best Woman—no doubt Cubby explained) and others. Then the bed was made. Being a bed shelf, like ours, it was incredibly difficult to tuck in on the wall side. Cubby's brightly coloured cover was rejected, and a suitably white lace alternative put on (it was a tablecloth present from sister-in-law, a bleached wonder from Athens—the sister-in-law, not the lace). The boy baby who was to be placed on the bed was asleep and had to be woken. Rice, money, and sugared almonds were thrown on the top of the bed and left until the next day. Eventually, Michali was left to sleep in the house—do you think he peeped at the wedding dress under its cover on the bed? Cubby came to spend the night and seemed to sleep very well.

By seven next morning, the boys had helped to lay a terrace table with flowers and very fair portions of fruit juice. So, the bride had fruit juice and a boiled egg. Cubby was still convinced that the church service was going to be long and that she was going to faint—after all, everybody knows that she always stands at the door, and at seven already, it was a simmering, still, heat that kept our cups of tea quite hot. Not long after, Cubby was in her own house receiving women and children bearing flowers and gifts, endless glasses and plates from Vasili's shop (only to be put back in Michali's shop a few days later—sounds like island economy, or is it economic Islanders?) Cubby handed round glasses of water, liqueur and soft squodgy jellies which my boys seemed invariably to have managed to get yet another one. At one point a group of unmarried girls arrived, giggling and nudging each other—their names were written on the bottom of the wedding shoes. They told Cubby that the first one to be totally rubbed off would be the next one to get married (by the end of the festivities all of the names had disappeared). The ladies looked round the room, looked at the dress on the bed, they looked in the kitchen, and after many days of Cubby being told she was doing it all wrong, they had to admit it looked lovely.

Then I went home, and there were hair washings, 6 white socks on 6 washed feet—all rather immaculate by our usual Amorgos standards—even Henry's one pair of trousers were proudly stiff with sun and air and could be worn straight off the line (that was lucky because he had no alternative). Then back to Anna's house—there were children on the roof, on the stairs to the terrace, on the walls to the courtyard. There in the courtyard, the musicians were playing —A light, happy tune closely resembling a Celtic jig —A lovely sound. So happy.

In came the candles—unlit—<u>huge</u>, ornate, surrounded by frills, flowers, organza, and lace—off-white and rather magnificent—but perhaps only in this environment. So, the numbers grew—

"Where's the Combara?"

"When am I going to get changed?"

The Combara arrived "I'm sorry I'm late I've been sick thirty times"—what else could she have said.

Little boys clambered at the lavatory window where a very hot bride was being got into a long-sleeved, high-necked, long-skirted white dress, veil, etc. Michali suddenly appeared having changed elsewhere. Everyone clapped (had they never seen him in a suit before?) But the suit was so thick it must have been incredibly hot. Out of his pocket he pulled a tie and gave it to the Best Man. He put it round his neck and started to tie it above his own tie—he then put it over a young man's head, beside him who completed the knot, loosened it and put it in turn over Michali's head and eventually, all was made to look as convincing as necessary. So seduced by

359

all the goings-on was I, that it took me a little time to realize that this part of the ceremony was due to the bridegroom not knowing how to tie a tie, rather than part of the folklore.

Suddenly a ribbon was called for and hastily produced by Zachary—an arrangement of white lilies and carnations was hurriedly made for the bride to carry. Henry was called to the lavatory, and arm in arm, Henry and Cubby appeared, obviously moved. Henry handed Cubby's hand into Michali's, and the procession began. The musicians ahead of the bride and groom with music so light that any long white dress would appear to float over the mule dung. The family and many others wound through the steep streets to the church. The service was short and full of humor. Four priests, exchanging of wreaths and rings, throwing of rice, drinking a large glass of wine, and ending in a circular dance of the priests, the candle holders and Michali and Anna, with rice pouring from heaven. An ecclesiastical hailstorm maybe. No stage management (Michali hissing to the priests "Please do not repeat everything twice") But a very good performance by all. Jason, Julian and Zachary found it fascinating.

Then, back to the bride's house with Henry dancing ahead of the musicians along the walls and rooftops to get photos of the procession as it wound its way back down to the house. The wedding guests poured over the roofs, onto the steps and into neighboring streets.

Out came the sweets, the liqueurs, and then a procession through the house to greet the bride and groom (yes, a lot of the paint came off the floor). Home to change then up to the Platia to the wedding dinner. In another dress—English material but designed by dressmaker and convincingly Greek smart looking. Cubby looked a little overawed but very happy. After a splendid, priestly grace, we ate, and then the dancing began. By three in the morning the Matthews family did a rather unorthodox family dance. Only shortly before this a little boy had been sent to wake the priest and asked him to go back to the house with the happy couple. This was the only moment that Cubby found difficult; she felt dizzy and tired and just wanted to go to bed, but she said the ceremony in the house seemed to go on and on, and every time she went for some fresh air she was called back into the house for yet another blessing.

Next morning Henry and Carolina went up to the Platia to do the washing up—the plates went through a first lot of water and a second and a third! Immediately after that was finished, they continued to help prepare the wedding breakfast, "batsa." A soup made from all the, as the boy's call it, "goat's-gut!" Disguised by mounds of ground garlic, lemon, and herbs, it is still unmistakably what it is: Everything that is left on the goat that has not been used in the previous night's stew. By midday, the bride and groom arrived (looking far more relaxed in a sparkling white shirt and a red and white gingham dress of her own design, at last). They had apparently been waiting in their house some time for the ceremonial group to come and make their bed and the musicians to play them back to the Platia. The musicians were asleep so Cubby and Michali just came anyway. Cubby looked radiant.

Cubby bravely made her way through half the "batsa" but it's not surprising, with all the things that she has adapted so well to, that this is the one thing she still finds impossible. Zachary cannot even sit in the same room as this soup—and we conducted our meal with him looking through a window at eye level! Then Michali started the dancing in his new shoes that were killing him by this time. And Cubby danced and danced and danced. By eleven in the evening, all the village lights were out. There was not a sound except the donkeys who wished they were getting married too— even all the dogs seemed to be exhausted and so were we.

We return on the 10th of September so we will be in touch. Your daughter has made this a very special summer for us. She is an amazing person. I must get this to a Mercury we have found.

Much love from all of us here, wishing that you could have just had a peep at some of the many happy moments.

- Catherine, Henry, Jason, Julian and Zachary.

Made in the USA
Monee, IL
11 July 2024